Contents

Politics and the Processes of Schooling

EDITED BY

STEPHEN WALKER AND LEN BARTON

Open University Press

Milton Keynes · Philadelphia

Open University Press
12 Cofferidge Close
Stony Stratford
Milton Keynes MK11 1BY

and
242 Cherry Street
Philadelphia, PA 19106, USA

First Published 1989

British Library Cataloguing in Publication Data

International Sociology of Education
    Conference (*10th: 1987: Westhill College*)
    Politics and the processes of schooling.
    1. Education.   Political aspects
    I. Title   II. Walker, Stephen, 1944–
    II. Barton, Len
    379

    ISBN 0-335-09546-1
    ISBN 0-335-09545-3 Pbk

Library of Congress Cataloging-in-Publication Data

Politics and the processes of schooling/edited by Stephen Walker and
    Len Barton.
        p.   cm.
        "Presented at the Xth International Sociology of Education
    Conference held at Westhill College, Birmingham, in 1987"—
    Acknowl.
        Includes index.
        ISBN 0-335-09546-1.   ISBN 0-335-09545-3 (pbk.)
        1. Educational sociology—Congresses.   2. Politics and
    education—Congresses.   3. Education and State—Congresses.
    4. Social control—Congresses.   I. Walker, Stephen, 1944–   .
    II. Barton, Len.   III. International Sociology of Education
    Conference (10th: 1987: Westhill College)
    LC191.2.P65 1989
    370.19—dc19   88-23671   CIP

Printed and bound in Great Britain by
Biddles Ltd, Guildford and King's Lynn

Contributors

Peter Aggleton	Department of Education, Bristol Polytechnic
Stephen J. Ball	King's College, University of London
Len Barton	Department of Education, Bristol Polytechnic
Steve Baron	Department of Sociology and Social Policy, University of Stirling
John Beynon	Department of Behavioural and Communication Studies, Polytechnic of Wales
Robert G. Burgess	CEDAR, University of Warwick
Gill Crozier	Department of Education, Bristol Polytechnic
Hilary Homans	Department of Nursing, Health and Applied Social Studies, Bristol Polytechnic
Judith L. Kapferer	School of Education, Flinders University, Australia
Marg Malloch	Ministry of Education, State of Victoria, Australia
Stephen Walker	Newman and Westhill Colleges, Birmingham
Ian Warwick	Department of Education, Bristol Polytechnic
Lois Weis	State University of New York at Buffalo, USA

Acknowledgements

The articles in this collection are all versions of papers presented at the Xth International Sociology of Education Conference held at Westhill College, Birmingham in 1987. The conference is supported by Carfax Publishing Company of Oxford.

Thanks for their help and support to Janet Cowsill, Newman College; and to Sandra Walker and Joan Barton.

Introduction: Management in Education

Stephen Walker and Len Barton

In the spirit of the main intention of the International Sociology of Education Conference, i.e. to provide a forum for the exchange of ideas between researchers working in different analytical perspectives and between researchers, teachers in higher education and school teachers, we selected the theme of the tenth Conference – 'Politics, The Teacher and Schools' – with the central idea of providing an opportunity for discussion on the ways the many policy initiatives and directives which had been targeted on education in the UK, the USA and Austral-Asia have influenced the daily lives of teachers in schools and classrooms. In selecting the theme, we anticipated that debates at the 1987 meeting would be chiefly concerned with policy analysis and policy impact. To our surprise, this is not what we got. Instead, attention was focused on how the ideologies which operate around schooling are being manipulated and transformed and how these 'power-play shifts' are influencing life in schools. Thus, the concern was with charting how social change gets enacted rather than with a concentration on political theorizing or perspective analysis. In the course of discussions during the Conference and in the papers selected for this volume, this concern centred on a single idea as the dominant issue. This is the rise of MANAGEMENT GOALS as a central strand of the ideological mechanisms currently at work upon and within education. As various writers and teachers reflect on their present experience of education, of educational policy shifts and of the political developments happening outside the system, they keep returning to a common observation, a shared recognition – the realization that in the political changes and policy shifts *people are being managed.*

This recognition constitutes the major theme of this book. It raises several crucial and related questions, including:

● What do we understand by the term 'managed'?
● How are the managed managing?
● How are the managed responding to the attempts to manage them?

The discussion of these questions is strongly related to the many instances of centralized intervention in the educational and welfare systems which characterize the 1980s. In previous ISEC collections we, along with other analysts (Baron *et al.* 1981; Bates *et al.* 1984; David 1983), have attempted to outline some of the political thinking on which these interventions rest, in short, the ideological movement that has come to be known as the New Right. Three particular features of New Right thinking seem pertinent to a consideration how people outside and inside education are being managed. These are:

Economic dogmatism based upon a belief in an efficient market-based economy in which market forces are allowed unimpeded free play. This involves an enormous increase in the direct use of economic principles, instrumentation and business ethic as a basis of educational planning and policy-making.

A concentrated endeavour to redefine the relationship between the individual and the social formation. This involves the establishment of ideological reformulation which includes a new morality and new principles of social cohesion. Particular types of subjectivities and forms of behaviour are being called for. For example, the reference point proclaimed as the essential basis of decisions about moral and social norms is unequivocally 'family life'. But for the main architects of New Right politics, family life and family relations are perceived in simplistic, non-problematic and prescriptive terms. 'Proper' family relations are hetero-sexual; they are only legitimated through marriage; they require family members to make social obligations a priority above individual needs and designs; they celebrate patriar-

chical and cultural dependency; and there is no alternative to
these definitions.

Economic dogmatism and authoritarian moral piety should
frighten people. It has to be said, therefore, that one of the
most impressive achievements of the New Right has been the
way in which new forms of social control have been defended
and sold. If the New Right is engaged in ideological
transformation, it is also engaged in a process of manipulating
popular opinion to facilitate the transformation. New
policies are defended through reference to increased choice,
higher living standards, more secure social discipline and the
right to gain maximum benefit from one's own economic
endeavour. In this manipulation, that individuals and
groups significantly differ in their capacity to exercise
choice, in their access to wealth, in their ability to influence
their community and in their opportunities to find work, is
successfully overlooked or obscured.
(Barton and Walker 1985; Walker and Barton 1986, 1987)

The fundamental concern is with *control* and this necessitates
viewing educational changes:

as not merely superficial changes in how educational control
is achieved and defended, but as fundamental changes in
what those in control wish to achieve through education,
goals which are inevitably related to their overall social
vision and ambitions.
(Barton and Walker 1985, Introduction)

The radicalism of the New Right vision has meant that teachers
have become a central management target for controlling the
impact and the outcomes of the education system. Teachers *have* to
be managed; and to secure a basis for achieving and legitimating
this requirement, in the UK, the USA and in Australia, we have
witnessed recently a relentless (though not surprising) process
through which teachers are systematically devalued and debased.
This process has involved the explicit and implicit promotion of a
view in which teachers are represented as:

Fundamentally responsible for the general crisis in education, including the decline in standards and discipline in
schools.

Teachers are thus not to be trusted and more visible signs of regulation and accountability need to be effectively introduced.

Teacher unionism is dangerous and inhibits the kinds of professional thinking and behaviour that are seen as desirable.

The power to define the nature of the curriculum and how it is monitored must never be given to teachers.

Teacher education at both initial and in-service levels needs to be more centrally and effectively controlled.

Analysis of developments in the United States (within official government reports on teachers and schools) offer a similar series of conclusions. The impact of interventionist measures can be viewed as an attempt to reduce the power of teachers to control their own working lives. These critiques also marginalize the question of the work-conditions of the teachers, and instead, present the issues of teacher attitude, motivation and skills as being the fundamental contributing factors of the problems within schools today (McNeil 1987; Weis 1987).

The papers in this volume do emphasize the ascendancy of management principles in the current attempts to both redefine and control the nature and method of schooling. Dominating state interest is the issue of the efficiency and effectiveness of existing provision. The establishment of management targets have been an increasingly major goal of social relations.

For the purpose of discussion, it is possible to distinguish three particular areas of educational concern which have become both target areas and battlegrounds of the kinds of managerial enterprise we have tried to outline above. These are the areas of:

- the management of the identity and evaluation of individual and groups in society (cultural, sexual, ethnic and economic), and of the norms used for evaluating people;
- the management of the locus of control of state enterprises, like education;
- the management of the ideological parameters through which certain crucial social relationships, like gender relations, are enacted and transformed.

We have used these three 'target' areas as a basis for the organization of the papers in this book.

The collection opens with three papers (by Burgess, Aggleton *et al.* and Crozier) which all explore different aspects of the relationship between normative evaluations of individuals and groups and schooling processes. Although the papers focus on different topics – pastoral care, sexuality and attitudes to ethnic differences – all three provide evidence and insights about how the management of school norms based on present ideological trends has implications for who gets 'cared-for' in school and for how 'care' gets put into practice.

In the peculiar rationale of New Right policy, the balancing of collectivistic and individualistic logic has been adjusted and freshly interpreted. Increased state intervention is defended in terms of increased individual autonomy and personal freedom. Clearly, this new logic raises questions about which cultural form is sponsored in education, about whose interests are extended through schooling and about how local communities and interest groups might understand and respond to state intervention and initiatives. These 'locus of control' issues are addressed in the articles by Baron and by Kapferer.

Contemporary political policy and ideological shifts challenge the parameter of social relationships which exist outside and within schools – the contradictions of class, gender, ethnic and power relations. The papers in this book by Weis, Malloch and Beynon all explore different aspects of how the 'lived contradictions' of, particularly, gender relations are manifest in schools and of how the situation in the 1980s is transforming these lived experiences.

In his contribution to this volume (Chapter 9), Stephen Ball suggests:

> The micro-political perspective provides a vehicle for linking individual careers, ideological commitments and actions with organizational structures, and forms of control with forms of resistance and opposition.

To the extent that we feel this book in total offers essential information for making links between forms of control and forms of opposition, it is appropriate that the collection concludes with Ball's discussion of school organization and micro-political analysis and action. In this spirit, we hope that all the papers in this book make some contribution to the struggle by 'the managed' to regain political and educational initiative and to re-establish a programme aimed at establishing democratic participation in schools and society.

References

Baron, S., *et al.* (1981) *Unpopular Education.* London, Hutchinson.
Barton, L. and Walker, S. (eds) (1985) *Education and Social Change.* London, Croom Helm.
Bates, I., *et al.* (1984) *Schooling for the Dole.* London, Macmillan.
David, M. (1983) 'Sex, education and social policy: a new moral economy' in S. Walker and L. Barton (eds) *Gender, Class and Education.* Lewes, Falmer Press.
McNeil, L. (1982) 'Exist, voice and community: magnet teachers' responses to standardisation' in *Educational Policy* Vol. 1, No. 1, pp. 93–114.
Walker, S. and Barton, L. (eds) (1986) *Youth, Unemployment and Schooling.* Milton Keynes, Open University Press.
Walker, S. and Barton, L. (eds) (1987) *Changing Policies, Changing Teachers. New Directions for Schooling?* Milton Keynes, Open University Press.
Weis, L. (1987) Introduction to 'The Crisis in Teaching' in *Educational Policy* Vol. 1, No. 1, pp. 3–8.

CHAPTER 1

The Politics of Pastoral Care

Robert G. Burgess

Writing just ten years ago Best, Jarvis and Ribbins (1977) commented on the paucity of literature from social scientists and educationalists on the topic 'pastoral care'. Indeed, they indicated that even when writers did examine pastoral care and related tasks and activities they were rarely defined or critically evaluated. Much of this work they argued was based on 'conventional wisdom' where writers such as Marland (1974) and Blackburn (1975) presented a portrait of pastoral care in terms of the care of children. Such accounts were not only normative in the sense of presenting what *ought* to occur rather than what *did* occur, but also failed to present a detailed portrait of pastoral care in action not only from the pupils' perspective but also that of teachers. This analysis was taken further by Best, Ribbins, Jarvis and Oddy (1983) when they remarked:

> One of the weaknesses of the 'conventional wisdom' ... is its failure to give adequate consideration to what 'pastoral care' means for those who are supposed to provide it on a day-to-day basis. As a result pastoral structures of roles and institutions ('Houses', 'Years' etc.) are all too often taken at face value and there is a danger that the tensions involved in the dynamic relationship between different dimensions of the school structure, and between the formal role-positions and the (very human) teachers who fill them are ignored.
>
> (Best, Ribbins, Jarvis and Oddy 1983, p. 55)

Such a statement points to a critical gap in our knowledge of the structures and systems of pastoral care – systems that not only include relationships with pupils but also the position of individual teachers and their career paths. In short, the material interests of teachers in pastoral care are omitted from view. This deficiency in our knowledge may be partly accounted for by the emphasis given to experiential accounts on the working of the systems rather than research based activities with teachers engaged in the pastoral system.

Nevertheless, some studies of pastoral systems have been conducted in the last decade that contribute to our understanding of this aspect of school organization (Ribbins and Best 1985). First, a study by Corbishley and Evans (1980) who provide a comparison of two schools that operated different pastoral systems (a vertical system based on houses and a horizontal system based on year groups). By focusing on the work of Marland (1974) and Hamblin (1978) they demonstrate how these writers underestimate the socio-historical contexts within which pastoral care systems are located. In turn, they focus on pastoral care within school organization and point to the ways in which both Marland and Hamblin underestimate the chance of internal conflict among staff and the career motivations and aspirations of teachers in the pastoral system. As a consequence of their critique, Corbishley and Evans (1980) focus attention on the teachers' perspective of the pastoral system in two schools and point to the way in which the organizational structure may provide a focus for teacher careers, teacher dissatisfaction and teacher turnover.

Some of these themes have been taken up in the only major case study on pastoral care by Best *et al.* (1983) where they focus on teacher perspectives of pastoral work in Rivendell, a large comprehensive school in the South of England. Here, the focus is upon the study of the pastoral organization and the ways in which teachers defined pastoral care. As such, their study is concerned with the structure and system of pastoral work focusing on teachers' roles, styles, ideologies and identities as members of the pastoral team. In turn, their work also points to some conflicts, divisions and tensions that were present among the teachers at Rivendell School.

It is this theme of social division that was taken up in my first study of a co-educational Roman Catholic comprehensive that I called Bishop McGregor School (Burgess 1983).[1] In particular, it was concerned with the way in which the structure of the school staff was a reflection of the internal organization of McGregor School; a situation that resulted in the allocation of allowances to teachers, and structured formal and informal relationships among the staff. Yet this study was conducted at a time (1973–4) of expansion in comprehensive schooling. As a consequence, we might consider how the situation may have changed ten years later.

It is, therefore, the purpose of this chapter to focus on data collected during a restudy of McGregor School in 1983–4.[2] In particular, I examine the way in which teachers' jobs and careers in the pastoral system became the subject of discussion during the academic year 1983–4 when the Head received a request from the governors to review the system. By focusing on this review we shall look at the ways in which Bishop McGregor School is managed and organized as well as examining the ways in which teachers attempt to define and defend the structures within which they work and their own material and ideological interests. Such an account therefore focuses not only on pastoral care but also on the micro-politics of school life that has been discussed by Hoyle (1982, 1986) and by Ball (Chapter 9, this volume). Micro-politics has been referred to by Hoyle as the 'dark side of organisational life' (Hoyle 1982, p. 87). However, he continues by defining it as:

> those strategies by which individuals and groups in organisational contexts seek to use their resources of power and influence to further their interests.
>
> (Hoyle 1982, p. 88)

In turn, Ball (1987) takes micro-political activity to include the interests of those people involved in the organization, the maintenance of organizational control and conflict over policy. In this sense, the school is perceived as an arena of struggle. However, Ball has pointed to the importance of examining the politics of teachers' jobs and careers in context. In this respect, it is important to understand the ways in which the pastoral system had been organized, managed and developed in McGregor School.

Systems of pastoral care

Since Bishop McGregor School was established in 1969 it has had a system of pastoral care, but it would be too simple to suggest that this has been one system. Over a fifteen-year period the pastoral system has been changed and the tasks that teachers have in that system have been modified (cf. Best *et al.* 1983). Furthermore, it is possible to identify three phases in the pastoral system.

1. Establishing pastoral care

When Bishop McGregor School was established in 1969 there was no opportunity for the Head and his staff to consider whether they would have a pastoral structure or what kind of system would be introduced as it was the policy of the local authority to have a pastoral structure in each secondary school. Bishop McGregor School was a purpose-built comprehensive based on a physical structure of houses – a system that was favoured by the officers of the local authority as a means of subdividing a large school into small manageable units. Indeed, this system was commonly used in many comprehensive schools established in the late 1960s as a way of allaying the fears of parents and teachers who were concerned about school size (Benn and Simon 1972).

At the time of his appointment, the Head was merely told by the governors and the local authority that the internal organization for pastoral care would be based upon a house system. Indeed, the local authority took this a stage further as Geoff Goddard (the Headteacher) explained:

> There was no question of any alternative – in fact, it wasn't on offer because in the first structure of staffing I was told that I had *one* Head of Department post and I had four Head of House posts, and I had a number of points which I could use to appoint teachers in charge. I was not given an option. And the advertisements for the Deputy Head went out first and the advertisements for pastoral Heads of House went out next, before the Heads of Departments. And, that was done – I was simply *told* that this was what they were doing. I wasn't asked did I want it. I was told. This is what they were doing and that was how they always proceeded.[3]

In this way, the pastoral system was considered of greater importance than the departmental system in McGregor School – a situation that was constantly reflected in the higher salaries and higher status that was given to those individuals who were House Heads (cf. Burgess 1983, pp. 52–83). Indeed their area of responsibility was defined by the Head as:

Social and academic welfare of each child within the house.

He (the Head of House) is expected to be involved in the implementation of agreed school policy and play a major role in helping to plan future school policy.[4]

This level of responsibility brought Heads of Houses into conflict with their colleagues in departments who considered that they had too much autonomy to develop their own position. Furthermore, they were critical of the extent to which House Heads could engage in policy making and contribute to the day-to-day running of the school along with the Head and his deputies (cf. Ball 1987). It was this situation that resulted in social divisions between House Heads and members of departments that contributed to a second phase in the development of the pastoral system.

2. From houses to super houses or mansions

Originally Bishop McGregor School was to have had ten vertical houses, but the pupil population never reached a sufficient size to justify more than eight houses being developed alongside the sixth form. From the Head's perspective this system worked well, as he remarked in an interview:

The pastoral system to my mind worked well even as we expanded it from four houses to six, and from six to seven and eight. Obviously it worked best when one had a good Head of House. Obviously it creaked when we had a weak Head of House.

However, staff gradually became sceptical about this system as the Head explained:

Quite a number of the staff had worked in other systems and their increasing disenchantment with the unevenness of disciplinary procedures became evident. Right at the heart of it, in my personal view, was the fact that the Heads of House could use the cane and the Heads of Department couldn't. A great number of people who came to the school saw a demotion of their ranks and standards. But they were second class citizens because they couldn't cane.[5]

It was for this reason that the Head considered there was a request to move away from a system where eight houses existed. Indeed, he pointed to the way in which attempts were made to change the pastoral system to something that the staff:

Thought would apply disciplinary procedures, more carefully, more evenly, and perhaps all for changes in discipline
generally. There was a small element which believed we
should abolish the pastoral system, even then, seeing it as an
interruption to the traditional pattern of English education.
The teachers were there to teach and not to molly coddle
children. I didn't want to change, but I recognized that by this
time I was one amongst 80 – I recognized that I wasn't a soul
source of wisdom. By this time there were a number of people
with a number of years' experience in comprehensives, and I
listened, and ultimately the compromise that we arrived at,
which got about 70 per cent of the full staff voting for it, was
to alter the vertical houses into half vertical houses. Con-
centrating 7 or 8 houses into four, with an upper and a lower
half each. And that was the structure that did us, and does us
to this day.[6]

Indeed, as far as the Head was concerned this pastoral system of
four 'major' vertical houses subdivided into upper and lower
divisions performed five major tasks which he summarized in the
following terms:

1. They care for each child in a more detailed way than
    would be possible without some division of school. This
    care shows in home visiting, liaison with parents and
    support services, written and telephone messages,
    medical care, progress and encouragement of students,
    parties, expeditions, discos are often house based.
2. They share substantially in the religious care and forma-
    tion of pupils through assemblies, special masses and
    services and by their participation in formal RE
    Chaplains work closely with house staff over problems
    with particular children and families.
3. They are an important part of the administrative
    structure of the school, monitoring registration, punctu-
    ality, sickness, class structures in much of first to third
    years, supervision of arrangements for dinners (both free
    and paid).
4. They act as the third stage in discipline procedures,
    stages 1 and 2 being class and departmental based.
    Outside classes they represent level 1 in matters such as
    bounds, behaviour at break and lunch-time. Both de-
    partments and houses are involved in such matters as

disciplinary meetings and recommendations for suspensions.

5. The system also carries major responsibilities in matters of assessment reports, transfers to other schools, and references for those seeking jobs. Tutors and house staff offer counselling on all aspects of adolescence and about their futures to students.[7]

However, this system had been designed for a developing comprehensive school whose pupil population numbered almost 1500. But by 1983 falling rolls were beginning to make an impression upon the system. No longer were there sufficient pupils coming from primary schools to enter each house. Instead, first year pupils were allocated to only two houses – a situation that some teachers argued resulted in a change being considered.

3. Considering change: from mansion (house) to year group

It was this third phase that constituted the main part of my enquiry on pastoral care when I returned to conduct a restudy of Bishop McGregor School in the academic year 1983–4. Indeed, the first schoolwide staff meeting that I attended consisted of a discussion of the pastoral system.

The formal origin of this debate can be located in a request to the Head from the governors in the summer term 1983 to arrange investigations on alternative pastoral structures with special reference to year groups. However, house staff considered this was far too simple an explanation. Many teachers told me how they thought this enquiry came to be initiated. In particular, their explanations were linked to the social context of Bishop McGregor School. While some of these explanations rested on local circumstances such as the appointment of a new Chairman of Governors who had experience of a year system, others were linked to demographic trends that confronted all comprehensive schools and made reference to falling rolls, the subsequent redeployment of teachers and the reallocation of scale posts.

Among the pastoral staff, Ian James summed up the main factors that had resulted in the review when he commented:

I think the Chairman of the Governors was very keen for a change. I think he has obviously experienced other places where they've had the horizontal system and felt it was a little bit of his, sort of influence that came to bear on the school, for us to look into the pastoral system and come to see – to see if we can come to any conclusions about it. I think because of falling rolls, falling numbers, this is a significant factor as well, that the numbers are falling so much. We have got four houses, and it was obvious that in the future you wouldn't be able to maintain those four houses. And we would have to either reduce to three houses or go to the horizontal, so there's a movement afoot there, and we were asked to review the situation, which we have done.[8]

Certainly, many staff agreed with this diagnosis; especially as far as falling rolls were concerned. Indeed, even the Chairman of Governors who was considered to be keen to move to a horizontal system perceived the exercise as a task in restructuring that followed from a decrease in the size of the school. However, many teachers were aware that a reduced pupil population and restructuring of the pastoral system could have far-reaching consequences in terms of redeployment and the allocation of posts.

The Head of Sixth Form outlined the way in which restructuring from a house system to a year system would hold implications for House Heads when he remarked that we were also talking about:

the possibilities of redeployment. We are also now going to have a look at ten people, and I'm not talking about those on (scale) 2's who are helping the pastoral system, but – sorry eight people, here including myself who have got to change their jobs and there is only six jobs to go into.[9]

While redeployment was never publicly mentioned as part of the discussion on restructuring the pastoral system it was often privately discussed. For example, two senior teachers outlined their concerns. In response to a question on the future of his job Brendan Shine responded:

Well, at the moment I just don't know. It might be that I might be a year head, it could be that under the present system that I might be redeployed. There is as you know, at the moment, on paper, twelve people from this school to be redeployed this year. In fact, it is unlikely to be anything like that. And with I think, sixteen/seventeen other schools in the City also having to redeploy people, there being no compulsory redundancy, I just cannot see where there will be anywhere to redeploy people to. But it is a problem at the moment rearing its ugly head, so people are feeling a little bit 'unsettled' and are wondering what is going to happen. Well, if redeployment does not occur, we have got four heads of house plus four deputy heads of house, and the discussion really, has not yet started, as to what will be happening.[10]

This view of a pastoral system that was heavily oversubscribed in terms of staff was also held by another senior teacher who maintained that all the factors relating to pastoral care would need to be examined by a range of people. He considered that the Head rarely imposed decisions on the staff. In an interview with me, Dick Wilkinson explained the mechanisms that he thought were involved in the decision-making process when he remarked:

It is a very interesting thing, I mean, how far decisions are actually taken by, say the Head, and we, the staff, then fit into those positions, or how much do people sort of weigh it up for themselves and come to a sort of bit of a conclusion perhaps, the odd, implied sort of thing here and there that has its influence that way. I think it is a two way thing. I don't think that one could – perhaps in any organization – well certainly not in any school that I know of, sort of say that this person is, you know, making those decisions, you know sort of how far decisions are – perhaps again the word I used earlier – evolved within a school, obviously pushes in certain directions, but I don't think really within the school decisions are made – of this nature – are sort of set down – someone doesn't sit down and take them. The Head I don't think sits down and thinks it all through and then puts whatever wheels into motion for that to happen. I think that he is very susceptible to other people's ideas and their influence.[11]

Dick Wilkinson had been at McGregor School since the day it had opened and had had the opportunity to watch Goddard (the Headteacher) at work – 'playing the system', 'manipulating staff' and 'playing politics'. Certainly, these were all micro-political strategies that teachers were accustomed to Goddard using when schoolwide issues were under discussion. In this sense, Goddard used what Ball (1987) has identified as an interpersonal style of headship as he relied on face-to-face contact to fulfil his role. Debates concerning school organization and reorganization did not just take place in public meetings because the Head was adept at having 'quiet words' with individuals, and requesting private meetings with staff. He was also prepared to see individuals who wished to put proposals to him. The result was a series of bargains, negotiations, manipulations, co-optations and 'side bets' that accompanied any 'public decision' that was taken in staff meetings. Certainly, this was the case with the events leading up to the decision to restructure the pastoral system. For anyone concerned to develop an ethnographic account of the debate, it is the public meetings that are open to observation, while the private exchanges where gossip is transmitted, bargains are made and negotiations developed rely on private accounts that are subsequently provided by the individuals or more often an individual who is directly involved. In this case, we turn first to the public debate about pastoral care before briefly examining some of the accounts of private exchanges that had taken place with the Head.

Public meetings and private accounts

During the late autumn of 1983–4 the Head arranged for a staff meeting to occur where the pastoral system was to be debated. At the meeting, reports were provided by teachers who had made six visits to other schools in the authority with a view to examining their pastoral systems after which the Head outlined the way in which they would proceed when he said:

> If there is a strong move towards one position (a vertical or a horizontal system) I would be happy to have it debated and a motion put. But if further work is needed I would be happy to have a further staff meeting. The initial idea was to have a special governors' meeting in January. Some think this is too quick in which case it could go on the normal agenda in February.[12]

This statement complemented a paper from Gill Davies, a Deputy Head, who advanced a set of recommendations on behalf of the management team. It was apparent to staff that the Head and his deputies were intent on slowing down the discussion and retiming the meetings principally because they had further restructuring work to do. However, the staff were engaged in a form of 'pseudo-participation' (Ball 1987) as they were led to believe that they were involved in a genuine public debate where a decision could be taken. Here, several teachers spoke against reaching a sudden decision or having a situation imposed on them. When a proposal was made to evaluate the McGregor system of pastoral care and a range of other systems the Head used it to suggest that more work needed to be done and further discussions should occur. In summing up this discussion from the chair he advanced three proposals:

> First, maintain the status quo (i.e. vertical groups). Second, decide to change and then go on to decide what change. Third, look at the changes that are possible and have a further discussion.[13]

It was the final proposal that was seized on by two Heads of Departments who subsequently told me that they had supported this move as they wished to discover the hidden agenda that was within this public presentation. Yet in doing so they had helped the Head and the management team to exercise control over the discussion.

After the Christmas break it became apparent that alliances were formed among staff who supported the vertical system and those who advocated the horizontal system. In the first two weeks of term the following discussion papers were issued:

1. *Evaluation of a pastoral system at McGregor* written by the Head in which the advantages of the vertical system (in terms of home-school links, family connections and competition) were shown to outweigh the disadvantages (of standardization, mixed ages and standards of behaviour).

2. *A revised vertical house system at Bishop McGregor School* by a senior teacher who argued that continued use of the vertical houses is most easily accommodated within our buildings, even if we ignore our new role as a community school, but with our added commitments in this new area of education it will probably also enable us to use our buildings to the best advantage of all. It would also help to remedy the imbalance which has arisen in the distribution of 'points' for pastoral and departmental responsibilities.

3. Two papers on *house systems* prepared by a Head of Department who argued in favour of creating 'a First Year House ... with three vertical houses, a community

area with access to fifth formers and a block for all 16–19 year old students as the most suitable in 1984 since it solves some of our more significant problems'.

4. *A possible horizontal system at Bishop McGregor Community College* by a Deputy Head who had just taken up this appointment having been a Head of Department in McGregor. This paper outlined some of the advantages (eighteen) and disadvantages (three) of a year system. In addition, this paper outlined a staffing structure where senior teachers, and current House Heads could be used. It was also proposed that year heads should rotate between years two and five with 'a stationary Head of First Year probably a "Mother figure" who has a large proportion of her teaching commitment in the first year. She will do most of the liaison with primary schools and build closer links than are possible when four people are liaising.'

All these papers were prepared for a special staff meeting in early February when the school closed for the afternoon so that a three-hour staff meeting could be held to debate the various proposals that centred around the vertical versus the horizontal system, the role of co-ordinators and the role of women in the pastoral system – all topics that were advanced by the Head and his deputies. While these issues were publicly debated at the meeting they were also the subject of common room discussion and examined in subsequent meetings of staff, Heads of Houses and governors. These themes were also raised with me in a series of interviews that I conducted with teachers who worked in the pastoral system. It is, therefore, to these issues that we now turn.

A vertical or horizontal system

The public debate centred around the system of pastoral care that was most appropriate for McGregor School. However, for some participants among staff and governors the terms 'vertical' and 'horizontal' were confusing, so much so that one of the deputies had to explain the difference which was summed up as:

Horizontal means year system.
Vertical means straight up and down.[14]

Yet it was not merely these two options that were under

consideration as alongside these was the notion of a first year house and a sixth form house. For staff who worked in the pastoral system the main debate concerned the introduction of year groups to replace houses as this would influence their jobs and their status in the pastoral system and in the school. By the end of the first staff meeting many teachers considered that it was fairly evenly balanced in terms of those who favoured the vertical as opposed to a horizontal system. However, after a collective discussion, staff were given a questionnaire to complete to express their preferences; a strategy used by the management team to subdivide staff and avoid collective decision making. When the governors' meeting was held the Head could report 80 per cent of staff favoured a first year house and 84 per cent a sixth year house. He could also report that while 94 per cent of staff favoured change they were divided over whether this should be a year system or a house system. This reflected a considerable change in mood as the Head indicated when he reviewed the debate on the pastoral system:

> I think taking it from last March to this March [1984], it went substantially in favour of going to a year system. We then sent quite a number of members of staff out to look at schools that had recently changed and it swung substantially away from change, and by – if the vote had gone at the end of November 1983; it would have been 70 per cent against the change, but it didn't go then; at the request of the staff it was postponed until January, and I think it is fair to say that the advocates of changes, mobilized their forces, perhaps not consciously but perhaps with a certain amount of thought. I don't think there was any malice in it at all, but they organized the presentation of their case such that when it came to the vote the vote showed – it is very interesting – it showed a very substantial group in favour of a first year house, a very substantial vote in favour of a sixth form house, and then we had to clarify the issue in between. And it came out not hugely substantial, with something like 60–40 in favour of a rolling year system. There is an increasing number of 'don't knows' as the questions get more sophisticated.[15]

It was these results that were reported to the governors who were not prepared to just implement the systems advocated by staff. Instead, the Head and the new Deputy who had advocated a horizontal system were asked to present the case for each of the systems. In the end the governors arrived at a classic trade-off and compromise in relation to innovation and change (MacDonald and Walker 1976; Ball 1987). Here, it took the form of a first year house coupled with a horizontal system: a decision that meant there were no outright 'winners' as the Head had obtained support for a first year house, while the Deputy Head and the Chairman of Governors had brought about a change to a horizontal system. Only those who had to work the system had 'lost' out, for House Heads had wanted to maintain the status quo as they argued it was an easier way to liaise with families and to control groups of pupils. But no individual publicly stated a concern about his or her job – yet this was a major issue as the old system had provided twelve posts while the new structure seemed to only have ten positions available. Once the decision had been taken to move to a horizontal system with a first year house the debate took a new turn as individuals became concerned with their prospects for employment and redeployment.

Co-ordinators, employment and redeployment

In the early part of March after the governors had announced their decision to shift to a system of a first year house coupled with year groups the Head issued a paper to all Heads of Houses in which he stated that they would all need to submit applications for positions in the newly constituted pastoral system after which interviews would be held. This document proved to be inflammatory as the House Heads were aware that they could not all gain posts in the new system, yet they would not lose financially. Status was at issue.

In the house system, twelve staff had held posts and it was apparent that with senior teachers being used in the new system there would be surplus staff. One attempt to 'balance' numbers came from the Head and his deputies who proposed co-ordinators of the upper and lower school; a structure that would successfully employ all former house staff. When this system was discussed at a meeting of house staff it met with opposition from all House Heads. The Head had not 'squared' the house staff but had entered into an adversarial stance which Ball (1987) defines in terms of public meetings and consultation. However, Goddard responded to their opposition by stating:

> I'm not a democrat but I'm not an idiot. You wouldn't object
> to Dick Wilkinson [a senior teacher who was hotly tipped as a

co-ordinator] being a co-ordinator. You wouldn't object to him would you?[16]

But they did object. As the meeting proceeded, each of the House Heads spoke against the use of co-ordinators, arguing that such a system had not worked in a neighbouring school. However, one of the Deputy Heads attempted to assist the Head in confronting opposition by arguing that:

There is a need for individuals to pull together things which people feel they are doing in splendid isolation. There is a need to take up the work of the tutors.[17]

Meanwhile, the other Deputy argued that if the role of co-ordinator was accepted it would 'prevent moving people out of the pastoral side'.[18] However, the House Heads were not prepared to shift their ground as they argued that the co-ordinator posts lacked specification and introduced a further level into an already hierarchical system. Furthermore, they would lose status in the school as they would no longer control day-to-day school policy. Indeed, they were prepared to say privately that they saw a further layer in the formal organization of the school where they would be 'supervised' by senior teachers. This would result in them having no direct route to the deputies and to the Head.

When the senior management team found that the House Heads were not prepared to change their view, a further attempt was made to confront opposition as one of the deputies said:

What you all thought was: 'What am I going to do?'[19]

But this remark made no impact. It was clear that the House Heads would not collectively agree to this system. By the end of the meeting no decision had been reached and the Head announced that he would like them to think about their current roles but he asked:

Will you feed into me what you as a post holder want to do. I will make available a period to listen to each member of the pastoral team to discuss what jobs are available for each individual. I may also have a further collective discussion and consultation before going to the governors.[20]

Individual meetings did occur but no collective meeting ever took place. Here, the Head's attempt at an adversarial style had failed and so he returned to an interpersonal strategy where he could control meetings with individuals (cf. Ball 1987). These meetings took place in the Head's office prior to the Easter holiday and were supposedly private, but by the last day of term one staff member in the pastoral team was able to tell me the staffing system for the new structure; a system that was eventually ratified by the middle of May.

By this time one teacher had been persuaded to take a post in a department which it was argued would enhance his professional development, while three teachers were grafted into the fifth year as the Head considered one of them would be leaving before the end of the summer term. All the staff involved in the house system were now successfully accommodated in the year system. They had all been seen by the Head either for a meeting in his office or a brief word in the corridor – the location often depending on whether a scale 4 or scale 2 position was being offered in the pastoral system (cf. Ball 1987, pp. 88–95).

All the pastoral staff knew the positions that they were to hold in the autumn term of the following year but they all had to be 'interviewed'. Each 'interview' was with the Head and three governors. Members of staff appeared, were thanked by the Chairman for their work, had a new job title read to them and were asked if they had anything to say prior to leaving the room. For most staff a word of thanks was as much as was uttered so that staff interviews for all those engaged in the restructuring of the pastoral system took just over an hour. The staff were very critical of this procedure. As one teacher put it:

> They are called interviews but in many ways it was just a charade. I mean we were in and out and so on. I think it was perceived by the Head and the Chairman of the Governors as 'going through the motions of something that was legal' and they were legally obliged to do.[21]

While another remarked:

> I was shocked by the fact that we had to go for an interview, you know, we just got this little note to say 'report at such and such a time and that was it'. I didn't see why... The whole pastoral thing is a bit of a façade because it has all been done in a sort of very backward clumsy way.[22]

Nevertheless, charade or façade, teachers in the pastoral structure thought their posts were now settled and that a redeployment exercise that was taking place would exclude them. However, the

new pastoral system was still slightly over staffed. The result was
that two teachers who held posts in the pastoral system
subsequently received letters from the governors indicating they
were to be formally considered for redeployment, not because they
held pastoral posts, but because there was insufficient work in the
History Department where there were two men in addition to the
two women who held posts in the pastoral structure. One of the
women questioned the Head of Department about redeployment
and she reported him as saying:

> 'Oh, well, I'm the Head of Department they wouldn't move
> me and Bill's the number two in the Department, and so if it's
> not you it will be Penny.' So I said, 'What about the fact that
> my scale point is pastoral and that this year I haven't taught a
> lot of history, and in fact if it helped I'd say OK I'll teach less
> history because there wasn't very much last year', – 'Oh,
> you're a member of the History Department.' I said,
> 'Suddenly! suddenly, I'm welcomed back in the fold! That's
> very peculiar.' And I said, 'Some of Penny's points go
> towards pastoral as well', so I said, 'If we are going for
> members of the History Department, if you turn your
> argument round it's you and Bill' – 'No, no, no, no, no', then
> 'Don't let's be silly, don't let's be silly, it's nothing personal
> in this, we are all vulnerable.' But he didn't really leave us in
> any doubt, it is going to be one or other of us.[23]

This teacher had been applying for several posts earlier that year
and it was widely assumed by many staff that she would be
successful. In her view the Head had also made that assumption
with the result that she had been wedged into the year system only
to find that she could easily be removed as she was subsequently
nominated for redeployment. The position was only retrieved as
one teacher gained promotion in Home Economics and she
subsequently took over part of her timetable together with
responsibilities in the History Department and in the pastoral
structure. Within a term, she gained promotion out of the school
but she regarded the events that had occurred were indicative of the
position of women in the school and in the pastoral structure – a
view that was shared by several teachers.

Women in the pastoral system

When the school opened, equal numbers of men and women had

been recruited for the house system. However, as these women had moved into domestic responsibilities or gained promotion or retired they had been replaced by men. Gill Davies, a Deputy Head, summed up the situation by saying:

> I don't think that there is enough women in the pastoral system. But that isn't because the opportunities haven't been there. There just simply haven't been the candidates. It does concern me. that the pastoral system here is now 'male dominated'; perhaps that isn't quite the right expression, but you know what I mean – there are far more men in it than women, and there are far more men in senior posts than there are women. Again that isn't anybody's fault, and it certainly isn't the policy of the governors or the Head or anybody else. It's just been that when posts have come up – there are few women – few mature women still available for that kind of post when they become available. Within the school itself, I mean the proportions of men to women here, probably – I think I'm correct in saying that at the moment – I'll look the figures up for you in a minute – we're forty-odd men and twenty-nine women, I think, now that in itself says something. Proportionately, of course, you can't have the number of women in top posts. I'm not happy that there are sufficient women of maturity and strength to support the girls here. That does concern me. That the women that we have are good and kind and helpful and so on, that is all fine – still doesn't compensate for the lack of one or two women with experience and knowledge and so on to really take a front line.[24]

However, it was not just the number of women in pastoral posts, but the kind of women that members of the management team preferred. For Gill Davies it was 'sufficient women of maturity' which some staff (both male and female) interpreted to mean a search for the archetypal good Catholic woman, married with two children: an ideal for female pupils (cf. Griffin 1987). Indeed, this was the kind of person who they thought was required for the first year house when reference was made to a 'Mother figure'. Here, many of the women in the house system were openly critical.

> *Penny Simpson:* Women are often palmed off in the lower shores of the school or the younger years, I mean, the

'Mother figure' and I resent that. I resent it because it's being – you know, the assumption, 'they are alright for younger ones, but anything particularly academic or career minded they can't cope with'.[25]

Maggie Childs: Well what image in your mind do you have of Mother figures? Really nice and rounded, in their fifties and perhaps a grandmother as well and... you know, I think it is a load of nonsense. I think if you have a man who is good with the younger children, there is no reason why a man shouldn't be head of first year.[26]

However, many teachers thought that the term 'Mother figure' had been deliberately chosen as this matched their public perception of Mary O'Dowd who was a grandmother who had worked in primary schools before coming to Bishop McGregor School.

Mary O'Dowd indicated that Phil Barlow, the Deputy Head who had written the paper in which the phrase 'Mother figure' was used, had asked her if she objected to the term. She explained:

He didn't ask me about inserting it because he had already put it but he asked me would I be offended and I said 'no'. But he was jumped on by some – well... I suppose they are feminists [laughs] who have this thing about, you know, that they don't like this idea of putting people in compartments and saying 'it should be a Mother figure'.[27]

This suggests that in the view of management, Mary O'Dowd was to be responsible for first year; a situation that Gill Davies confirmed when she said:

Mrs O'Dowd was I think in everyone's [i.e. senior management's] judgement a first class person to take the first year.[28]

When Mary O'Dowd saw the Head he suggested she should write her own job description; a task that she did in consultation with the two deputies. In addition she was also asked about teachers who would be most appropriate for the position of Deputy. It was, therefore, to the position of Head of First Year that Mary O'Dowd was appointed, but unlike other year Heads she was only to be paid a scale 3 salary. To obtain a scale 4 post, in common with the male year heads, she was also required to take on the post of Head of the Remedial Department; a situation that the Head explained would give her access to the same number of pupils as her male counterparts.

The micro-politics of pastoral care

But how might these ethnographic data be interpreted? What do they tell us about the process of schooling? Both Hoyle and Ball have pointed to the importance of micro-politics in the organization of schools. Hoyle argues that:

> Micro-politics can be said to consist of the strategies by which individuals and groups in organizational contexts seek to use their resources of authority and influence to further their interests. (Hoyle 1986, p. 126)

Central to the study of micro-political processes are the strategies that are deployed by groups and individuals not only in meetings but also in corridors and staff rooms. In turn, these strategies also indicate the relative power of the parties involved. In Bishop McGregor School it is the power of the Head that defines the reality of reorganization and restructuring. It is the Head who is the critical reality definer in determining teachers' careers (cf. Riseborough 1981) just as he was when establishing school organization in a period of expansion (cf. Burgess 1983). However, in a church school the head is also accountable to the governors who are able to exercise power over the pattern of restructuring. In part, the Head and his management team together with the Chairman of Governors established different interest sets who pursued strategies especially in relation to those staff in the pastoral system. Among the strategies that Hoyle (1986) has identified are the following:

1. Dividing and ruling where private deals were eventually struck between the Head and different teachers within the pastoral system.
2. Co-optation where an individual such as Mary O'Dowd is co-opted into the system. Her willingness to be involved in establishing a first year house was central to the Head being able to advance this argument in favour of this system. Similarly, in the case of a pastoral teacher who could have mounted strong opposition to restructuring; co-optation involved diverting him into the departmental structure.

3. Controlling meetings where the Head utilizes his position from the Chair to summarize positions in such a way so as to impute consensus or to generate opposition. Certainly, this can be seen in the initial staff meeting when opposition to any change in the pastoral system was apparent. But the Head's summing up resulted in the possibility of change being kept on the agenda and referred to a future meeting.

4. Controlling information whereby the Head uses his power to make sure that only certain information becomes available for staff to take informed decisions. Often, as in this case, staff are able to piece together information about the procedures to be adopted. For example, the matching of staff to posts. However, the control of information also resulted in the restructuring of the pastoral system being kept separate from the redeployment of teachers within the school.

Conclusion

This ethnographic account of the restructuring of the pastoral system in a comprehensive school has provided another dimension to the study of pastoral care and to school organization. Indeed, it has allowed us to look at the way in which pastoral structures are intimately related to teachers' status positions, as well as to their financial rewards and material prospects. Secondly, this study has provided further evidence on school organization and the relationships established between a Head, his governors, his management team and his pastoral staff. Thirdly, it has also helped us to examine the way in which decisions are taken (or not taken) and how gender relations are maintained within the school. Finally, it has helped us to look behind the consensus and continuity implied in a joint letter written to parents by the Head and the Chairman of the Governors who claimed that:

> The Year Heads will act in the same way as the present House Heads and will co-operate with each other to ensure continuity and maintenance of the strong family links enjoyed by the school.[29]

To anyone reading this letter, the year-long discussion between the Head, governors, and staff would appear to have been little more than a process to bring about a cosmetic change rather than a debate in which teachers' interests, job prospects and status positions were at the centre of the political stage.

Acknowledgements

The research that is reported in this chapter was made possible by grants that I received from the University of Warwick Research and Innovations Fund and the Nuffield Foundation to whom I am most grateful. I am indebted to Stephen Ball and Hilary Burgess and to participants at the Xth International Sociology of Education Conference at Westhill College for their comments on an earlier draft of this chapter. I am also grateful to Sally Venables for efficiently producing a clean copy of the text.

Notes

1. All the names in this study are pseudonyms.
2. The main study follows on from a previous study conducted ten years earlier in 1973–4. The principal methods of investigation in the restudy included observation and participant observation and unstructured interviews. For a discussion of the study and the restudy see Burgess (1987).
3. Extract from an interview.
4. Job description contained in a set of further particulars written in 1973–4.
5. Extract from an interview.
6. ibid.
7. Extract from a document entitled 'Evaluation of pastoral system at McGregor' written by the Head of Bishop McGregor School in January 1984.
8. Extract from an interview.
9. ibid.
10. ibid.
11. ibid.
12. Extract from field notes.
13. ibid.
14. ibid.
15. Extract from an interview.
16. Extract from field notes.
17. ibid.
18. ibid.
19. ibid.
20. ibid.
21. Extract from an interview. For further analysis of such symbolic events see Ball (1987), p. 184.

22. Extract from an interview.
23. ibid. For further examples of this strategy see Ball (1987), especially Chapter 8.
24. Extract from an interview.
25. ibid.
26. ibid.
27. ibid.
28. ibid.
29. Letter from the Head and Chairman of Governors to parents in July 1984.

References

Ball, S.J. (1987) *The Micro-Politics of the School: Towards a Theory of School Organisation*. London, Methuen.

Benn, C. and Simon, B. (1972) *Half Way There*. Harmondsworth, Penguin.

Best, R., Jarvis, C. and Ribbins, P. (1977) 'Pastoral care: concept and process', *British Journal of Educational Studies*. Vol. XXV (2), 124–35.

Best, R., Ribbins, P., Jarvis, C. and Oddy, D. (1983) *Education and Care*. London, Heinemann.

Blackburn, K. (1975) *The Tutor*. London, Heinemann.

Burgess, R.G. (1983) *Experiencing Comprehensive Education: A Study of Bishop McGregor School*. London, Methuen.

Burgess, R.G. (1987) 'Studying and restudying Bishop McGregor School' in G. Walford (ed.), *Doing Sociology of Education*. Lewes, Falmer Press, pp. 67–94.

Corbishley, P. and Evans, J. (1980) 'Teachers and pastoral care: an empirical comment' in R. Best, C. Jarvis and P. Ribbins (eds), *Perspectives on Pastoral Care*. London, Heinemann, pp. 210–24.

Griffin, C. (1987) 'Review of schooling as a ritual performance', *British Journal of Sociology of Education*, 8 (1), 87–90.

Hamblin, D. (1978) *The Teacher and Pastoral Care*. Oxford, Blackwell.

Hoyle, E. (1982) 'Micropolitics of educational organisations', *Educational Management and Administration*. 10, 87–98.

Hoyle, E. (1986) *The Politics of School Management*. London, Hodder and Stoughton.

MacDonald, B. and Walker, R. (1976) *Changing the Curriculum*. London, Open Books.

Marland, M. (1974) (ed.) *Pastoral Care*. London, Heinemann.

Ribbins, P. and Best, R. (1985) 'Pastoral care: theory, practice and the growth of research' in P. Lang and M. Marland (eds), *New Directions in Pastoral Care*. Oxford, Blackwell, pp. 14–49.

Riseborough, G. (1981) 'Teacher careers and comprehensive schooling: an empirical study', *Sociology* 15(3), 352–81.

CHAPTER 2

Health Education, Sexuality and AIDS

Peter Aggleton, Hilary Homans and Ian Warwick

Introduction

By the beginning of January 1988, 1,170 men and women in Britain had been diagnosed as having AIDS and an estimated 50,000–100,000 others had been infected by the Human Immunodeficiency Virus (HIV), its putative cause. In the United States, some 49,000 people have been diagnosed with AIDS and an estimated $1\frac{1}{2}$ to 2 million others have been infected. In central African countries such as Zaïre, Uganda and Zambia, it has been estimated that some 5 to 10 per cent of the population has already been infected by the virus (Institute of Medicine, National Academy of Sciences, 1986).

In early 1986, the first government information campaign relating to AIDS and costing £2.5 million was announced. In November of the same year, a further £20 million was earmarked for a more co-ordinated and substantial programme of health education aimed at enhancing people's understanding of AIDS and making available options for minimizing the risk of its further spread. Both of these campaigns have aimed specifically to increase public awareness of the *sexually transmitted aspects* of the disease, and have tried to bring about behavioural change as a means of containing its further spread.

Unfortunately, the preliminary evaluations of the first of these two campaigns (which took the form of full page newspaper and magazine advertisements) carried out by both the Department of Health's own specialist advisers (DHSS, 1986) and by Mills *et al.*

(1986) at the University of Southampton indicate that if anything, people were *more* anxious and *less* knowledgeable about AIDS after the first of these campaigns than they had been beforehand. The second of these two investigations found that only 31 per cent of respondents in Southampton were aware of the advertisements and concludes somewhat pessimistically that the campaign:

> seems to have had little effect on the public's knowledge of AIDS, and the increased publicity may have caused some confusion about the principal causes of AIDS.

It is too early to predict what the outcome of the most recent campaign will be. In addition to newspaper advertising, it uses television, radio and billboard announcements in order to enhance public awareness of AIDS, as well as the steps that can be taken to minimize the risk of infection. However, research into the effectiveness of mass media campaigns in general as an approach to changing behaviour should make us less than optimistic about the possible outcomes. Gatherer *et al.* (1979), for example, argue that the most effective way of spreading health-related information is through word of mouth and personal contact, *not* through the mass media, and our own research (Aggleton, Homans and Warwick 1988) would seem to suggest that one of the unintended consequences of the recent campaign has been to suggest that *everyone* is at risk of AIDS, whether or not they involve themselves in activities likely to result in the transmission of HIV. This has tended to confuse people and raise their levels of anxiety, rather than inform and reassure.

Such a situation is clearly serious, not only for levels of public health but also for the members of those groups which have been quite erroneously identified by the popular press as the *causes* rather than the *first people to develop* AIDS. In Europe and North America, groups singled out for attention in this way have included gay and bisexual men, prostitutes and injecting drug users, as well as the residents of central African states such as Zaïre, Zambia and Uganda.

In this chapter, we intend to raise a number of questions about the role that health education can play in helping people respond to the challenges posed by AIDS. In order to do this, we will examine three rather different sets of issues.

First, we will focus on some of the assumptions and ideologies which underpin the way in which sex education in schools and elsewhere currently takes place. In doing this, we will identify some of the barriers which conventional sex education strategies create for effective education about AIDS.

Secondly, we will consider media representations of AIDS and the possible consequences of these for popular perceptions of risk. Reference will be made to preliminary findings from research carried out in connection with the project *Young People's Health Knowledge and AIDS*. As part of this work, a series of in-depth semi-structured interviews have recently been conducted with heterosexual and homosexual young women and men. These interviews have attempted not only to explore popular understandings of AIDS, but to locate this health knowledge within the broader context of lay theories about the causes of health and illness in general.

Finally, we will consider the relevance of four more general health education paradigms for effective AIDS education. These four *models of health education* emphasize information-giving, self-empowerment, community-orientation and social transformation respectively.

Education about sexuality

Reading the popular press today, one might be forgiven for assuming that the curriculum of British primary and secondary schools is awash with teaching about sexuality, and that in every classroom there is a sexually 'permissive' teacher preaching the virtues of polymorphous perversity and criticizing traditional 'family values'. In reality, of course, nothing could be further from the truth. Teaching about sex and sexuality is most usually conspicuous by its absence, and when sex education has been on the agenda, it has most often been within the context of concern about morals, social hygiene, sexual purity and the promotion of motherhood (Bland 1982).

In the present century, there have been, and there continue to be, perennial debates about who should teach sex education – whether this should be the prerogative of parents, the task of the education system or the duty of the state. However, the grim reality for many young people today is that either sex education does not take place at all or, if it does, it appears in a strangely contorted and token form. As Lee (1983), a sex educator working in London schools, has put it, the common reaction of teachers, parents and politicians has been to adopt a response of 'nervous neglect'.

Amongst parents in particular, sex education is afforded low priority.

> Well over 80% of the roughly 1500 teenagers I have seen in eight years of teaching say they have had *no* sex education *whatsoever* within the home. No member of their family explained to them how sexual intercourse takes place, how a baby is born or *why* sexual intercourse takes place.
>
> (Lee 1983, with emphasis added)

A recent survey of parents' attitudes to sex education conducted by the Policy Studies Institute (Allen 1987) has also found that parents do not see themselves as good sex educators. In this study, many parents stressed that they did not know how to express themselves when talking about sexuality with their teenage children, and most were very critical of the inadequacy of their own education in this respect. Of those surveyed, 96 per cent said that schools should provide sex education and over a quarter wanted schools to take sole responsibility for teaching their children about sex.

In the majority of schools, on the other hand, sex education makes spasmodic and sporadic appearances, most frequently under the guise of 'biology', 'personal hygiene' and 'physical education' and, more occasionally, as part of the personal and social education curriculum. As a teacher in Marshall and Smith's (1986) recent study explained:

> Sex education was taught in the third form in *one week* at the end of the summer term. During this week, a whole programme of films and specialised talks were organised by the head of Home Economics. It was a terribly limited programme which covered up the subject of sex education under the heading of 'health education'. It was very clinical. The whole stress was on hygiene and the prevention of misbehaviour... The whole emphasis was on VD and the pill. It relied very much on hidden notions of sin to keep the children clean.

It should come as little surprise to learn, therefore, that there is still a great deal of confusion in young people's minds about sex and sexuality. Lee (1983) cites examples of boys who believe that masturbation can cause sexually transmitted diseases, and who think that the word 'lesbian' means prostitute. She also quotes girls who know about the workings of the contraceptive pill but who believe that it should be inserted into the vagina, and others who believe that they cannot become pregnant the first time they have intercourse.

Ideologies of sexuality

Of course, such confusions are not simply the result of inadequately reconciled debates about whose responsibility sex education is. They also relate to contradictions between the ideologies and assumptions that underpin modern approaches to sex education.

From the beginning of the twentieth century, sex education in schools has been closely linked to a moral agenda whereby girls in particular should be directed 'away from promiscuity' towards parenthood (Bland 1982). The early proponents of sex education in Edwardian Britain argued that a certain amount of sexual knowledge was necessary to *protect* girls and young women and to ensure that they sought sexual 'satisfaction' within monogamy, motherhood and marriage. As Dr Elizabeth Sloan Chesser put it at the turn of the century:

> The longing of every normal woman is to find happiness in sex union, and to exercise her functions physically and psychically in marriage and motherhood is an eradicable instinct.
>
> (cited in Bland 1982)

In retrospect of course it has been shown that these early moves for sex education in schools had less to do with protection than with the *regulation* of female sexuality, something deemed essential at the time in order to protect racial purity and social hygiene (Bland 1982). Hygiene education (which was the most usual context within which sex education took place) thereby became an important forum for discussing not only hygiene itself but also moral and social restraint: the latter being particularly linked to the inculcation of respect for motherhood and domesticity (Davin 1979).

Prior to the late 1940s when the first official literature for use in schools was produced, teachers were dependent largely on popular sources for their teaching materials. Many of the early texts available were written by medical writers but subsequently these authors were joined by an ever-expanding number of sexologists. Within the tracts they produced, Marcell (1982) has identified the operation of two dominant modes of discourse. The first of these, which he calls the *obfuscatory paradigm* emphasizes the mystery of life itself at the expense of clear understanding.

So, for example, in response to the question 'Where do babies come from?', the wise parent or teacher in 1910 was advised to reply,

> This baby grew in mother's body. *God* has made a little room in mother's body purposely to hold a baby.
>
> (Hall and Hall 1910)

Nevertheless, accounts such as these were frequently linked to women's future role within the family as a nurturer of and provider for the child which 'God' had given her.

Looking at sex education materials available during the mid-twentieth century, the Birmingham Feminist History Group (BFHG 1979) has identified the beginnings of a disjunction between official ideologies relating to sex education in schools and those operating in popular literature at the time. While school-based sex education remained preoccupied with women's future role within the family, books and magazines for popular readership became more concerned to provide explicit information about the sex act itself. This brings us to the second of Marcell's paradigms – that which emphasizes *scientific* explanation.

This sought to blend evolutionary theory with botanical and zoological explanation to provide accounts of sexual activity which were none the less obscure. Many of the explanations offered within this logic began by describing the ways in which plants and animals reproduced, and made copious reference to 'seeds' and 'eggs'. In some of these accounts, there is only *one* 'seed' or 'egg'. Hence adults might claim:

> You began your life as a tiny egg that was inside your mother's body. This egg was not at all like a chicken's egg. It was not like any egg you have seen, but was just a tiny speck of an egg.
>
> (Levine and Seligman 1949)

In others, procreation involves both a *mother* seed and a *father* seed which 'meet' by some mysterious process to produce a baby. Thus,

> The daddy puts a little seed, that grows inside him, right inside the mother, and when the daddy's seed and the mother's egg get together the baby begins to grow.
>
> (Groves and Groves 1929)

Explanations such as these were frequently couched within

scientific-sounding terminology to give parents and teachers the chance to, as Hall and Hall (1910) put it, 'eliminate the personal element': something deemed eminently desirable within this objectivist mode of discourse. Furthermore, children were frequently introduced to the sexual activity of humans in a graded manner contingent upon their age. Hence, it was often presumed that younger children would have an easier time understanding the reproduction of simple organisms such as plants (via a consideration of the functions of stamens, pistils, anthers, calyxes etc.) than that of animals. A little later, the sexual behaviour of molluscs, oysters and fish might be explored more fully, but only at an advanced age were the wonders of human reproduction considered to be fully comprehensible.

These evolutionary and biological perspectives were subsequently superseded by a 'new realism' within scientific explanation in the 1960s and 1970s. Here, and perhaps stimulated by Piagetian research into the conceptual limitations of concrete operational thought, children were taught that,

> The penis consists of two [*sic*] long sausage like structures (and) the female anatomy can best be imagined as a person standing with two footballs one under each arm, and leaning slightly forwards. The footballs are the ovaries which produce the ovum (egg) each month, and are separate from the rest. The ovum crosses into the fimbriae (the fingers) and up the Fallopian tubes (the arms) into the body of the uterus (the body of the person). If it is not fertilised, the ovum is swept out into the vagina (the legs) and into the menstrual flow.
>
> (Bevan 1970, with emphasis added)

Pfeffer's (1985) more recent study of the ways in which women's and men's reproductive anatomy is portrayed in scientific and medical texts shows clearly how the language used to describe these organs is clearly gendered – the male reproductive system is frequently described as an *efficient factory* for the production of spermatozoa whereas the female reproductive system is most frequently described in terms of its *pathology*. Similarly, spermatozoa are frequently represented as active and competitive, in contrast to the passive and docile ovum.

> As cells, spermatozoa are in a class by themselves . . . It is an *actively mobile* cell, in many ways resembling a free living

micro-organism, whose only function is to race in the direction where an ovum may be *waiting* to be fertilized – and to be the first of some 300 million competitors to reach the ovum.   (MacFarlane-Burnett 1973, with emphasis added)

To these two dominant paradigms about sex education (the obfuscatory and the scientific) must be added a third more *romantic* one which has sought to link sexual expression to untheorized and unproblematic notions of heterosexual love and desire. Thus, it has been claimed that,

> When a man and a woman who *love* each other go to bed, they like to hug and kiss. Sometimes, if they both want it, the man puts his penis into the woman's vagina and that feels really good for both of them. Sperm comes out through the man's penis. If one sperm meets a tiny egg inside the woman's body, a baby is started, and the man and the woman will be the baby's parents.
> (Gordon and Gordon 1974, with emphasis added)

Within the romantic paradigm, which incidentally operates blithely unaware of women's and men's very different experiences of penetrative sexual intercourse, sex education becomes tied once more to a moral agenda emphasizing personal responsibilities and commitments usually expressed within the context of *love* and *marriage*.

Sex education and familialist ideology

This third approach to sex education was the one which most informed early official documents relating to sex education in schools. One of the first of these, *Sex Education in Schools and Youth Organisations* (Board of Education 1943), for example, argued that the 'difficult and delicate task' of sex education should not only provide information about the physiology of sexual activity, but should aim to help young people gain 'control of (their) sexual impulses and emotions in preparation for the ultimate goal of marriage'.

Implicit in its recommendations were normative and function-alist conceptions of family relationships, in which appropriately regulated sexual behaviour was intimately linked to procreation and childcare for girls, and to the no less thorny question of heterosexual fidelity (after marriage) for boys.

The Handbook of Health Education (Department of Education 1956) was the first official document in Britain to recommend that sex education should be a subject in its own right. Underpinning the approach it took to sex education was a peculiarly

> Freudian view of sexuality as a series of stages ultimately resolved in heterosexual monogamy, with motherhood as an additional obligation for mature femininity.
>
> (BFHG 1979)

Notions like these were consolidated by both the Crowther (1959) and Newson (1963) Reports. The Crowther Report, in particular, argued that schools had a special role to play in preparing academically less able girls for marriage and parenthood. In keeping with the pervasive dual standard in this respect, it had little specifically to say about the sorts of preparation for adult life that less able boys should receive. The Newsom Report on the other hand while acknowledging the existence of 'profound differences (of opinion) in society about (the value of) pre-marital intercourse and about the permanence of marriage' pre-empted all debate about these in favour of the view that boys and girls should be offered 'firm guidance on sexual morality based on chastity before marriage and fidelity within it'.

It was not until 1977 and the publication of *Health Education in Schools* that a severing of the connections between sexual activity, marriage and procreation can be found in official statements about sex education. Its authors argued that sex education is best viewed as a complex phenomenon,

> bound up with the physical, emotional and mental development of children, especially in adolescence, and for *many* with their not too far distant prospect of parenthood.
>
> (DES 1977, with emphasis added)

Nevertheless, in keeping with what by now was a well-established tradition, this report too had little concrete to say about the nature and value of either non-genital modes of sexual expression or non-heterosexual relationships.

This breaking of the links between heterosexual activity, marriage and procreation proved to be short-lived, however, and the most recent statement on health education *Health Education from 5 to 16* (HMI 1986) once again argues that sex education should be, presented in the context of family life, of loving relationships and of respect for others: in short, in a moral framework.

And not just *any* moral framework it would appear from reading between the lines of this pamphlet, but one which values above all other forms of sexual expression those that are linked most closely to normative conceptions of family life.

Health Education from 5 to 16 is also relatively explicit for the first time in its treatment of non-heterosexual relationships. While arguing that 'there has been a marked shift away from the general condemnation of homosexuality', a claim which is itself questionable, this document adopts a patronizing and neo-Freudian tone in arguing that an attraction to members of the same sex is no more than, 'a *phase passed through* by many young people' (emphasis added).

Sex education and heterosexism

Within these three competing paradigms concerning how teachers and parents might best approach sex education (the obfuscatory, the scientific and the romantic) are a number of recurrent themes which seek to *privilege heterosexual activity* above all other forms of sexual expression. The first of these argues forcefully for both the 'naturalness' and 'inevitability' of heterosexuality: be it amongst daffodils, strawberries, oysters, lions, elephants, dogs or humans. Homosexuality, bisexuality, let alone other non-genital forms of sexual expression are, above all, conspicuous by their absence. When reference is made to these other forms of sexual expression, and this tends to occur only in those sex educational materials that have been prepared specifically for an *adult* readership, they are relegated either to the realms of *perversion:*

> the word perversion should only be used ... where heterosexual intercourse is consistently bypassed in favour of other sexual activities.
>
> (Cauthery, Stanway and Stanway 1984)

or of *handicap:*

> Like their male counterparts, lesbians are handicapped by having only half the pieces of the anatomical jigsaw puzzle.

Just as one penis plus one penis equals nothing, one vagina plus one vagina still equals zero.

(Reuben 1969)

Alternatively, they may be described as phases to be 'passed through' or 'got over' en route to the El Dorado of heterosexual bliss.

Why are some people homosexual? The short answer is that no one knows. As we have seen the vast majority of boys go through a developmental stage around puberty during which some degree of homosexual behaviour is normal, and many experts believe that most adult homosexuals have remained frozen at this stage of their development.

(Cauthery, Stanway and Stanway 1984)

A second theme is that which equates sexual expression narrowly and *genitally* with procreation. Thus, biological reproduction, which is logically the *consequence* of certain forms of heterosexual activity, comes to be seen as the *cause* and motivating principle behind all 'natural' forms of sexual expression.

A third theme seeks to establish clear-cut differences between the two partners involved in 'valid' sexual acts. In doing this, it sets up different roles for each to play within the pre-ordained and highly conventional heterosexual scenario. These usually assign to men the role of initiation within sexual activity and to women the supposedly complementary role of acquiescence (see Dworkin 1981 and Jackson 1984a for critical reviews of these accounts). They also suggest the desirability, indeed the near inevitability, of bodily penetration in 'authentic' sexual encounters (Jackson 1984b). All other forms of sexual expression are thereby presented as preliminaries (foreplay), optional extras or substitutes for the 'real thing'.

Pollock (1985) has recently extended this analysis to suggest that modern heterosexual activity has become increasingly geared to male pleasure. Evidence for this can be seen in the widespread adoption of contraceptive practices which are deleterious to women's health (the IUD, the contraceptive pill), but which are less likely to interfere with men's enjoyment of penetrative vaginal intercourse.

So pervasive is this third theme, and so powerful is it in naturalizing particular social and sexual scripts, that in books such as Comfort's (1972) *The Joy of Sex* (sub-titled 'A Gourmet

Guide to Lovemaking'), it is little coincidence that vulvas, penises and beds are listed under 'Starters', the missionary position under 'Main Course', and bisexuality, excesses and safe sex under 'Problems'. Indeed, as Jackson (1984b) has pointed out:

> the very term 'sexual intercourse' which could in theory mean any form of sexual interaction, is in practice synonymous with coitus in everyday speech as well as in the scientific literature.

Modes of sexual expression which are non-genital in character, or in which the relations between partners, be they physical or otherwise, are less unequal, are rarely to be mentioned in readily available educational materials.

In the light of the preceding analysis, any concern that the images and understandings of sexuality commonly available to young people in modern sex educational materials might pose a serious threat to 'conventional' sexual practices and 'established' moral values would seem premature, to say the least. Official prescriptions about sex education, as well as those materials readily available to parents and teachers, operate with an almost uniform commitment to heterosexuality, procreation and 'traditional' role relationships between women and men. Any inroads that the recent 'positive image' education policies of a few education authorities (such as the Inner London Education Authority and the London Boroughs of Haringey and Ealing) may have made into this state of affairs would seem so far to have been minimal in their effect. Indeed, in a recent survey of the experiences of young lesbians and gay men in *London* schools, 60 per cent said that the topic of homosexuality had *never* been mentioned in any lessons at school, and of those who said that the topic *had* been mentioned, 80 per cent said that this had been in a way which was unhelpful to them (Warren 1984).

Some problems for AIDS education

At this point it would seem useful to consider some of the implications of the approaches to sex education so far identified for effective AIDS education. By equating 'authentic' forms of human sexual expression narrowly and genitally with penetrative vaginal intercourse between a woman and a man, official ideologies informing modern styles of sex education are likely to militate against the adoption of 'safer' forms of sexual expression within the context of AIDS. Unprotected vaginal intercourse is of course one of the most effective means of transmitting HIV from man to woman (Institute of Medicine, National Academy of Science 1986) and woman to man (MMWR 1985; Calabrese and Gopalakrishna 1986).

Moreover, if non-penetrative forms of sexual activity are represented as somehow lacking in 'authenticity', or as 'pre-liminaries' or 'substitutes' for the 'real thing', and if forms of contraception which limit male pleasure (but which also prevent the transmission of HIV) come to be seen as somehow less 'acceptable' than those which do neither of these things (the IUD and the contraceptive pill), then there may be real problems for programmes of health education which seek to re-orient hetero-sexual expression away from those activities which are likely to result in the exchange of body fluids between two partners.

Popular representations of AIDS

Before considering the varieties of health education intervention possible within the context of AIDS, it is important to identify a second set of factors which may militate against the widespread adoption of safer forms of sexual practice. These relate to the popular understandings that people operate with in making sense of health and illness in general and AIDS in particular. Some of these are likely to relate to recent media representations of AIDS. Others will have their origins in the folk and lay understandings that people operate with in making sense of health and disease.

Media responses to AIDS

Until very recently media representations of AIDS in Britain have identified it as a predominantly *gay* issue. Even supposedly 'quality' newspapers such as *The Times* have fallen prey to this common misconception. To quote from an editorial published in 1984:

> The infection's origins and means of propagation excites repugnance, moral and physical, at promiscuous *male homosexuality* ... Many members of the public are tempted

> to see AIDS (as) some sort of retribution for a questionable
> style of life.
>
> (*The Times* 1984, with emphasis added)

More recent reporting has done little to remedy early inaccuracies
such as these. The *People*, for example, recently claimed to have
'discovered' that:

> AIDS is not *just* a gay disease – victims now include a
> rocketing number of heterosexual men, women and children.
>
> (*People* 1986)

But by using the word 'just', the report effectively reinforces the
misperceptions that many people have. It should come as little
surprise, therefore, to find that 44 per cent of the respondents
questioned in Vass's (1986) study of public opinion and AIDS felt
that homosexuality *per se* was the cause of AIDS. Only 14 per cent
identified a viral etiology for the syndrome. In the light of this
evidence, there would seem to be good reason for supposing that
popular perceptions of AIDS are presently bounded by an agenda
which, in Watney's (1986) words:

> blocks out any approach to the subject which does not
> conform in advance to the values and language of a
> profoundly homphobic culture – a culture, that is, which
> does not regard gay men as fully or properly human.

Further evidence supportive of such a claim can be found in recent
statements by popular journalists:

> We are constantly invited to feel sorrow for individuals who
> suffer from the disease (AIDS) and for the *homosexual
> community* in which it flourishes... Those who choose
> unnatural methods of sexual gratification choose thereby to
> put themselves at risk... It is more important to protect the
> lives of those who might *innocently* and accidentally catch
> the disease than to protect the reputation of those who have
> caught the disease through their own self-indulgence.
>
> (Gale, in the *Daily Express* 1986)

and conservative social commentators:

> The attempt to suppress the moral aspects of AIDS won't
> work as anyone who looks at leaflets such as those from the
> Terrence Higgins Trust can see... *Homosexuals* appear to

get up to a range of ... bizarre and revolting practices which
are particularly unsafe if the skin is broken.
        (Anderson, in *The Times* 1986, with emphasis added)

Comments like these display levels of ignorance and prejudice
which are almost unbelievable in a modern supposedly rational
society, since they seem *ignorant* of the fact that AIDS is not
specifically a homosexual disease, *ignorant* of the fact that the
virus responsible for AIDS can be transmitted by any act (sexual or
otherwise) which involves the bodily exchange of blood, semen or
vaginal fluid, and *prejudiced* in their efforts to privilege above all
other forms of sexual expression those that are narrowly linked to
received notions of (again, ill-defined) 'normal' heterosexual
intercourse.

Media attempts to portray AIDS as a predominantly gay issue are
likely to be far reaching in their consequences, not only for
heterosexual perceptions of risk but also for societal reactions
towards a section of the community which has been scapegoated as
the 'cause' rather than the first to be affected by a life-threatening
disease. But in order to understand popular responses to AIDS
more fully, we must also take into account the effects that lay
perceptions of health and illness may have in disorienting
professional health messages.

Lay understandings of AIDS

Co-existing with the professional understandings of health and
illness generated within medicine are popular or lay beliefs about
health. These operate so as to 'make sense' of an individual's state
of illness or well-being. Lay beliefs about health are generally
syncretic in origin (Fitzpatrick 1984), being derived from a variety
of sources. The claims that they make may also be contradictory in
some respects (Blumhagen 1980). Additionally, there is often some
degree of overlap between lay and professional explanations of ill-
health, with health professionals themselves subscribing to both
these sets of beliefs, and lay beliefs being influenced by those
advances in medical knowledge that are popularly known about
(Helman 1978).

In our work associated with the project *Young People's Health
Knowledge and AIDS*, we have begun to explore the nature of
popular perceptions of AIDS. Amongst those that we have
interviewed, we have identified generally high levels of awareness
with respect to the nature and transmission of AIDS.

Most young people we have talked to recognize that AIDS is a disease for which there is, at present, no cure – 'a killer disease' as many describe it. What is more, amongst these same young people there seem to be reasonable levels of awareness concerning the principal ways in which AIDS can be transmitted – via blood, shared needles and unprotected sexual intercourse.

But co-existing alongside health beliefs such as these are other less accurate perceptions. In particular, there would seem to be some scepticism about the accuracy (or otherwise) of official explanations of AIDS. Some of our respondents go so far as to suggest that there have been attempts to cover-up the 'true' incidence of AIDS within the general population and the ease with which the disease can be transmitted.

In making sense of these perceptions, our enquiries have led us to identify the existence of three powerful *lay models of causation* which underpin the ways in which young people and others 'make sense' of AIDS. Although we are only just beginning to identify the internal dynamics of these models, we would suggest that *miasmatic, serendipitous* and *endogenous* lay theories of causation may serve as important disorienting devices in mediating the impact of official health education messages.

We have, for example, frequently encountered the miasmatic belief that:

> There's a lot of it around, this AIDS. It's everywhere. You get it from the environment you live in, the people you mix with and what have you.

Coupled with this, many of those we have interviewed believe that whether or not they personally are likely to fall prey to infection depends very much on chance or luck. In making sense of these views, it is important to recognize that these same respondents make similar claims about the likelihood of their contracting sexually transmitted diseases in general.

> 'Why do some people get AIDS and not others?' Uh, luck. OK, there's a little bit of limiting or trying to limit the amount of risk... But I think with everybody it's just luck.

Concurrent with both miasmatic and serendipitous lay theories of causation are others which suggest that AIDS (like cancer, so some of our respondents claim) may already be present within us all. Like the creatures in the film *Alien*, AIDS may lurk endogenously within us, simply awaiting the right combination of circumstances to appear.

AIDS? Oh people are born with it. It's in them from the start.
It's something you can carry and not get it.

The complex relationships between these lay theories of causation, the states of well-being and illness to which they relate, and AIDS itself, is only just beginning to be unravelled in our work. Nevertheless, before examining in detail the approaches to health education that can be used to help people learn about AIDS, it is possible to make some preliminary comments about some of the issues that any effective programme of educational intervention relating to AIDS will have to address.

Some further problems for AIDS education

In the light of our discussion so far, it would seem essential that health educators working to develop effective AIDS education strategies recognize the importance of a full discussion of sexuality within the initiatives they develop. At the present time, popular perceptions of 'authentic' forms of heterosexual expression are bounded by an agenda which ascribes highest status to those activities which in fact carry the *greatest risk* of transmission so far as HIV is concerned (penetrative forms of intercourse involving the exchange of body fluids). As we have seen, these perceptions are reinforced and reproduced by the narrow way in which human sexuality is portrayed within the three major paradigms in which sex education is currently carried out.

Secondly, people working in AIDS education will need to anticipate the disorienting effects which media representations of the syndrome and 'common sense' understandings of health and illness can have on official health education messages. Miasmatic, serendipitous and endogenous lay theories of causation, as well as the media-propagated belief that AIDS only affects certain groups of people, can powerfully influence the extent to which individuals perceive themselves to be at risk of infection. Health educators will clearly need to identify strategies to circumvent these effects if their interventions are to be successful.

So far, via a critique of existing forms of sex education and by an examination of the ways in which AIDS has been popularly represented, we have tried to identify some of the factors which need to be taken into account within future approaches to AIDS education. In the final section of this chapter, we intend to move beyond critique to explore some of the options open to those who would seek to move beyond the difficulties we have identified.

Towards effective AIDS education

In recent years a number of writers have begun to differentiate between the different styles or *models of health education* around which programmes of health education intervention can be organized (Tones 1981; Ewles and Simnett 1985; French and Adams 1986). These differentiate between the *goals* and *means* of particular health education initiatives. Amongst the better known models of health education of relevance to those working in AIDS education are those which emphasize *information-giving, self-empowerment, community-orientation* and *social transformation* (Aggleton and Homans 1987; Homans, Aggleton and Warwick 1987).

Information-giving approaches to AIDS education

Information-giving is by far the most familiar health education strategy and has underpinned many of the recent AIDS education initiatives devised by the Department of Health in Britain as well as those of many local health and education authorities. In a recent article identifying health education priorities to do with AIDS, a Medical Officer at the Health Education Council argued that:

> The first aim of education must be to *make information widely available* about the size and characteristics of the epidemic... Information about the numbers and types of cases and carriers of AIDS is important for professionals and the public in order to combat ignorance and unrealistic fear... Further information about the way infection is transmitted is crucial in taking steps to contain the epidemic.
> (Kurtz 1986, with emphasis added)

In its own work, the Department of Health has felt it important to alert people to the 'facts' about AIDS – its signs and symptoms as well as the ways in which it is 'spread'. As part of its 1987 campaign, every home in Britain has received a leaflet on AIDS, and newspapers, radio and television have been used to disseminate 'public information' messages such as 'AIDS: Don't

Die of Ignorance' and 'The Longer You Believe AIDS Infects Others, the Faster It'll Spread'.

Local health education initiatives within this paradigm have aimed to increase public awareness of AIDS via the use of posters, leaflets and talks by physicians, health education officers and other 'experts' (Griffiths *et al.* 1985). Many of these have identified as their first priority, information-giving exercises in which factual information about AIDS is made available to as many people as resources allow.

By and large, information-giving models of health education operate from the assumption that women and men are rational decision-makers and posit a relatively direct relationship between three supposedly discrete variables – knowledge, attitudes and behaviour. They take individual behaviour change as their primary goal, and advocate the use of relatively didactic pedagogic strategies while recognizing that 'knowledge' may need to be packaged differently to meet the needs of particular client groups.

There are many reasons though why we should be sceptical about the likely effects of health education interventions which use information-giving as their sole means of bringing about behavioural change. First, although these strategies have been widely used in tobacco, drugs and alcohol education, there is little evidence that they produce immediate or lasting effects (Gatherer *et al.* 1979). Second, information-giving approaches to AIDS education have to contend with difficulties created by the fact that they advocate those very forms of heterosexual expression which have been rendered *inauthentic* by the discourse of modern sex education – those which do not involve bodily penetration or which, by ensuring that there is a physical barrier to the exchange of body fluids, interfere with male pleasure during the sexual act. Finally, of particular importance in determining how people respond to health education messages are lay beliefs about health (Helman 1978; Fitzpatrick 1984; Herzlich and Pierret 1986). From our earlier analysis of young people's beliefs about AIDS, there is every reason to believe that lay beliefs about the syndrome may act as powerful filters of official health education messages.

Such an analysis is supported by findings from a recent study amongst sexually active heterosexuals conducted for the San Francisco AIDS Foundation (NYN 1986). This concluded that although those surveyed seemed generally well informed about AIDS and its modes of transmission, 40 per cent of them were in fact at 'high or medium' risk for infection: having had sex in the last twelve months with four or more different people, with prostitutes, gay or bisexual men or intravenous drug users. Of the men interviewed 15 per cent said they had had sex with 10 to 20 different female partners during the last year and 10 per cent of the women reported having had 8 to 20 different male sexual partners. Yet 66 per cent in total reported that they did not use condoms during oral or vaginal intercourse and few felt themselves personally threatened by AIDS. In a city in which publicity about AIDS is marked by its omnipresence and sophistication, and in which there have been truly remarkable shifts amongst gay men to safer forms of sexual expression, such findings are quite alarming.

The most effective interventions within the information-giving paradigm tend to have been those linked to discrete and identifiable behavioural changes, and in which information is spread through personal contact and word of mouth, *not* through the mass media (Gatherer *et al.* 1979). In this respect, there may be much to be learned from the AIDS health education campaign developed by the Los Angeles Co-operative risk-reduction service. Using the theme 'LA Cares . . . like a Mother', the campaign utilizes posters, public service announcements, display advertisements as well as a wide variety of handout material (calling cards, pamphlets etc.) to communicate a number of simple health education messages linked to *discrete* and *specific* behavioural changes. These messages include 'Say "NO" to Unsafe Sex', 'Don't Forget your Rubbers', and 'Don't Use Needles'. One of the most striking aspects of the campaign has been its use of a positive figure – MOTHER – who is seen in the publicity material (and at live appearances) giving sound advice to her various SONS on what they should and should not do. MOTHER is played by the distinctive actress Zelda Rubinstein and her SONS were deliberately chosen so as to project, in the words of the advertising agency handling the campaign, 'a slight sexuality as an attention-getting device'.

In contrast to present British campaigns, the *LA Cares* initiative has sought to *personalize* its messages. MOTHER attends small group meetings around the city of Los Angeles and throws parties at which she urges her favourite SONS to spread her health education messages on a one-to-one basis. While the campaign was devised to address the specific health needs of the Los Angeles gay community, there is no reason to believe that similar approaches might not prove effective amongst other client groups.

Self-empowerment approaches to AIDS education

In contrast to information-giving models of health education, self-empowerment approaches aim to be more experiential and client-centred in their operation. In particular, they argue that individuals should be provided with opportunities in which to explore the extent to which their anxieties and feelings about a particular issue may block the ability to act rationally. The major aim of self-empowerment models of health education is to identify and work with individuals' personal needs so as to extend the range of existential choices open to them. Self-empowerment approaches to AIDS education are likely to advocate the use of group-based and participatory styles of learning whereby each person's knowledge and feelings about a particular issue can be made available and used as a resource for the group as a whole. Ideas like these have underpinned the approaches to AIDS education advocated by writers such as Spence (1986) and to a lesser extent Tatchell (1986).

In our view, however, the concept of self-empowerment is highly problematic since it seems to suggest that the process of self-empowerment and the skills thereby developed are *sufficient* for the individual to actually become more powerful. The major problem with this approach is that it marginalizes the effects of *systematically structured inequalities* between people in limiting the expression of personal power. Someone who has been through an experience which enables them to 'reclaim their power' or their sense of 'personal efficacy', for example, may *feel* more stronger, more self-important and more confident, but unless the original conditions which led to their feeling powerless in the first place are changed, then these enhanced feelings are likely to evaporate on the next occasion that their real cause is encountered. For example, people may leave a workshop on 'safer' forms of sexual expression with every intention of adopting these in future, but may then find their options blocked by the expectations of their sexual partners.

It is not enough for individuals to participate in their own learning experiences. They need also to participate in the decision-making processes that affect day-to-day life (and which make resources available). Self-empowerment can therefore be a *first step* in enabling people to gain greater self-confidence, but action to tackle the fundamental causes of disability and ill-health is also needed if this approach to AIDS education is to be anything other than a device to placate and 'cool out' members of the communities who have suffered most from the epidemic.

Community-oriented approaches to AIDS education

Community-oriented approaches to health education attempt to move away from the idea that individuals are responsible for their own health to suggest that people should act collectively to identify and act upon the environmental and community-based factors which affect their well-being. A distinction can usefully be drawn between community-oriented initiatives which have their origins in issues which health educators and policy makers have defined as important and those which arise from the concerns of self-help groups organized around particular health issues (Beattie 1986).

Within the context of AIDS education, the Terrence Higgins Trust is a good example of a self-help group which arose originally to meet the educational and counselling needs of gay men, but whose activities have been extended dramatically in recent months to provide services to intravenous drug users, women and church-goers (amongst other groups). The success of this and other groups in providing realistic and appropriate information on 'safer' sex and health education more generally has been widely recognized as a significant factor in slowing down the rate of HIV transmission amongst gay men. There is some evidence therefore that community-oriented approaches to AIDS education can be relatively successful in meeting a wide range of needs. However, for AIDS-related health education to have long-term effectiveness, there is growing recognition that it must be linked to changes in legislation and resource allocation as well as to interventions which will ensure a more balanced media reporting of the issues. These changes can be seen as part of a more socially transformatory approach.

Socially transformatory approaches to AIDS education

In contrast to information-giving and self-empowerment models of health education, which operate largely at the level of the individual, and community-oriented initiatives, which tend to be relatively limited in their goals, socially transformatory approaches to health education aim to enhance health and well-being by bringing about far-reaching social change. It is possible to identify four inter-related aspects of society which AIDS educators working with a commitment to social transformation will need to address in their work – ideologies about health and sexuality, the social relations to which these give rise, the micro- and macro-politics of AIDS, and resource allocation. Within the context of this article it is only possible to begin to spell out what this alternative approach to health education might look like. A more complete analysis of the issues involved can be found in Aggleton and Homans (1987).

With respect to ideologies, a socially transformatory approach to AIDS education might seek to challenge both the medicalization of the syndrome and the extent to which popular understandings of AIDS have been informed by racism and homophobia. Much of what presently counts as medical knowledge about AIDS would need to be de-mystified and replaced by more accessible medical understandings in which scientific arguments are clearly separated from moral considerations. For example, present medical knowledge does *not* suggest that it is the number of sexual partners *per se* which increases the likelihood of contracting HIV infection. Rather, the particular acts that are engaged in with these partners are crucial in determining whether or not the virus is transmitted. Non-penetrative forms of sexual expression which do not involve the exchange of body fluids do not result in the transmission of the virus. Yet relatively few people seem aware of this, believing instead that it is *medical* evidence (rather than moral proscription) which suggests that a high number of sexual partners will itself increase the risk of infection.

Similarly, many popular understandings of AIDS seem currently to be influenced either by the view that AIDS is 'caused' by gay men or that it has 'spread from Africa'. In a situation where we simply do not know what the origins of the virus are (and where quite possibly we never will know this – how many viruses do have clearly identified origins?) views like these can be used to advocate the unequal treatment of gay men (through quarantine) and people entering the country from Africa (through immigration control). Health educators committed to social transformation would very quickly find themselves involved in struggles to counter the racism and homophobia generated by these sorts of interpretations.

In terms of social relations, one of the greatest challenges to be faced by health educators working with a socially transformatory model of health education will be that of encouraging increased understanding and concern for those who have (or are assumed to have) HIV infection. Already, criteria identifying the 'innocent' and 'guilty' victims of the disease have achieved wide circulation. Increasingly, health educators may wish to act politically as the advocates and allies of particular client groups.

Additionally, health educators working with this model may have to consider the extent to which they can restrict their activities as health educators simply to the professional sphere of practice. At least four additional arenas of intervention are open to those who would wish to extend their role in this way. *Personally*, health educators may have to make changes in their own lifestyles and sexual practices. *Professionally*, they may wish to establish contact with groups and organizations routinely perceived as beyond the remit of conventional health education practice (trades union, gay and lesbian community groups, body positive groups etc.). At a *peer group* level, it may be necessary to educate colleagues and friends who feel uncomfortable with socially transformatory approaches to health education in general and AIDS education in particular. Finally, for some health educators there may also be an arena of *parental* intervention within the home and elsewhere. All four of these arenas provide opportunities for interventions to re-orient popular understandings of sex and sexuality away from those which privilege the status of penetrative vaginal intercourse between one woman and one man.

Socially transformatory approaches to AIDS education also advocate the development of a more genuinely *participatory politics of AIDS*. Opportunities may therefore need to be provided for members of the popular constituencies most affected by AIDS to meet and systematize their experiences and insights. As a result, people may become more critically conscious of the possibilities and limitations associated with existing forms of health and social service provision. Health educators may also have a role to play in fostering popular alliances between health care workers and community groups involved in work to do with HIV infection and AIDS. These alliances may subsequently generate new approaches to health education intervention and health care provision.

Last but not least, socially transformatory models of health education would advocate that health education be directed at those who currently control access to resources such as housing, health and social service provision and insurance benefits (amongst other things). Attention might also need to be focused on priorities to do with central government resource allocation and the extent to which the development of vaccines, therapies and treatments for AIDS should be left to private sector initiatives.

At the present time, it is only possible to spell out schematically the main features of this fourth model of health education since as yet there have been few concerted attempts to allow principles such as these to inform AIDS education in practice.

Conclusions

In this chapter, we have tried to spell out some of the issues which need to be addressed by those seeking to develop effective initiatives within the field of AIDS education. We began by first identifying some of the barriers posed by present sex education practices in schools and elsewhere for effective education about AIDS. We then explored some of the ways in which popular and lay understandings of the syndrome may further disorient the impact of official health education messages. Finally, we have considered some of the strengths and limitations of four rather different styles of health education for present and future approaches to AIDS education. If this chapter stimulates debate and constructive criticism amongst those who have a responsibility for AIDS education, our intentions will have been achieved. If in turn this leads to new and effective AIDS education initiatives, then our aims will have been more than realized.

References

Aggleton, P.J. and Homans, H. (1987) *Educating about AIDS: a discussion document for community physicians, health education officers, health advisers and others with a responsibility for effective education about AIDS*. Bristol, National Health Service Training Authority.

Aggleton, P.J., Homans, H. and Warwick, I. (1988) 'Young people's health beliefs about AIDS' in P. Aggleton and H. Homans (eds) *Social Aspects of Aids*. Lewes, Falmer Press.

AIDS Newsletter (1986) *Condoms and their Sales*. (Item 433). London, Bureau of Hygiene and Tropical Diseases.

Allen, I. (1987) *Education in Sex and Personal Relationships*. London, Policy Studies Institute.

Beattie, A. (1986) 'Community development for health: from practice to theory', *Radical Health Promotion*. 4, 12-18.

Bevan, J. (1970) *Sex, the Plain Facts*. London, Faber and Faber.

BFHG (Birmingham Feminist History Group) (1979) 'Feminism as femininity in the 1950s?' *Feminist Review*. 3, 48-65.

Bland (1982) ' "Guardians of the race" or "Vampires upon the nation's Health"? Female sexuality and its regulation in early twentieth century Britain' in E. Whitelegg (ed.); *The Changing Experience of Women*. London, Blackwell.

Blumhagen (1980) 'Hypertension: a folk illness with a medical name', *Culture, Medicine and Society*. 4, 3, 197–227.

Board of Education (1943) *Sex Education in Schools and Youth Organisations*. London, HMSO.

Calabrese and Gopalakrishna (1986) 'Transmission of HTLV-III infection from man to woman to man', *New England Journal of Medicine*. 344, 15, 987.

Cauthery, P., Stanway, A. and Stanway, P. (1984) *The Complete Book of Love and Sex*. London, Guild Publishing.

Comfort, A. (1972) *The Joy of Sex*. London, Mitchell Beazley.

Crowther Report (1959) *15 to 18*. London, HMSO.

Daily Express (1986) George Gale column cited in T. Sanderson Mediawatch. *Gay Times*. October.

Davin (1979) ' "Mind you do as you are told": reading books for Board School girls'. *Feminist Review*. 3, 89–98.

Department of Education (1956) *The Handbook of Health Education*. London, HMSO.

DES (1977) *Health Education in Schools*. London, HMSO.

DHSS (1986) Press release 86/244.

Dworkin, A. (1981) *Pornography*. London, The Women's Press.

Ewles, L. and Simnett, I. (1985) *Promoting Health: A Practical Guide to Health Education*. Chichester, Wiley.

Fitzpatrick, R. (1984) 'Lay concepts of illness' in R. Fitzpatrick *et al.* (eds), *The Experience of Illness*. London, Tavistock.

French, J. and Adams, L. (1986) 'From analysis to synthesis', *Health Education Journal*. 45, 2, 71–4.

Gatherer, A. *et al.* (1979) *Is Health Education Effective?* Monograph No. 2. London, Health Education Council.

Gordon, S. and Gordon, J. (1974) *Did the Sun Shine Before You Were Born?* New York, Okpaku.

Griffiths, C., *et al.* (1985) 'AIDS – a health education approach in West Glamorgan', *Health Education Journal*. 44, 4, 172–3.

Groves, E. and Groves, G. (1929) *Wholesome Parenthood*. New York, Houghton Mifflin.

Hall, W. and Hall, J. (1910) *Counsel to Parents*. Chicago, Howard-Severance.

Helman, C. (1978) ' "Feed a cold, starve a fever": Folk models of infection in an English suburban community and their relation to medical treatment, *Culture, Medicine and Psychiatry*. 2, 107–37.

Herzlich, C. and Pierret, J. (1986) 'Illness: from causes to meaning' in C. Currer and M. Stacey (eds), *Concepts of Health, Illness and Disease*. Leamington Spa, Berg.

HMI (1986) *Health Education from 5 to 16*. London, HMSO.

Homans, H., Aggleton, P. and Warwick, I. (1987) *Learning about AIDS: Participatory health education strategies for health educators with a responsibility for effective education about AIDS*. London, AVERT/Health Education Authority.

Institute of Medicine, National Academy of Sciences (1986) *Mobilizing Against AIDS*. London, Harvard University Press.

Jackson, M. (1984a) 'Sexology and the social construction of male sexuality (Havelock Ellis)' in L. Coveney *et al.* (eds), *The Sexuality Papers*. London, Hutchinson.

Jackson, M. (1984b) 'Sexology and the universalization of male sexuality (from Ellis to Kinsey and Masters and Johnson)' in L. Coveney *et al.* (eds) *The Sexuality Papers*. London, Hutchinson.

Kurtz, Z. (1986) 'AIDS – a health education challenge', *Health Education Journal*. 44, 4, 169–72.

Lee, C. (1983) *The Ostrich Position*. London, Readers and Writers Publishing Co-operative.

Levine, M. and Seligman, J. (1949) *A Baby is Born*. New York, Simon & Schuster.

MacFarlane-Burnett (1973) *Genes, Dreams and Realities*. Harmondsworth, Penguin Books.

Marcell, M. (1982) 'Sex education books: an historical sampling of the literature', *Children's Literature in Education*. 13, 3, 138–49.

Marshall, J. and Smith, D. (1986) 'Birds, bees and babies: the real scandal of sex education', *Gay Times*. October, 44–46.

Mills, S. *et al.* (1986) 'Public knowledge of AIDS and the DHSS advertisement campaign', *British Medical Journal*, 293, 1089–90.

MMWR (1985) 'Heterosexual transmission of HTLV-III/LAV' 34, 561–563.

Newsom Report (1963) *Half our Future*. London, HMSO.

New York Native (1986) 'Study reports 100,000 SF straights at risk for AIDS'. 13 October.

People (1986) 'Put AIDS victims in holiday camps': doctor's shock remedy', 28 September.

Pfeffler, N. (1985) 'The hidden pathology of the male reproductive system' in H. Homans (ed.), *The Sexual Politics of Reproduction*. Aldershot, Gower.

Pollock, S. (1985) 'Sex and the contraceptive act' in H. Homans (ed.), *The Sexual Politics of Reproduction*. Aldershot, Gower.

Reuben (1969) *Everything You Always Wanted to Know about Sex* (*But were Afraid to Ask)*. New York, Bantam Books.

Spence (1986) *AIDS: Time to Reclaim our Power*. London, Lifestory.

Tatchell, P. (1986) *AIDS: A Guide to Survival*. London, Gay Men's Press.

The Times (1984) Editorial. 21 November.

The Times (1986) 'Facts that Stay Concealed (Digby Anderson'. 19 August.

Tones B.K. (1981) 'Health education, prevention or subversion?', *Journal* of the Royal Society of Health. 3.

Vass, T. (1986) *A Plague in Us*. Cambridge, Venus Academica.

Warren, H. (1984) *Talking about School*. London, London Gay Teenage Group.

Watney, S. (1986) 'AIDS, moral panic theory and homophobia' in P.J. Aggleton and H. Homans (eds.), *Social Aspects of AIDS*. Lewes, Falmer Press.

CHAPTER 3

Multi-Cultural Education: Some Unintended Consequences[1]

Gill Crozier

> Outside and within education one of the key debates in race relations has been, since the turn of the decade and will most probably continue to be throughout the '80s, the debate between on the one hand anti-racism and on the other multiculturalism.
>
> (Mullard 1984)

The intention of this chapter is to add to that debate by reference to my empirical research.[2] My research interest was prompted mainly by my experiences as a teacher for seven years in a 'multi-cultural education centre' in Bristol and my involvement during that time in political activities campaigning for what I thought then was 'better multi-cultural education' (MCE) but now understand to be anti-racist education (ARE). I was concerned not only that the growth in MCE which was taking place at that time failed to facilitate an improvement in the educational life chances of black children, but also that the quality of MCE appeared trivial and at times insulting.

The particular focus of my research was to look at MCE in the context of the school and classroom and to enquire into what was actually happening there: to explore the social processes and to seek to understand the concerns of the actors in order to make some sense of it all. Although the research write-up is not yet finished and the thesis is incomplete, this chapter represents an attempt to indicate a number of issues arising out of the practice of MCE.

Before doing so, however, I would like to locate the analysis of MCE within a wider framework. The academic debates, of which it is assumed Mullard speaks, have been represented on the one hand by the advocates of MCE such as Bolton (1979) and Jeffcoate (1979), and on the other, its critics voiced for instance by Carby (1979), Dhondy (1982) and Mullard (1982). These debates, however, have taken place within a context of struggles against racism by young black people in the inner cities; the campaigns of black parents, children and anti-racist teachers in Bradford, Brent, Berkshire, Newham and elsewhere. Moreover, these and other similar struggles have served to put racism firmly on the agenda. So much so that the government has had to take a stand against it, not just by use of the police and the media which has been their usual response but through direct intervention, for instance, in the Honeyford affair, the Savery case in Bristol and more recently the McGoldrick case. Kenneth Baker was asked on television recently in relation to the McGoldrick case if he thought that people should not challenge racism. He said he thought that they should – so long as they did not go too far. Of course Brent went too far not only with regard to McGoldrick but also in their proposal to employ 116 teachers under Section 11 with a specific brief to develop anti-racist strategies. Baker has now threatened to withhold their Section 11 funding. Presumably, just in case anyone else goes too far, the DES have let it be known that they will not support any in-service courses that are entitled 'Anti-racist education' and a CNAA working party which had written some 'Notes on multi-cultural education' for visiting CNAA officials was instructed to remove any reference to the term 'anti-racist' (*The Teacher* 1987).

On the other hand the government is giving positive (albeit limited) encouragement to the development of MCE. An indication of this is its recent allocation of £1 million for the development of MCE. Much of this money has gone into Education Support Grants to employ temporary MCE advisory teachers in predominantly white areas like Sussex and Gloucestershire (*TES* 1987). Here we are seeing a mushrooming of activity in MCE just as we saw in the late 1970s and early 1980s in areas where there were sizeable black populations. In the light of this the words of Hazel Carby in *Multi-cultural Fictions* (1979) resound: 'The need for MCE is not merely regarded as an ideal but as practically necessary.'

She went on to suggest, among other things, that MCE was a form of 'social engineering', an attempt to incorporate black people into the system, designed to promote tolerance between social groups and aimed at containing the effects of racism and the resentment which it produces.

At Mill Lane School, in Middleshire (where I undertook my research), the debate that existed there primarily focused on MCE and whether or not MCE should be their concern at all. The debate between ARE or MCE had not (yet) impinged. Why MCE as opposed to ARE is not directly within the scope of this paper. However, I am suggesting that in order to develop an understanding of this it is, first of all, necessary to examine and analyse some of the practice of MCE that was undertaken in the school.

One of the issues I identify is that contrary to the commonly held view that there is no agreed definition of MCE (Troyna and Ball 1985), there does exist a 'common code' or 'ideology' of MCE which has been taken on board by teachers uncritically but in the belief that it is both pedagogically and ethically sound. With the use of empirical data I attempt to illustrate that the aims espoused within the 'common code' fail, giving rise to unintended consequences. I propose to discuss this with reference to two recurrent themes that emerged from my data. These are the marginalization of black people and the reinforcement of negative stereotypes. I shall begin, therefore, by giving a brief description of the research methodology and setting, followed by a description and discussion of the 'common code' and finally I will make an analysis of its practice.

It is important to state that although the postion of this chapter may take a critical stance it is not a personalized attack against a group of individuals. Furthermore, while I do not ignore the necessity for each of us to take responsibility for our own actions, the problem of racism is primarily structural and political. An underlying premise here is that we live in a society highly differentiated along class, gender and race lines and that society is thus characterized by various forms and manifestations of classism, sexism and racism. The structures and processes within the school, the behaviours and attitudes of teachers and pupils (and anyone else for that matter) will be informed and influenced by these divisions and ideologies. This chapter is offered as a small contribution to the continuing struggle against racism.

Research methodology and setting

The research field work was carried out between the summer of

1983 and the summer of 1985. I was looking at teachers' interpretations and practice of MCE and focused on two secondary schools in two local authorities which I call Middleshire and Northgate. In this article, however, I will only refer to Middleshire.

It is an ethnographic study using interviews and participant observation. I was in school for an average of four out of five days over three terms. I interviewed teachers, pupils, school governors, education officers, a very few parents, the Community Relations Officer for education, a Labour councillor (none of the other Parties' councillors replied to my letters) and some representatives of black organizations. I observed classroom situations, the staffroom, playground, dining hall and meetings and responded to what I saw rather than having a fixed schedule. I have also examined documents.

The school, which I shall call Mill Lane, is situated in an affluent town, Middleton, which is a commercial/business centre. Middleshire, situated in the south of England, is a predominantly rural area with two major and several lesser urban areas. Out of the total population 10 per cent[3] are black and most of these people live either in Middleton or the other major urban centre. Mill Lane School is situated to the north of Middleton quite a way from the town centre in a white middle class locality. It is a mixed comprehensive of 1500 pupils, approximately 10 per cent of whom are black. Most of the black children live to the south of Middleton, having to cross the town to get to school.

Middleshire had a Conservative-led council when, in 1978, a group of parents and teachers launched a campaign and took the LEA to the Commission for Racial Equality on the grounds of racial discrimination. Out of this campaign came the demand for an adviser for MCE and for a policy statement, both of which were won. The LEA set up lengthy procedures to write a policy and a strategy for implementation. It set in motion a countywide process of consultation with black groups, teachers, parents, unions, head teachers and governors. Two external black consultants were also employed. During this time the council became a hung council.

The policy which I shall call Racial Equality in Education (REE)[4] took an explicit stand opposing racism and was regarded by its authors as having disassociated itself from the cultural pluralist model (Mullard 1982) of MCE.

Multi-cultural education at Mill Lane School

By the time Middleshire had produced its policy on REE in 1981, Mill Lane had been implementing MCE in some areas of its curriculum. This of course was not surprising since MCE in the form of 'saris, samosas and steel bands' had been around for quite a long time. In Integrated Humanities for the lower school (first and second years) and World Development Geography for fourth, fifth and lower sixth years, their MCE courses were firmly established, well resourced and written by the teachers themselves. There was also an attempt to implement aspects of the LEA's RE syllabus on world religions. Other courses were more ad hoc. For example in Music, one teacher taught the history of pop music including jazz and blues to third years; some English teachers occasionally used Afro/Caribbean or Asian literature and one Home Economics teacher said that she sometimes let the children cook 'their own cultural dishes'.

The approach was piecemeal. There were no departmental policies on MCE and no school policy. Teachers' overwhelming response to the REE document was to dismiss it, though not out of hand. The Adviser for Multi-cultural Education was invited to address the staff, some of whom chose not to attend, while others, according to the Adviser himself, made sound arguments both for and against the policy. Also, the Humanities Faculty invited the Adviser to return to the school to talk with them about their own particular needs for Humanities and in relation to the REE policy.

The teaching staff's response to the REE policy could be broadly divided into three categories:

1. those who were opposed to it or indifferent to it;
2. those who were not opposed to it entirely but objected to aspects of it and also thought it to be irrelevant; and
3. a very small minority of teachers who thought the policy was a good thing to have but did not think it was very useful.

The second group which comprised some of those teachers who had written and were teaching on the Integrated Humanites course, World Development Geography and multi-faith Religious Education, regarded the document as irrelevant because they said they were 'doing it already' and that they had heard it all before. They also felt that the work they had been doing on MCE had not been taken into account by the LEA and they resented this.

The first and second group felt that the document accused them of being racist and blamed them and schools generally for the 'ills of society'. The response of one teacher was: 'When I read th? document it made me angry. I got the feeling [it was saying] white people were all wrong.'

Overall I believe they felt threatened by the implication that all they had been doing as teachers was racist, discriminatory and therefore unjust. They were in fact very defensive about racism and reluctant to acknowledge its existence within the school. According to the Head of Lower School: 'the document was over done. We didn't see it [racism] happening here. There's no need for it [the policy] here.'

A senior mistress added: 'This was the unanimous feeling amongst the staff. Besides we were way ahead of the document, much further on than the document.'

The Head of English insisted that there was no evidence of racism in the school. He, as a representative of the NAS/UWT, wanted the Authority to instigate an inquiry for such evidence but he didn't think they would ever do this because 'they'd given into black pressure and already agreed to the document'.

The defensiveness at other times was replaced by what seems to be naïvety. For example, the Head of Lower School, on a later occasion, described to me an incident when, on first coming to this school, she reprimanded a black boy by saying: 'We don't have the law of the jungle here.'

She said she had not meant any harm by it, it was just what she might have said at her previous, predominantly white, school. She said she did not realize that she had said anything offensive until the Middleton Council for Racial Equality who had heard about the incident complained to the school.

When they did acknowledge the existence of racism they accepted it or recognized it only as pupils' negative attitudes towards each other. Neither was this taken very seriously. When the Head of Lower School was asked about the manifestation of racism she replied: 'There is a bit. I don't think its very serious. Only, he called me a wog. He called me a nigger. You get the odd comment but you'd get that anyway.'

This last statement was a common response from the staff although many of them said they would not tolerate racialist[5] abuse and if it occurred they 'stamped on it'. How hard they stamped is open to question, for according to black pupils themselves, they got little support from teachers when they were racially abused. They were usually told to ignore it. The older pupils said they dealt with it themselves. This is illustrated in the following extract from an interview with some black sixth form girls. They had been talking about experiences of racism in school and I went on to ask them about racialist[6] behaviour from pupils.

> GC: What about racism from pupils?
> Tina: You just have to sort them out.
> [laughter]
> GC: Was that your experience?
> Joan: Not so much now but when you first come they all, sort of, you know and try – You just had to slap their mouth and they just shut up. Well that's the only way you can do it . . .
> Tina: Well you go to the teachers, they just come back again.
> Tina: Yeh 'cos all they [the teachers] say to you is, you know, 'just take no notice.'
> Joan: And you just have enough of it one day.
> GC: So did the teachers take it up with the pupils?
> Tina: Some of them did but they're gonna still come back and give you the same thing . . . They [the teachers] never took it up seriously.
> Joan: No, it was always like: 'don't do that', you know, a little tellin' off . . .
> Tina: It was more like, you know, just like if someone bullies you. It was more like that. Not taken up as a special, as a special – You just have to deal with that yourself.

The third group of teachers referred to above, however, were opposed to 'racism' and wanted to do something about challenging it. They were responsible for setting up a working party which attempted to discuss the implementation of REE. This working party also involved some of those teachers characterized by group 2 which perhaps gives an indication of the sorts of contradictions that the struggle against racism throws up. The working party folded after a short series of protracted meetings, primarily due to industrial action mounted by the two major teaching unions. However, from its inception, it was dogged by a lack of certainty about what to do and how to do it and also perhaps a lack of time in which to do 'it'. In particular they too had little understanding about racism, how it manifests itself and how to deal with it. Nor was there any apparent awareness of the differences between Anti-Racist Education (ARE) and Multi-cultural Education (MCE).

Multi-cultural education and teachers' ideology

Teachers did, however, have an understanding of MCE. As stated above I found that when teachers talk about MCE they hold a shared philosophy, a common code which underlies and informs their practice.

The following statements illustrate this 'common code'. According to a teacher of Integrated Humanities:

> If you broaden their outlook and increase their understanding of different communities then in the long run that can only help foster the right kind of attitudes . . .
>
>   I think it's about fostering an understanding because ignorance is quite often the main cause of racism and that they [the white pupils] don't understand why they [the black pupils] are different and they don't understand why they wear different clothes, why they act in the way they do, so we try to solve these problems for them.

Specifically with reference to the multi-faith RE syllabus the RE teacher said:

> [It's] to try to help kids to have an understanding of other beliefs hoping that will make them more tolerant; to relate better to each other; to build better understanding between groups. We are trying to relate to them [black children] and for their benefit. The Muslims and Sikhs have got a lot out of it. It gives them identity within their peer group.

A teacher of English whose interpretation was broader than that of her colleagues, explained the purpose of MCE:

> to make black children take pride in their culture; to counter negativeness of books etc.; to educate all children about society; to educate teachers; to counter attitudes.

And the Head of Lower School gave the main reasons for doing the Integrated Humanities course:

> because we were taking more of these kind of children. It's been wonderful for them. It has integrated them much more quickly. Their friends have accepted them more.

Out of these statements a number of common aims can be identified:

1. to promote and develop tolerance;
2. to improve black children's self-identity, to develop 'cultural pride';
3. to break down the ignorance of white children and through this to put an end to 'racism' which is (sometimes) fostered by ignorance; and
4. to give value and respect to 'their' cultures.

This 'common code' should come as no surprise since these views have been perpetrated through the plethora of writings on MCE over the last decade. The popularized notion of poor black self-concept can be partly attributed to the publication of the pamphlet by Coard (1971) 'How the West Indian Child is Made Educationally Sub-normal in The British School System', a view which is given much credence in the literature, such as *Multi-cultural Classrooms* by Cohen and Manion (1983); *The Multi-cultural Curriculum* by Lynch (1983) and a recent book of readings edited by Cohen and Cohen (1986) *Multi-cultural Education*. The literature has also made great play of the so-called underachievement of black children and prejudice based on ignorance. In very few of these books are counter-arguments represented by black or even white researchers, such as Stone (1981) and Louden's (1978) critiques of 'poor black self-concept' or Reeves and Chevannes' (1983) demolishing argument against the notion of black underachievement.

Moreover, the view of the need for tolerance, breaking down of ignorance and so on is clearly evidenced by their reference and exposition in government and (the former) Schools Council documents. *Education in Schools* (1977), for instance, included in its eight aims for education: 'to instil respect for moral values for other people and oneself and tolerance for other races, religions and ways of life' and 'to help children understand the world in which we live and the interdependence of nations'.

Furthermore, except for the slight change of a few words, these aims were repeated in: *A Framework for the School Curriculum* (1980); *The School Curriculum* (1981); *The Curriculum 5–16* (1985); and *Better Schools* (1985).

Also, in 1982 the Schools Council issued a six-page leaflet written by Alma Craft entitled 'Multi-cultural Education'. The leaflet included an explanation of the School Council's view of MCE:

In a society which believes in cultural pluralism, the

challenge for teachers is to meet the particular needs of pupils from different religions, linguistic and ethnic sub-cultures; to prepare all pupils for life in a world where they will meet, live and work with fellow citizens of diverse religions, languages and ethnic origins and also to seize opportunity to enrich the lives of all their pupils by taking account of the cultural diversity around them . . . All pupils need to acquire knowledge and sensitivity to other cultural groups through a curriculum which offers opportunities to study other religions, languages and cultures . . . At all stages this may enhance pupils' attitudes and performance at school through development of a sense of identity and self-esteem.

During this same period there were numerous INSET courses on 'cultural background studies' and LEA policy statements expounding this perspective.[7]

What *is* remarkable is how strongly the words of the teachers echo the pronouncements in these documents. Bullivant (1981), however, in his comparative study of cultural pluralism in five countries observed that: 'An outstanding feature of all these case studies is the broad similarity between the languages in which their ideologies of pluralism are expressed.' (p. 238) He attributed this to 'intent' and went on to suggest that amongst other things 'the ideologies of pluralism, for which we can take multi-culturalism as a prime example' legitimates (in this case) the government's authority which is then taken for granted (pp. 238–9). Furthermore, in discussing primary education Alexander (1984) also refers to a set of common sense assumptions amongst primary teachers. He calls this the 'Primary Ideology' and also, suggests that it serves to legitimate practice. Drawing parallels with this a similar claim could be made for the function of the 'common code' of MCE. While the ideology of MCE may be a fairly recent phenomenon Williams (1986) has argued that it is based upon or parallels the solution that was constructed to deal with the perceived problem of white working class children, a 'problem' which has been around longer. Predicating the existence of a deficit model of white working class children which has become transposed through a process of racialization to fit the black child, Williams states: 'Not only have key policy themes remained identical but earlier explanations and solutions are still being reproduced.'

She cites Flude (1974) as one who categorized existing

explanations of working class underachievement in terms of four paradigms. These included cultural deficit and cultural difference. The 'solution' to these perceived problems, she asserts, was compensatory education paralleled today by MCE.

Teachers in this study saw the main problems (with regard to black children) in terms of cultural deficit and cultural difference also. They believed that by implementing MCE they were in some way, as indicated earlier, improving the relationship between black and white pupils and creating benefits for black children themselves. Moreover, since teachers' interpretation of 'racism' was at the level of name calling and the root of that (for them) was ignorance by alleviating this 'ignorance', the 'racism', therefore, would also be dealt with. Having said that, with the possible exception of those whom I characterize as group 3, racism was not seen as a central issue. (In the case study that follows only Ms Green is of that group.) Indeed the focus on culture serves to mask recognition of the structural and institutional manifestations of racism. As Bullivant (1981) says:

> the adoption of multicultural [education] is question-begging because it defines other interpretations out of consideration and analysis ... The danger is that important issues which are promoting dissension and conflict in British society will be defined away as objects of legitimate concern. (p. 230)

Furthermore, the lack of analysis which is intrinsic to 'common sense' assumptions, gives rise, as I will show, to a number of consequences which in terms of the 'common code' were not intended.

I would now like to illustrate the operation of this 'common code' with reference to some case study material from Mill Lane School.

First year integrated Humanities at Mill Lane School

In the first two years Humanities comprises an integrated theme-based course. In year 1 the theme taken is 'Community'. The course is resourced by work-sheets (no text books are used), occasional visiting speakers; video and artefacts and a few visits are organized. The materials are plentiful. The worksheets are written by the teachers themselves who work as a team. In the first year there are five teachers who teach on this course: two historians; two geographers and one RE teacher. Four of these teachers were white and one of the history teachers was black. All were women. The team met fortnightly to discuss the course. According to the Head of Lower School Humanities Ms Gray, the theme of 'Community' was inspired by a Schools Council project. It provided a 'good umbrella' for History, Geography and RE, and 'things we thought we ought to be doing. It gave scope for looking at communities in the past and contemporary communities'. They also already had the appropriate resources. The course was established in 1981 and the element on Islam was introduced in 1982. The aims of the course included those already outlined in the 'common code', above. They began the course by creating their own community on an imaginary island and then looked at the communities of the Saxons; Monks; Eskimos [*sic*]; India; North and South [*sic*]; Islam and finally, in the last term, the local community where the school is situated; the school itself and a nearby old English village.

India was chosen because they 'happened to have a few materials on it that looked interesting ... we had an Oxfam pack ... Islam because we had some Muslims and we thought, what a good idea!'

For this case study I want to discuss aspects of the work on India. The reasons for this choice coincide largely with the lessons that I observed. 'India' and 'Hinduism' was the part of the course that was in progress at the time when I began my research in the school. Since I did not focus my attention solely upon Integrated Humanities it was not possible to observe all aspects of the course. Later in the third term I did have the opportunity of observing the work on 'The local community'. Regrettably because of the limitation of space here it is not possible to include an analysis of that also.

The observations were carried out in three of the five first year classes. None of these three teachers, Ms Green, Ms Rose and Ms White, had been teaching for more than three years.[8] Ms Green and Ms Rose were members of the working party referred to earlier. I would like to give examples from lessons taught by Ms Green and Ms White. Both of these teachers were white. The size of the classes were 26 and 23 respectively. In Ms Green's class there was one black child, Lakshmi, who was a Hindu and whose parents originally came from India. In Ms White's class there were two black children of Afro/Caribbean origin. All the other children were white.

The work on India took as its focus Hinduism and rural village life. There was much enthusiasm from the teachers involved for this part of the course. Ms Green was particularly taken by the colourfulness of the topic which she said acted as a stimulus for the children. This would account for the emphasis placed upon exoticism and display.

> India has got a really colourful religion and the kids find it unusual and interesting and so once you've got them engaged its easier to get over ideas, I think. And also because its so different to our own way of living. It's such a contrast that I think it's a real eye opener for the children . . . I think they've [the children] been really interested in it and surprised because it was so new to them they didn't realize it was so colourful and so bright and so interesting.
>
> (Ms Green)

In fact great store was placed upon the use of resources and making a 'show of things'. Ms White describes one occasion when:

> One of the mothers came in. She works in the Civil Service but she came in wearing a sari and talked to all the children about India. And that was marvellous because her daughter's in the first year and she got some of the girls, the Asian girls, to try the saris on. And they've been bringing in saris. She's going to come back in and bring in some food for us as well. We're going to have a whole session of food.

And in Ms Green's class:

> There've been a lot of practical things for the kids to do and they've had people coming in and talking to them. They've had things for instance, you know, actually doing Puja themselves.

The brilliance of the Hindu shrine, set out in the school hall and the simulated practice of Puja which I observed in Ms Green's class undertaking was certainly a seductive experience. They all seemed to enjoy it and for the time I was there so did I. It was not until I stepped out of this illustrious setting that I reflected upon its exoticism and asked what purpose this served either to fulfil their original aims or go anyway towards fighting racism. The focus on some aspects of Hinduism which some British children of Asian origin may experience are represented here as exotic artefacts, novel, unreal museum pieces. This subtly reinforces the notion of white homogeneous culture, 'our way of living', which is very different from this 'colourful unusual one'. The implications are that it separates off black people as 'strangers' failing to recognize that most black children in this school and indeed most black people in this country are at least second generation British. It fails to recognize black people as part of this society and the role they have played and do play in contributing to society. Furthermore, it divides black people themselves, focusing upon their ethnicity and ignores their mutual experience of racism (Sivanandan 1985).

As stated earlier, this theme of marginalization was a recurrent one. The perpetual use of the terms 'our' and 'their', 'them' and 'us' is just one indication. Similarly, the reference above made by Ms White to 'the girls, the Asian girls' trying on saris may be construed as a subconscious slip displaying a view that saris are not for 'English' girls.

Some black children also expressed the feeling of being singled out or set apart from their peers. During their work on India, Ms Green decided to use Lakshmi as a resource, someone with 'first hand experience of Hinduism' and 'Indian culture'. Ms Green also believed it would make Lakshmi 'feel good' and that it would 'boost her self-confidence'. When I interviewed her, Lakshmi did say that she enjoyed the work on India and Hinduism, as did a number of other children of Asian origin from other classes. However, she also said that when she was asked questions (about her religion or cultural practices), by the teacher and the children, in class she felt 'a little bit left out'.

An extract from the observation of another of Ms Green's lessons illustrates Lakshmi's experience further. The lesson topic was 'Food and the Sacred Cow' [*sic*].

> *Ms Green:* What do most Indians eat?
> *A white pupil:* Lentils and beans.
> [*Silence*]
> *Ms Green:* Is that the only thing they eat?
> *Various white pupils reply:* Curries. Maize. Millet. Peas. Chapattis.
> *Ms Green:* What is the biggest difference between what they eat and what we eat?
> *A white pupil:* Meat.
> *Ms Green:* Right!

There was further discussion about food and then the teacher introduced the topic of the 'sacred cow'.

Ms Green: Why are most Indians vegetarians? Are there any
  vegetarians in this class?
Lakshmi [the only pupil to reply]: I'm a vegetarian because
  I've got the same religion.
Ms Green: Why? Can you explain why?
Lakshmi: I eat eggs but not meat.
Ms Green: What kind of food do you eat then?
Lakshmi: Lots of vegetables. Chapattis. Indian food.
Ms Green: What do you mean by Indian food?
Lakshmi: Curries.
Ms Green: Who eats Indian food?
[One boy said he ate Vesta curry].

The 'them' and 'us' is perpetuated here, but who is Lakshmi? Is she
one of 'them'? Or is she one of 'us'? At one point, it seems that she
tries to assert her identity as a Hindu ('I've got the same religion')
and as an Indian when she says she eats Indian food. But she is
thwarted in this when Ms Green implies that anyone, whether
you're Indian or not, can eat Indian food. Towards the end of the
lesson Lakshmi is put into a dilemma when Ms Green instructs
them to: 'Draw a plate of your own food that you like to eat and
label it. Then draw a picture of food that an Indian person might
like to eat and label it.'

Ms Green talked to various pupils while they did this. She
eventually spoke to Lakshmi who explained that she was drawing
'an English meal that an English person would like' and then she
would 'draw a picture of what an Indian person would like.'
Lakshmi seemingly identified with neither and nor could she. Ms
Green had set up a polarization between 'Indian' and 'English'
people ('What is the biggest difference between what they eat and
what we eat?). Lakshmi is marginalized on both accounts. She does
not seem to be allowed to be one or the other, or indeed to make her
own synthesis of the two.

I talked to a lower sixth form pupil, a seventeen-year-old boy
whose family are from Pakistan and who is a Muslim, about his
school experiences. He recounted RE lessons in which they studied
world religions. He echoed Lakshmi's feeling of being 'left out' or
singled out when he said: 'The teacher would say something and
then start staring your way and then ask you some dumb
questions.'

He explained he didn't like this and why it troubled him: 'The
kids would find out about one custom and to them it would be

funny and they'd start laughing.'

Neither Ms Green, nor any of the other teachers, had considered these consequences. She had not considered that to ask Lakshmi about her religion and cultural experiences was to ask her to talk about something very personal to her which none of the other children were asked to do. She did not consider that in doing so she was marginalizing her, not simply emphasizing a difference but presenting the 'difference' in such a way that it has no place in 'our English society'. And neither did she consider that she might be exposing a black child to further racial abuse. Lakshmi had on occasions been racially abused in the playground.

The perceived need of having to make special provision for promoting the positive self-concept amongst black children legitimates that separation in the eyes of the teachers. They were convinced that they were doing something worth while. Ms Green talking about Lakshmi again:

> I think it's made her more interested in her own religion and home life and I think it has made her feel she's got something to offer the rest. She's certainly more talkative and she enjoys bringing things in. She brought in a couple of saris the other week which were absolutely gorgeous that her mum had done herself. The fact that she's got things to show and the fact that she is different. So if it has affected her I think it's in a positive way rather than a negative way...But it's also difficult to capitalize on this at times because Lakshmi doesn't really understand a lot about it. You can only go so far. It has helped in a way but um, not to a great extent.

Her only doubt is expressed in relation to what she perceives as Lakshmi's inadequacy. Indeed 'inadequacy' must confirm her in the need to promote black self-concept and 'cultural background studies'.

Perhaps Lakshmi didn't 'understand a lot about it' – how many eleven year olds would understand the intricate details or underlying premises of their religion? In fact Ms Green bases this assumption on Lakshmi's reticent responses, an explanation of which were offered above. However, it is little more than arrogance on the part of this teacher to suggest that the brief encounter with Hinduism in some Integrated Humanities lessons has 'made her more interested in *her* religion and home life'. There is also an implication here that Ms Green knows more about Lakshmi's culture than she does herself. In the words of Sivanandan (1983) such arrogance amongst white teachers is 'based no longer on feelings of superiority about their culture but on their superior knowledge of mine', or at least the superior knowledge that she thought she had.

The course moved on from the study of Hinduism to that of rural village life. Ms White, one of the other Integrated Humanities teachers, saw this as an opportunity to draw comparisons:

> We start to bring in people who are living at the moment and so we do a lot of comparison... We compare our community with a community that exists at the present because so far we've been looking at the past and the differences that exist in our world (and ask the pupils) how they feel about it... We do comparisons between – these are the jobs your mother does in a day, these are the jobs this particular family does.

In keeping with the use of resources one lesson was conducted with the aid of artefacts and a slide sequence, illustrating the use of the artefacts. The slide sequence depicted an eleven-year-old girl, Meena, who did not go to school but worked in a brick factory and earned a small amount of money. Her family were poor farmers who lived in a clay house. While teachers claimed that they made some attempt to refer to the rich and to city life most agreed that their emphasis was on rural poverty. The comparison was unfavourable. Meena carried five bricks at a time from the brick factory; the shoes people wore were sandals made from car tyres; cow dung was used as fuel; the dishes were washed on the earthen floor. The images and associations were in opposition to all that is valued in an advanced technological, materialist society.

Teachers had expressed some awareness of the possibility of reinforcing negative stereotyping but they felt that attempts were made to minimize this. Ms Green said that she aimed at getting the children to think about and question such concepts as 'primitive', 'luxuries' and 'necessities'. There was also some attempt to look at the interdependency between the developed and developing world in the two weeks (one double and one single lesson per week) spent on 'North and South'. However, there was no analysis of why there was poverty in the developing world and India in particular. Neither was there any mention of poverty in Britain. On the contrary in the final term the focus of the course was on the local community: a middle class, white, affluent leafy suburb and a quaint English village. The juxtaposition of poverty stricken rural India with this was to say the least insensitive. Nor did it do anything to challenge (it may have even given rise to) the sentiments expressed by these white children:

> People came from India etc. came to Britain because they have a good impression in their minds. They think they'll be able to get jobs and will be better off and that there'll be a better way of life... They obviously want to get away from India because they don't like it.

> It's really bad over where some of them come from originally. They came over 'ere so they can get a job.

One of the original intentions of this course was to break down pupils' ignorance, to broaden their outlook. When I interviewed some of the white children from these classes about the course their strongest impression of India was one of poverty.

> The poor people live in small huts with a pig outside. The cow lives inside.

> Life is hard for the poor people. The mother had to collect water and wood.

One boy compared their life with his own. When he thought about 'all the electric gadgets and TV and eating sweets', in his own life, 'it made you think their main enjoyment was singing in church'. He couldn't imagine there being any electricity in India at all, let alone 'electric gadgets'. Those who did speak of the existence of rich people believed that they did nothing all day and were afraid of the poor.

Naseem, the Muslim boy I mentioned earlier describes his experience of a similar course. He was taking the lower sixth World Development Geography course in which they also studied India, and the relationship between 'North' and 'South'. While the teacher acknowledged that they studied the poverty of India and 'the South' she said that they attempted to explain the exploitation by 'the North'. According to Naseem, however, all that was put across to them was the poverty of the South. He said that whenever the teachers wanted to talk about anything like that 'they always take a poor country like India or Pakistan – rather than anywhere else. One of the consequences of this for him, he felt, was that his friends wouldn't take what he said about Pakistan seriously. He once told them, for instance, that Pakistan had a better airforce than Britain but he said nobody believed him. They just said:

' "Yeah, an elastic band one. You wind it up and then let it go." And they start taking the micky out of it'.

And so instead of increasing the children's understanding and respect it could be seen to reinforce their ignorance and fuel their disrespect.

If the passing reference to 'North–South' interdependency was designed to offset negative stereotyping a glaring contradiction existed in the course with the solution to poverty being presented in the form of Aid – financial aid raised and distributed by the 'North's' charitable voluntary trusts. Each year a speaker from one of these organizations was invited to address the Lower School pupils. Following the talk the children carry out fund-raising activities. The purpose of this Ms Gray enthused was so that the children got 'the idea they could do something worth while to help... the idea you could do something about it... it's not a totally insoluble problem.'

Conclusion

While MCE is not widespread nationally (Little and Willey 1981; Swann 1985) it is none the less gaining credibility in a variety of areas, including the predominantly white areas referred to earlier. I contend that the government, also, is actually promoting MCE in order to stem the tide of ARE. Further, it would appear (certainly from my own research) that teachers find MCE more acceptable than ARE.

The case study that I have outlined is only a small part of a very complex picture of the processes and practices being acted out in the school. Nevertheless, we have here some committed teachers, pursuing a course which has been well resourced and well planned and yet according to my analysis has some disturbing, albeit unintended consequences.

The establishment of an ideology – the 'common code – (of MCE) and the legitimation of its practice has meant that teachers accept it as given. If they had questioned it they might have asked how a course that focuses upon the rural life of India bringing out the negative connotations (of which some teachers said they were aware) and reinforcing the stereotypes could enhance black children's self-image (irrespective of the validity of the need to do so); in relation to this they also might have asked how this could 'give value and respect to their cultures'. If they had done so they might have considered the unequal power relations between black and white people that already exist in this society where black people and their various cultures are less valued and are discriminated against because of being black. When the children in Ms White's class saw the taped slide sequence of Meena's way of life they saw it from their own value system based on a life in which they take little, if any, responsibility for providing for *their* family and a life where material goods and high technology are not only valued but also coveted as symbols of success and wealth. It seems hardly surprising then that children thought that India was 'really bad over there' and 'they wanted to get away from it'. Sivanandan (1983) explains the relationship of this with racism:

> Just to learn about other people's cultures is not to learn about the racism of one's own. To learn about the racism of one's own, on the other hand, is to approach other cultures objectively.

Conversely, the study of Hinduism and practice of Puja as part of that could be said to provide positive images despite its consequence of marginalizing Lakshmi. It might be argued that the purpose of positive images is in part to 'promote and develop tolerance'. But to tolerate something or someone is, however, to endure it (or her), not to respect it (or her). It could be said that by presenting Hinduism as exotic and novel rather than presenting black peoples and their cultures as integral to this society (after all most – if not all – of the black children in the school were Middletonians), the (unintentional) intention was to make black people easier to endure.

These questions and their answers illustrate, I suggest, the erroneous assumptions upon which the common code is founded and expose the unintended consequences of the teachers' actions. If the teachers in the study believed, as they seemed to do, that the absence of 'other cultures' was a reason for racialist behaviour by white children and poor self-concept of black children themselves, it is not enough to inject some of this 'other culture' into the system, for to do so is to fail to consider why those 'other cultures' were left out in the first place. If black people have been ridiculed, debased and hidden from history, as they have, then it is patronizing and trite to simply assert that somehow they now matter (Sharp and Green 1975, p. 226).[9]

Jeffcoate (1982) argues that criticisms of MCE are not valid for there is no 'identifiable enemy' to attack. The analysis in this chapter leads to the conclusion that the 'common code' constitutes such an 'enemy' and that as teachers we have a responsibility to question and develop a critique of this ideology. If we fail to do so the 'unintended consequences' will continue to be reproduced. In which case how much longer it could be maintained that they are 'unintended' is another matter.

Acknowledgements

I would like to record my gratitude to the teachers and pupils of Mill Lane School who so generously gave me their time; to the Economic and Social Research Council for funding the research from which this chapter comes; to Ian Menter and Barry Cooper whose comments have been extremely useful and to those who offered constructive criticism at the International Sociology of Education Conference at Westhill College, January 1987, where an initial draft of this paper was presented. I am also grateful to Len and Stephen for their helpful comments on an initial draft of this chapter.

Notes

1. It is not my intention here to develop the theory of 'unintended consequences' but rather to use the paradigm to explore some aspects of multi-cultural education. For the purpose of this chapter I shall use a simplified explanation of 'unintended consequences', that is: 'the existence of effects that the actors did not explicitly intend' (Boudon 1982).
2. The research was carried out for a D.Phil. between 1983 and 1985 which is in the process of being written up. The research is registered at the University of Sussex and was funded by the Economic and Social Research Council.
3. 1981 Census data. The term 'black' in this instance refers to people of Afro/Caribbean and Asian origin.
4. The REE policy warrants a full discussion in its own right. There is not, however, the space to have that there. Such a discussion would invariably provide further explanations of the practice of MCE.
5. 'Racialism' refers to individuals' prejudiced beliefs and behaviour. Racism refers to the structural and institutionalized exploitation and discrimination of black people.
6. In the interview I used the term 'racist' rather than 'racialist' as that was the term the girls used.
7. Middleshire's Director of Education was emphatic that their policy had moved beyond cultural pluralism and, as part of that, cultural

background studies. The LEA's INSET, however, after the adoption of the REE policy, continued to comprise courses on for example 'Multi-Cultural Music' and 'Afro/Caribbean and Asian Literature'.

8. I would also have liked to have observed other more experienced teachers but it was not possible at that time to gain access to their classrooms.

9. With reference to Matthew Arnold and the social crisis of the nineteenth century Sharp and Green (1975) actually said:

> If the lack of culture is the cause of our social crisis, then merely to advocate culture to cure the crisis ignores the reasons why culture was absent or had become so degraded in the first the individual, it is not enough merely to assert that the individual matters but to attempt to transform the character of the institutional framework (p. 226)

References

Alexander, R. (1984) *Primary Teaching*. London, Holt Education.

Bolton, E. (1979) *Education in a Multi-racial Society. Trends in Education*. London, HMSO.

Boudon, R. (1982) *The Unintended Consequences of Social Action*. London, Macmillan Press.

Bullivant, B. (1981) *The Pluralist Dilemma: six case studies*. London, Allen and Unwin.

Carby, H. (1979) *Multi-cultural Fictions*. Centre for Contemporary Cultural Studies, University of Birmingham.

Coard, B. (1971) *How the West Indian Child Is Made Educationally Subnormal in the British School System*. New Beacon Books.

Cohen, L. and Manion, L. (1983) *Multi-cultural Classrooms*. London, Croom Helm.

Cohen, L. and Cohen, A. (1986) *Multi-cultural Education* – a source bok. London, Harper Education.

DES (1977) *Education in Schools*. London, HMSO.

DES (1980) *A Framework for the School Curriculum*. London, HMSO.

DES (1981) *The School Curriculum*. London, HMSO.

DES (1985) *Better Schools*. London, HMSO.

DES (1985) *The Curriculum 5–16*. London, HMSO.

Dhondy, F. (1982) *Black Explosion in British Schools*. Race Today Publications.

Dorn, A. and Troyna, B. (1982) 'Multiracial Education and the Politics of Decision Making', *Oxford Review of Education*. 8, 2.

Flude, M. (1974) 'Sociological Accounts of Differential Educational Attainment' in M. Flude and J. Ahler, *Educability, Schools and Ideology*. London, Croom Helm.

Jeffcoate, R. (1979) *Positive Image: towards a multi-racial curriculum.* Writers and Readers Publishing Co-operative.

Jeffcoate, R. (1982) *Ethnic Minorities in Education.* Block 4, Unit 13–14, Open University Course, Milton Keynes, Open University Press.

Little, A. and Willey, R. (1981) *Multi-ethnic Education: The Way Forward.* London, Schools Council.

Louden, D. (1978) *Self-Esteem and the Locus of Control: some findings of immigrant adolescents in Britain.* New Community. Vol. 3.

Lynch, J. (1983) *The Multi-cultural Curriculum.* Batsford.

Mullard, C. (1982) 'Multi-racial Education in Britain: from assimilation to cultural pluralism' in J. Tierney (ed.), *Race, Immigration and Schooling.* London, Holt, Rinehart and Winston.

Mullard, C. (1984) An extract from a talk he gave to the national conference of the National Association of Multi-racial Education in Bath.

Reeves, F. and Chevannes, M. (1983) 'The Ideological Construction of Black Underachievement', *Multiracial Education.* Vol. 12 No. 1.

Sharp, R. and Green, A. (1975) *Education and Social Control: a Study in Progressive Primary Education.* London, Routledge & Kegan Paul.

Sivanandan, A. (1983) 'Challenging Racism: strategies for the '80s.' *Race and Class* XXV, 2.

Sivanandan, A. (1985) 'RAT and the degradation of black struggle', *Race and Class* XXVI, 4.

Stone, M. (1981) *The Education of the Black Child in Britain.* London, Fontana.

Swann, M. (1985) *Education for All.* London, HMSO.

The Teacher 23.2.87.

Times Educational Supplement 13.3.87.

Troyna, B. and Ball, W. (1985) 'Views from the Chalk Face: school responses to an LEA's policy on multicultural education.' Birmingham Centre for Research in Ethnic Relations.

Williams, J. (1986) 'Education and Race: the racialisation of class inequalities.' *British Journal of Sociology of Education.* Vol. 7 No. 2.

CHAPTER 4

Community Education: From the Cam to the Rea

Steve Baron

Introduction

In this chapter I want to trace something of the trajectory of 'community education' from its inception in rural Cambridgeshire in the 1920s to its current practice in the inner city; from the broad reach of the Cam to the rather nasty, culverted brook, the Rea, which runs through the Educational Priority Area of Balsall Heath in Birmingham; from the idyll of Granchester Meadow to the seediness of Calthorpe Park.

I want to ask whether this trajectory is one of a 'brilliantly argued' text having to wait over half a century for its full repercussions to be appreciated, the position adopted by Cyril Poster (1982) in his review of community education, or whether, during its rolling route from the Fens to Balsall Heath, 'community education' was transformed into a qualitatively different phenomenon from that enunciated by Henry Morris in 1924. My intent is not to examine any gap between the 'ideals' and the 'practice' (a rather unsatisfactory epistemology) but to ask whether the rhetoric of 'community education' is, today, obscuring a practice with a political logic different from, and contradictory to, its avowed logic.

The literature on community education is remarkable for its repetitive disavowal of precise definitions or for its proposal of tautological definitions. For example Midwinter (1973) in his review of community education opens by suggesting that 'the two words – community and education – must be among the most difficult in the language to define', while Poster (1982) argues that 'with the likelihood of as many definitions for education as Hillery found for community [94]... the product of the mathematic permutation is alarming'.

Should this lack of clarity worry the analyst? Midwinter (1973), in typical style, suggests not: 'there is an academic school of thought which implies that, if objectives and areas of operation cannot be strictly drawn, then there should be a reluctance to move into the field... One cannot afford the luxury of so pristine a view. Perhaps we should not, in education, be so terrified of the intangible, the immeasurable and the visionary. Perhaps, in any event, we should continue the quarrying of community education/action in an attempt to outline more lucidly the definitive statements for which the academics beseech us.'

While this view has many robust virtues, especially its rejection of the trivializing tendency of the 'aims and objectives' school and of a preference for linguistic neatness rather than practical action, it provides the cover, all too often used, for a lack of clarity about the political strategy of community education. This chapter is an attempt at clarifying the field somewhat not by trying to produce the 'definitive statements' against which Midwinter rails, but by trying to understand 'community education' (accepting the label at face value) as a series of practical interventions into specific political contexts and by trying to conceptualize the continuities and discontinuities between these interventions.

Ree (1985) in his assessment of the relevance of Henry Morris's work suggests that community education came to Britain in three distinct waves – the inter-war rural crisis to which Morris originally responded, the post-war adoption of community colleges by LEAs such as Devon and Leicestershire in response to the 1944 Act's proposing county colleges for the compulsory, part time, education of school leavers, and finally the post-Plowden establishment of community schools in areas of urban crisis. Now that the continued 'education' of the sixteen-year-old school leaver is a reality, practically compulsory but entirely remote from community colleges, I think it is not uncharitable to suggest that the inter-war period and the post-Plowden period are those of greatest significance.

I Henry Morris and the Cambridgeshire Village Colleges: The 1924 Memorandum

The origins of 'community education' are, with justice, usually traced to a paper submitted by Henry Morris, Secretary for Education of Cambridgeshire, to his Committee in 1924 – 'The Village College: Being a Memorandum on the Provision of Educational and Social Facilities for the Countryside with Special Reference to Cambridgeshire.'[1]

The details of his Memorandum can be outlined briefly. Morris started by noting the poor relation status of rural education both in its formal, statutory provision and in its provision of adult education. The loss of able rural children to schools in the towns meant that the countryside was losing its leaders ('the ablest of them . . . stolen by the town') and it was not able to keep pace with innovations necessary for its reconstruction. Morris thus suggested that 'the first essential is that the countryside should have a localised and indigenous system of education in its own right'. The conclusion Morris drew from this was that the current chaotic organization of rural education with Church and State competing to provide equally inadequate small elementary schools needed to be replaced with a two-tier system of junior and senior schools under unified administration.

These arguments it must be noted were ones which Morris had already quite brilliantly won in the space of two years against the prejudices of Church and backwoods County Council. Riding on this success, showing that reform was economic, Morris extended the argument 'there must be a grouping and coordination of all the educational and social agencies which now exist in isolation in the countryside' into 'a new institution, single but many sided. This would not only incorporate existing provision but meet hitherto unmet needs – 'room for reading during the long winter evenings when the small cottage is filled by the family and the light is none too good for reading'.

He went on to describe, and to give a ground plan for, a Village College in which there would be a Nursery Class, an Infant Welfare Centre, a Primary School, a Secondary School serving a group of villages, administrative offices, the Village Hall, the Library serving both school and village, an Agricultural Education Centre, two or three rooms for adult education, sports facilities, Careers centre and the Warden's house.

It was perhaps in his specification of the architecture of the

Village College that his vision was best encapsulated. The
'remarkable synthesis' needed 'imagination and administrative
courage'. The aim is:

> a building that will express the spirit of the English
> countryside which it is intended to grace, something of its
> humaneness and modesty, something of the age-long and
> permanent dignity of husbandry; a building that will give
> the countryside a centre of reference arousing the affection
> and loyalty of the country child and country people, and
> conferring significance on their way of life.
>
> It would create out of discrete elements an organic whole;
> the vitality of the constituent elements would be preserved,
> and not destroyed, but the unity they would form would be a
> new thing. For as in the case of all organic unities, the whole
> is greater than the mere sum of the parts. It would be a true
> social synthesis – it would take existing and live elements and
> bring them into a new and unique relationship.
>
> As a community centre of the neighbourhood it would
> provide for the whole man and abolish the duality of
> education and ordinary life. It would not only be the training
> ground for the art of living but the place in which life is lived,
> the environment of a genuine corporate life. The dismal
> dispute of vocational and non-vocational education would
> not arise in it... The Village College would lie athwart the
> daily lives of the community it served; and in it conditions
> would be realised under which education would be not an
> escape from reality, but an enrichment and transformation of
> it.

The 1924 Memorandum: an interpretation

How then are we to understand and assess 'community education'
at its point of origin? To anyone brought up in the dominant
tradition of the 'History of Education' the reflex is to start
searching for 'influences' – the influences on, and influences of, an
innovation. While a certain amount can be gained through this
route the results are not insightful.

We can learn a very little about the elementary school boy from
Southport, about his contact with the nineteenth-century adult
education tradition of Preston Mechanics Institute, about his
strong moral convictions and socialism, his Jude-like attachment

to the 'ideal' University and the privileged place of aesthetic education in social affairs, and about that curious mixture cᶠ horror, mobility and enlightenment offered to the officer class by the 1914–18 War. We certainly can trace continuities and themes from these experiences to his proposals for Village Colleges.

We can learn a little about the second and third wave of community education by tracing themes, teleologically, from Cambridgeshire; the coordination and co-location of different services, the area-based definition of constituency, the tensions over unified or multiple management, the diminution or abolition of strict age categories and the aspiration to the intermingling of education and life.

Such a history is strictly limited in its interpretive scope – we can gain little insight into why some themes pervade, others wither away. We can gain little insight into the significance of the innovations in their structural context and the possibly different significance of the 'same' practice in a different context.

Perhaps this is most graphically illustrated by Ree's (1985) explanation of the stuttering history of community education:

> One explanation for this might be called the *Innovation Time Lag* (emphasis added), the process by which new ideas about education are often locked away for at least a generation, and then are suddenly rediscovered and presented to the world, often in a new language. The community schools, community colleges and neighbourhood centres which are springing up today in widely different parts of the country bear a distinct resemblance to Morris's village colleges. It is not important to prove consanguinity, but their conception can very often be traced to Morris.

In this formulation we are to assume that the phenomenon is static throughout the period, that it is unitary across different contexts and that its waning and waxing is a matter of being 'locked away' and being 'suddenly rediscovered'. Ree's explanation of this, the Innovation Time Lag, is, frankly, no explanation at all.

Taken at this level of analysis the 'community education' tradition appears very thin indeed – a few, not very earth-shattering, administrative changes, the ever economical joint use of facilities plus unspecifiable hopes about the relationship between school and community. This does not, in my view, do justice to the innovations of Henry Morris nor to the potential of 'community education' today.

It is important to understand something of the political context and logic of Morris's intervention. As the authors of 'Unpopular Education' (Centre for Contemporary Cultural Studies 1981) note, the 1920s were a pivotal period in the politics of education, particularly in the balance struck by radical and reformist groups between 'statist' and 'substitutional' strategies. The former 'have centred on agitation over the public provision of educational facilities and the state's regulation of adjacent spheres' while the latter 'may take a "counter-educational" form and, where successful, constitute a challenge to established modes of cultural reproduction that is open, broad, combatative and capable of a really close connection with popular educational needs'.

The years up to the 1920s had been one of the two periods when substitutionist strategies had been widespread while the 1920s were the period when statist strategies, later to fuel the 1944 Act, were being developed. For example, Tawney's crucial 'Secondary Education for All' was published in 1922, the year Morris became Secretary for Education in Cambridgeshire. I want to suggest that the Village Colleges must be understood as responses to *that* context, bearing *that* stamp, and not as models of educational organization and ideals floating free from context and history.

Understood in this way, the Village Colleges represented an ambitious and brave attempt to advance popular educational interest at the limits of the statist strategy. Above all they represented an attempt to make education available for all. For children of statutory school age Morris aimed to make secondary schools available throughout the county with the provision of 30 to 40 Senior Schools and 10 Village Colleges, thus alleviating the educational poverty of the countryside. At the head of this Memorandum Morris quoted from a TES article of 13 December 1924:

> The rural problem is one that successive governments have ignored in despair. The elementary school buildings are inadequate and insanitary in an appalling proportion of cases; the lack of facilities for continued and secondary education is a disgrace to a highly organised community. All the necessary things can be done. What we wish to emphasise is the fact that in rural districts they are not being done, and do not seem likely to be done.

> (Ree 1985)

The Village Colleges played a strategically central role on Morris's plan, radical enough in its aspiration of secondary education for all. He was faced with a small, poor county with, at its heart, a major educational centre. Unsurprisingly there was, at least in educational terms, a clear centre–periphery relationship: 'Educationally the countryside is subordinate to the towns and its schools are dominated by, and subservient to, the urban system of secondary and higher education' or more graphically 'our ablest children . . . stolen by the town' (Ree 1985).

The Village Colleges were clearly intended to be the showpieces of the new system of secondary education – purpose built with good facilities and new modes of education to match. If we map Morris's proposals their logic appears – the Village Colleges were to be located in a circle around Cambridge, astride main roads, providing an educational cordon sanitaire around the city so that rural children tempted to school in Cambridge would have to journey past a showpiece rural school.

The Village Colleges were not, of course, to be restricted to secondary school age children with their aspiration to lifelong education 'there would be no leaving school – the child would enter at three and leave college only in extreme old age'. Self-consciously Morris wanted to import his version of popular adult education into the countryside – 'the most vigorous and systematic popular movement for adult education, the Workers' Educational Association, is an urban movement with comparatively little influence in the villages'.

Morris's proposals were radical in terms of the control of the Colleges. As Ree describes it the major obstacle in his path on arrival at Cambridge was the power of the Church which controlled three out of four schools in Cambridgeshire. The power of the Parson was one of the major popular targets in educational politics in the first two decades of the century. Morris, appointing a body of famous divines to advise, manoeuvred the Church into surrendering control of 'their' schools and proposed a new system of Government for the Village Colleges – there was to be one unified body consisting of County Council appointed elementary school managers, County Council and Parish Councils members representing higher education, one representative of the Senate of University of Cambridge plus an unspecified number of representatives of 'other interests' exemplified by the Parish Council.

In his proposals for the content of education and its relation to the surrounding social context Morris was both deceptively and startlingly bold. His proposals for the curriculum of the school element of the Village College appear modest enough – the concentration of resources would enable classes to be organized according to age and ability and would enable some facilities for handicrafts, domestic subjects, general elementary science and gardening. The Village Colleges would have the advantage of having the local Branch Library in-house and Morris proposed that new modes of learning be initiated around the Library as what we would now call a Resource Centre. The aim for Morris was 'an education which will fit boys and girls for life (in the widest sense) as countrymen and countrywomen'.

So far as adult education was concerned Morris's proposals appeared modest – a mixture of existing elements, the W.I., British Legion, Agricultural Education plus the range of village societies already operating with a nod in the direction of the WEA.

It was in the vision of what these different elements combined to make that the radicalism of Morris lay. Having disposed of the Parson elegantly (or as the Rector of Stretham, Ely, protested 50 years too late 'I consider that Henry Morris quite cold-bloodedly set out to destroy the influence of the church in village life'), Morris spent little time mourning the passing of the Squire under the impact of wider economic changes. This had created a crisis of leadership and of the 'maintenance of liberal and humane traditions in our squireless villages'. To Morris the Village College was the answer: 'the seat and guardian of humane public traditions in the countryside ... without some such institution as the Village College a rural community consisting largely of agricultural workers, small proprietors and small farmers will not be equal to the task of maintaining a worthy rural civilisation ... The Village College would provide the chance for creating for the countryside a new type of village leader and teacher with a new status and a wide function embracing human welfare in its biggest sense – spiritual, physical, social and economic.'

Essentially this task of leadership for Morris was a popular one: the tasks 'will fall on a larger number of shoulders – they will fall on the whole community'. This was no narodnik Utopia, but a practical proposal to prevent new forms of capital from filling the vacuum left by the decline of old agricultural capital. This can best be seen from the earliest conflict of community education – the issue of the Sawston Cinema where Morris attempted, with some success, to wrest control of film shows from Spicer, the local paper-making magnate. As he wrote to potential donors: 'What I, and especially the intelligent working people of Sawston want, is a Sawston Cinema Society. The cinema would be used in schoo! time for lessons in geography, nature study, travel etc. Once or twice a week an evening show would be given ... In addition to entertainment films, in which a high standard would be secured, there will be other films of a really interesting and fascinating character shown ... My fear is that if we do not act quickly some commercial travelling film exhibitor will appear and spoil our field ... It is a fine chance to show how a rural community can organise its own entertainment on a cultural basis, and to show how the cinema can be redeemed.'

How then are we to assess Morris's innovation with the benefit of sixty years' hindsight? His Village College proposals represented bold, imaginative initiatives at the edge of the statist strategy and thus reveal some of the ambiguities of that strategy. The victory over access was double-edged. The plan for opening up secular secondary education to all children in a poor rural county was at the forefront of educational politics and brilliantly conceived. Yet in his Memorandum we can see a weakness which was later to be written large over reformist politics of education – a concern with access at the expense of other issues. While Morris weighed the politics of access up to a fine degree, his touch was less sure with the other issues necessary to a popular education.

Faced with a rural county undergoing major structural change and wanting to keep commercial capital at bay, Morris fell prey to a version of the 'Golden Age' myth delineated and demolished by Williams (1975) in his *The Country and The City*. In trying to establish a radical education system for the country Morris took as his reference point the organic village way of life which was (as ever) just disappearing, in need of resurrection. As Williams warns: 'it is clear, of course, as this journey in time is taken, that something more than ordinary arithmetic and something more than ordinary history is in question. Against sentimental and intellectualized accounts of an unlocalized "Old England" we need, evidently, the sharpest scepticism.'

The revolt against both old and new forms of rural capital was, ironically, made possible by, but at the expense of, positing the rural population as a changeless cultural unity. Morris's proposals had little conception of the differences of class and gender in the countryside, how these generated ways of struggle rather than ways of life[2] and how these different ways could, or perhaps could not, inhabit the new Village College.

The consequences of this radicalism without struggle were fundamental. In trying to establish new forms of education and new forms of relationship between education and 'life' Morris took as his reference point the preparation of 'countrymen and countrywomen' without seeing these positions as contradictory both within themselves and between themselves. Only through positing 'the age-long and permanent dignity of husbandry' could Morris hope to abolish the 'dismal dispute of vocational and non-vocational education'. This led Morris into a practical version of that peculiar combination of the celebration of assumed folk ways and High Art being formulated at the time in Cambridge[3] as a critique of the perceived cultural crisis of industrial capitalism.

In trying to ensure that the new Village Colleges were under popular control Morris's strategy was less assured than over the issue of access. He felt certain of popular support for his proposals ('institutions already planted deep in the habits and affections of the people') yet in formulating his proposals for the Government of the College he equates the Parish Council and the County Council with 'representing local interests'. Given his experiences with his own Committee and his sense of the wide-ranging cultural dominance that could be established by capital in the countryside the equation of the formal constitution of state bodies with popular control is surprising and represents another of the limits of the statist strategy.

Sixty years on how are we to assimilate the Village College proposals of rural Cambridgeshire? Current 'community education' often traces its lineage back to Morris, but I want to suggest that the continuities are far fewer than normally assumed. While the institutional form of contemporary community education may bear some resemblance to the Village College proposal the political logic seems to me to be very different. In the Village College Morris was able to condense different political themes – they were to give access to secondary education for all, they encircled Cambridge to thwart the centre–periphery relationship, they were to take over the leadership functions of Parson and Squire to the denial of capital. The rationality of the proposals was a situated one – an intervention into the specific context of the time and not an abstract model to be applied universally. I take it as highly significant that, in another context, in the new towns, not only did Morris attempt to establish community schools but, in keeping with his celebration of folk ways and Art, centres for community organization based in a pub (Hilltop in Hatfield) and in a community of artists (Digswell in Welwyn Garden City).

II Community education in the 1970s and 1980s

Understood as situated interventions into a specific economic and political context Morris's Cambridgeshire proposals begin to look less plausible forerunners of contemporary community education. If we try to understand this latter form in a similar manner the continuities lessen further. The community education of the 1970s and 1980s is rooted in the social democratic politics which originated in the 1950s, flourished in the 1960s and early 1970s and which has been disorganized but not eliminated during the late 1970s and 1980s.

Access for all to secondary schools, the main prize of the inter-war politics of schooling, was won in the 1940s but in such a way as to vitiate many of the hopes of those demanding it. In the 1950s the new subdiscipline of the Sociology of Education grew largely through demonstrating the bitter result of the tripartite system and the failure to tackle the commercial sector in education: the resistant pattern of class reproduction through education. These findings connected with, and helped form, a nascent political agenda in which education was central – the modernization of British industry and the social structure simultaneously through the establishment of a technological meritocracy in education. The problem of working class 'failure' presented this agenda with one of its most difficult problems – the seeming inability of those at the sharp end of the British social structure to take the 'opportunities' for personal escape.

The Plowden Report of 1967 provided both the condensation of these themes and a practical politics for their resolution. The Peaker regression analysis located the problem of working class 'failure' in parental attitudes to education and thus identified a class, and specific fractions of it, as being in need of cultural interventions to make them more amenable to the state. The practical politics was, of course, the EPA community school to cover, initially, the 10 per cent of the child population living in the worst areas of multiple deprivation (Central Advisory Council for Education 1967).

Such interventions represented limit cases of the social

democratic politics – the education system was the central mechanism for realizing a capitalism which was both just and efficient by *reducing* class, understood as obstacles to the friction-free rise and fall of talent and as antagonistic attitudes. The community school was where the education system self-consciously tried to breach the process of class reproduction through altering parental attitudes and (hence) pupils' attainments. As has been noted elsewhere 'Halsey's own progress along the road to Balsall Heath provided a courageous case of social democratic policies taken to the edge' (Centre for Contemporary Cultural Studies 1981).

If we take community schooling as a limit case of social democracy and ask of it the question I asked earlier of Morris, its political logic in the structural context, then we can begin to see both the continuities/discontinuities between the two and some of the limits of social democracy. In what follows I will report, in schematic form, on a case study of one major community education intervention in a British city (The Project) involving some sixty person-years of work in the mid 1970s and early 1980s in areas with a national reputation for social problems.

I want to offer two lines of critique of this intervention: first that, despite the avowed aim of the intervention to facilitate the educational and social development of the areas involved, the logic of the Project in action was substantially to other ends. Secondly, I want to suggest that, in so far as the Project did operate on the reproduction of class, gender and racial divisions, its logic was to intervene and *better to secure* their reproduction.

Taking the first line of critique it is important to note that the Project was externally initiated and very actively propounded to the relevant local authority. The Authority showed no great enthusiasm for the Project but produced a very brief proposal on the basis of which substantial extra funding was secured from the external agency. Given the largely rhetorical analysis contained in the proposal it was unsurprising to find that the Project, once under way, became a vehicle for the contemporary debates over management practices in local authorities, for changes in the management and practice of the Project to be demanded from outside the authority and for these changes to be taken as 'models' for wider changes. In a real way the Project, by its very vacuity, provided the opportunity for bodies external to the local authority to intervene in the day-to-day operations of the local state.

This use of the Project was not restricted to external bodies – at the time the local authority was bitterly divided over the introduction of corporate management. The Project provided the vehicle for many of these issues to be fought both at the level cf policy and also at the level of detailed policy implementation. As the literature on corporate management shows, with a blurring of departmental boundaries, there arises a need for some alternative practical focus by which the local authority can structure its activities. The literature of the time also shows that, again and again, local area interventions were used to this end. In this specific case the rejection of the proposed merger of Education and Social Services departments left a legacy of departmental bitterness and insecurity in which context the Project enabled the boundaries to be fought over and re-established through a particular instance.

Within the Education department the Project provided the vehicle for a reformulation of the relationship between central administration and the teachers in the schools. A major theme of the Project was the need for Headteachers to surrender some of their traditional autonomy in the name of better coordination of services. In particular the Project enabled a testing of a 'Super-Head' model of management whereby a group of schools was subjected to the detailed intervention of one person located somewhere between the central office (and in that, between the Advisers and Officers) and the individual school. In the classrooms the labour process of class teachers was affected by the Project – new forms of pedagogy were demanded, unpaid teaching assistants (in the form of parents) proposed and working hours made longer and more flexible.

In these ways I suggest that the Project was substantially 'not about' community education and the improvement of life in several areas of crisis but that it provided a vehicle for contemporary struggles within the state and thereby the covert reformulation of state practices – less than frankly named Area Management Trials.

My second line of critique is concerned with the logic of the Project to the reproduction of race, gender and class. Here my suggestion is that the Project was the educational equivalent of the Handsworth mugging as analysed by Hall *et al.* (1978). In *Policing the Crisis* the authors describe how a crisis of hegemony emerged in the early 1970s and how economic, political and ideological factors combined to condense the themes of youth, race and the inner city into the figure of the mugger. On the back of a panic about mugging and law and order new forms of repressive state control were developed. In the terms of the time the 'depraved' could be controlled by such means, but that left the problem of the control of the 'deprived'. My suggestion is that the Project, and the post-Plowden community school in general,[4] provided the vehicle for developing such control. In particular I want to suggest three processes of community education as leading towards the more pacific reproduction of critical class fractions.

First, the Project developed new surveillance practices in the inner city. Specific class fractions (particularly the women of the underclass) were drawn into the ambit of the school through community events, afternoon groups, involvement programmes, play groups and nurseries etc., and assessments were made of them. The school went out into the local area actively gathering information through developing community profiles and home visiting schemes. The results of these practices were recorded and disseminated as necessary through the developing procedures of inter-agency cooperation, particularly between social workers and teachers. While these practices only developed in a primitive way in the Project they were part of a wider and still incoherent process within the local state to gather and collate information in a more intrusive manner.

The Project was not simply a recorder of information – it, secondly, developed forms of direct intervention into the cultural processes of reproducing class structures with their gender and race based inflections. The child was a major object of reform, particularly through the mediation of the child rearing practices of the mother. The Project attempted to develop a seamless web of intervention from birth (via the Health Visitor) through the first three years (by way of Mother and Baby groups, Toddler groups, Toy Libraries, Home Visiting etc.) and into school (by way of Play Groups and Nursery). The focus of these interventions was 'proper play'. This was thought to be a crucial lack in the residents of the inner city – either through the absence of play altogether or through the 'wrong' form of play being encouraged. Specifically West Indians were held to encourage destructive play while Asian boys were held to be too bookish to play and Asian girls too withdrawn.

The mother was the reference point of virtually all the interventions either in the capacity of childrearer or in a personal capacity. In the capacity of childrearer she was the centre of reform, to change self and thus to change children. In a personal capacity the mother was variously inserted into the Project – either to bring her into the public realm as in the case of women depressed through the isolation of the home and in the case of Asian women or to take her out of the public realm in the areas of kerb crawling by way of afternoon groups, craft groups etc.

Thirdly, the Project developed its own hidden curriculum – the representation of the people of an area to themselves. The local population was represented to itself as a community despite the many manifest differences between groups. The unity constituted was one of pathology – the community as united in needing help. Implicit in this representation was the power relation of professional and lay people and the more or less disguised play of the microphysics of power. As one officer put it: 'West Indian families are often very strict with corporal punishment regularly inflicted, Asian families are withdrawn, following their own culture, have serious communications problems, Irish are restless, violent, nomadic, undernourished, poorly clad.'[5]

In so far as differentiation within the community was allowed it was articulated in terms of 'leadership' – groups were recognized as legitimate through attributing leaders to them, classically the priests of certain religions. Thus the Anglican vicar, the Imam or the Secretary of the Temple reflexively constituted their various communities. This constitution of communities was selective with the explicit exclusion of the Rastafarians and the 'Asian Mafia' (a group of high status Asian men not directly connected with the Mosque) from the realms of the legitimate.

Culture was represented to the people of the areas by a series of community events. In these, culture was displayed not as existential struggles for survival in a hostile society but in the terms of a certain type of anthropology – the artefacts, formal traditions and rituals of groups as defined by powerful outsiders. The selective legitimation of groups noted above served to incorporate certain groups while disqualifying others.

All of these forms of intervention, surveillance, direct reform and representation, pointed in the same direction – the increasingly systematic inspection of the cultural context of reproduction, the selection of specific cultural forms for sponsorship and the reform or marginalization of non-sponsored forms. This sponsorship was, of course, directional – the adjustment of local cultures to that of the school and other state agencies.

Understood in this way, through this example, the post-Plowden community school bears little resemblance to the Village College of Morris's proposal. Both were at the limits of the politics of the time but where Morris rooted his proposals in a carefully weighed analysis of the economic and political context of rural Cambridgeshire and in popular pressure for access to secondary education, the Project was based on a rather facile version of the fecklessness of the underclass. There is every reason to believe that the Project was not untypical and that it highlights the limits of the social democratic politics of education.

The Project was an imposition on the inner city areas by the state which was predicated on the superior knowledge of professionals/ the pathology of the local people. There was little or no connection made with the existing or emerging struggles of the areas to deal with the problems as perceived locally; indeed the Project actively discouraged and disorganized such struggles. There was little or no understanding of the divisions of what was understood as 'the community' and of the roots of these divisions. There was little or no sense of the structural processes at work creating the inner city as it was nor of the order of action needed to challenge such processes. As has been suggested elsewhere these are features central to the social democratic settlement, features which constitute the politics as unpopular (Centre for Contemporary Cultural Studies 1981).

As I have suggested the logic of the action of the Project was towards securing the more *pacific* reproduction of the existing class structure with its gender based and racial inflections through bringing the cultural processes of the underclass into the ambit of the state and reforming them into closer conformity to state sponsored definitions. Predicated on the problematic of 'mobility' (ensuring fair conditions for the battle of talents) the Project could not contemplate the class *structure* let alone work to change it. Predicated on the 'mother' the Project more firmly rooted women in childrearing while smoothing the consequences. Predicated on an anthropological definition of race the Project could not grasp the systematic nature of racism nor the lived experience of black culture.

III Community education: into the 1990s

Community education viewed thus is not the long march of an idea from the Fens to Balsall Heath but a series of interventions held together by little more than two ill-defined words. What does seem consistent is the use of community initiatives at times, and in places, of structural change and at times of change within the state itself. It is these features, and the potential of community education for exploring what a popular education might look like, that make it an important category. Here I will restrict myself to three implications of the analysis presented.

First, I have suggested that community education should be understood as specific interventions into specific contexts and not as an itinerant, rather timeless, educational strategy looking for a home. This suggests that community education should start from a detailed analysis of the political economy of an area, the struggles engendered and how an 'education' can connect with these processes (if at all). This runs counter to the top–down nature of community education in social democracy in which community education has been imposed on areas with little understanding of the problems and less connection with the lives of local people. The pathology model which seems to underlie the post-Plowden initiatives (despite their protestations) provides a poor starting point for community education in the tradition of Morris.

This implies, secondly, that substitutionalist strategies can provide better starting points for community education – if we understand culture as ways of struggle then areas of 'multiple deprivation' present, not voids, but a rich field of opportunities to work *up* a community education from existing issues. In the example of the Project spontaneous organization was taking place in terms of the problems of kerb crawling, of policing practices, of changing land use and the renewal of housing and of the inappropriateness of local educational provision for local cultures. These spontaneous movements were either ignored by the Project or actively disorganized and disqualified.

Finally, although the direction of my argument is away from seeing the state as the locus for community education, schooling represents perhaps the most intrusive state institution which no community education can ignore. Here the emphasis on substitutionalist strategies propels community education into a guerrilla war against the reproduction of oppressive structures of class, race and gender so that the multiple sites within schools where this reproduction is fostered could become the sites of contestation. Such a strategy could both reveal the precise nature of schooling under capitalism and change it. It is in providing insights for these struggles that the Sociology of Education might find a renewal of its vigour given the intellectual demise of its social democratic origins and the political impasse of the 'New' sociology.

Notes

1. Available as an Appendix in Ree (1985) and in Ree, H. (ed.) *The Henry Morris Collection,* Cambridge University Press (1984). All references are to the more readily available *Educator Extraordinary.*
2. See the seminal critique E.P. Thomson, Review of The Long Revolution, *New Left Review*, May/June and July/August, 1961.
3. See Francis Mulhern *The Moment of 'Scrutiny'*, London, Verso, 1981.
4. A generalization based on fieldwork and literature reviewing but which can be taken as an heuristic.
5. Personal communication.

References

Central Advisory Council for Education (1967) *Children and their Primary Schools.* London, HMSO.
Centre for Contemporary Cultural Studies (1981) *Unpopular Education.* London, Hutchinson.
Hall, S., *et al.* (1978) *Policing the Crisis.* London, Macmillan.
Midwinter, E. (1973) *Patterns of Community Education.* London, Ward Lock Educational.
Poster, C. (1982) *Community Education: its Development and Management.* London, Heinemann Educational Books.
Ree, H. (1985) *Educator Extraordinary.* London, Peter Owen.
Williams, R. (1975) *The Country and The City.* London, Paladin.

CHAPTER 5

Schools for the State: The Complementarity of Public and Private Education

Judith L. Kapferer

This chapter is a revised version of a paper originally presented at the 1986 conference of the Australian Association for Research in Education at Melbourne University, and subsequently expanded and rewritten for the Xth International Sociology of Education Conference at Westhill College, Birmingham in January 1987. My thanks are due to participants at these conferences, and to Judith Sachs of the University of Queensland and Bruce Kapferer of University College London, for a number of helpful comments.

The ideology of individual choice is a fundamental issue in western education. From it arise a number of contentious questions and dilemmas centring upon the provision of schooling by the State. These include concerns about funding, curriculum content and design, the training of teachers and the relation of educational institutions and outcomes to other instrumentalities of the State.[1] Most particularly, and with increasing passion, the relation of education to the national economy has provoked heated debate, focusing upon the relative power, influence and authority of the parties to the formal educational act (students, teachers, parents, government) to determine who benefits from it.

Over the last decade the various Australian[2] governments have prosecuted strongly the claim that it is 'The Nation' which should have first call upon the fruits of education. Young people, it is said, are 'our finest natural resource' and an investment in them and their education and/or training is an investment in the future of the country. That this future is seen in entirely economic terms is little to be wondered at, especially in the difficult economic circumstances with which Australia is contending. Schools, and young people themselves, have been blamed for Australia's poor economic performance relative to 'our trading partners'. Low secondary school retention rates (with for example, only 51 per cent of an age cohort in South Australia in 1984 completing twelve years of schooling), a perceived neglect of 'the basics' of literacy, numeracy and technical competence, and a failure to instil the set of attitudes collectively known as 'the work ethic' are the most cited culprits. Schools are seen to be failing in both their instructional tasks and in their role of enculturating the new generation. It should be noted, however, that these strictures are much less frequently applied to those schools which are not wholly funded by the State. In South Australia the Catholic schools retain 70 per cent of their intake to the end of Year 12, the Protestant and non-denominational private schools, 124 per cent. Public schools, on the other hand, have a retention rate of 43 per cent.

The variegated terminology employed by Australian educationists to distinguish fee-charging from non-fee charging schools, and religious from secular foundations, is indicative of the range of parental interests which the different types of school purport, or are believed, to serve. It is common to refer to the three major types of schools as Government, non-Government Catholic, and non-Government non-Catholic (e.g. Karmel 1971). Others (e.g. Hogan 1984) use the terms State, Catholic and Independent. In common parlance, the pretentious 'college' is often used to distinguish fee-charging institutions from 'high schools' which charge no fees. Furthermore, it is easy to overdraw the distinctions between fee-charging and non-fee charging schools, as internal differences among schools of the same general type demonstrate. For instance, elite public high schools – those with academically selective entry and/or those situated in the more affluent parts of large cities–often appear to have more in common with non-Catholic private schools than with other public high schools. This is a mistaken impression however. The major distinction that I wish to draw is that of schools being open or not open to the general public, regardless of the ability to pay fees. This enables a more fundamental distinction to be made, between education mediated by the State bureaucracy on the one hand, and education provided through consumer patronage on the other. Since I want to develop the argument here that *all* schools serve the State (i.e. that all schools are State schools) I have chosen to use the simplest terms, public and private, to designate the basic distinction, despit:' possible confusion for some readers.

The argument I want to pursue here is that the only clear beneficiary of the Australian dual education system is that State which so assiduously supports it. While individual graduates of any type of school may and do achieve worldly success, as might be expected from a meritocratic ordering of educational provision, what supports the production and reproduction of the capitalist order and the hegemony of capitalism itself is the *maintenance of* a system which serves *complementary* rather than competing ends.

The Australian State actively encourages a formal educational arrangement whereby most children attend free secular public schools, and a small but disproportionately influential number (about 25 per cent of the total) attends private schools. What needs to be explained is why and how the State in the face of constant (if diminishing) egalitarian critique, and despite its own egalitarian rhetoric, insists on providing financial and, much more important, ideological, support for the private, fee-charging schools.[3]

Such ideological support is constituted within, as it is constitutive of, Australian historical experience. The pre-eminent role of the State in the surveillance and rehabilitation of convicts and later settlers has a symbolic identity with the ideology of transformation central to post-war immigration policies and the education of immigrants. More recently, however, the ideology of transformation and achievement of autonomy and self-determina- tion – an ideology central to the generation and maintenance of egalitarian ideals – has shifted its focus away from the solidarity and communalism of the 1950s and 1960s to an individualist and populist orientation more in keeping with the nationalist protectionism of the altered economic and geopolitical circum- stances of the 1980s.

Communalism and individualism can be seen to form two poles of Australian egalitarian thought (see B. Kapferer 1987) with emphasis oscillating between them according to changes and differences in social conditions. Thus, rather than representing opposing forces, the two poles both contribute to an understand- ing of social welfare and social justice whereby the private is conceived of as superior to the public, and more worthy of moral approbation. In this light, privatization, now rife throughout the western world, can be seen as more than 'de-nationalization' of erstwhile State-owned facilities and services. Increasingly, autonomy and independence from State control, long 'rights' of the dominated and powerful, and long conceived of as inherent in private provision and free enterprise, come to be claimed as 'rights' by the less dominant and the less powerful. The latter come to equate autonomy and personal freedom and high quality, with the *private* provision of welfare services in general, and education in particular.

The perception of a social order as founded in natural difference, producing notions of leaders and followers as possessing greater or lesser natural abilities, is fundamental to commonsense understandings of social equality in Australia. But more than this, it lies at the heart of the practices of selection which operate in schools and in the wider community. Academic selection, grounded in an interpretation of the comparative worth of natural abilities, provides a foundation for, and a legitimation of, class and status distinctions in the wider world. Individual autonomy and equality of opportunity are concepts which thereby refract different moments in the ideology of egalitarianism.

Thus, while the dual education system is often treated as an oppositional structure, it is as often seen as reflecting natural (and therefore legitimate) differences. Within such common sense understandings, those who can afford, or 'deserve', a private education for their offspring, have both a right and a duty to provide it, leaving the State to organize a residual welfarist provision for the indigent. At the same time, and given the interest of dominant fractions of the ruling group in maintaining the current social order, the State is also required to support (financially *and* ideologically) the provision of private schooling. It is also required to support the continuing hegemony of those conceptions of egalitarian individualism which dominate educational thinking about academic instruction and social selection.

The first provision of formal education in Australia was that of the Church, financed by fees and colonial governments. Between the 1850s and 1895, the financial support of colonial governments was withdrawn, leaving the private church schools and a handful of non-denominational private schools to fend for themselves, but the 1960s saw a return to limited aid in the form of Commonwealth government grants for school libraries and science facilities (see Hyams and Bessant 1972). Since that time, federal state aid for private schools has increased, and become a taken-for-granted aspect of overall educational provision. Indeed, Commonwealth aid has also increased in proportion to that provided for public schools:

> Between 1974–5 and 1982–3 Commonwealth expenditure on private schools in the states rose by 97.7 per cent while expenditure on public schools fell by 20.5 per cent. State Governments' expenditure on private schools rose by 125.9 per cent while their expenditure on public schools rose by 25.7 per cent. The Commonwealth has introduced an eight year funding plan which will see subsidies to private schools rise by at least one third ... by 1992.
>
> (Marginson 1986; p. 23)

The reasons for the renewal of Commonwealth support for private schooling are not necessarily the straightforwardly political ones advanced by Hyams and Bessant in 1972, i.e. the concern of the (conservative) government of the day to harness the Catholic vote and the parliamentary support of the Democratic Labour Party.

Rather, they are to be found in a concerted ideological push by the State to maintain and reproduce the capitalist relations of production upon which the Australian State depends for its survival in its current form. In this, the ideological apparatus of the family (certainly a major focus of Catholic and fundamentalist rhetoric) has become ever more closely connected to the educational apparatus through an elevation of the concept of individual choice as the 'lynchpin of democracy'. As well, the notion of community (which also achieves religious validation) has been brought into the ideological mix, perhaps in an attempt to drain individualist action of unpalatable connotations of self-seeking and to appeal to the communalist interpretation of equality of opportunity. The State's ideological (and economic) support for private property, which includes formal educational qualifications and cultural capital, has in fact led to greater government intervention in schooling, with the active connivance of those families who benefit most from the action of the State. The schools of the ruling group, which are greatly dependent upon consumer patronage, are accorded monetary support, while retaining their much lauded 'independence'; the public schools remain to facilitate the mediation of education by the State to the children of the rest.

The dual structure of education in Australia is such as to promote a common goal through means which are tailored to the perceived differential commitment of various class fractions to the social relations and practices of capitalism. While the attachment of the ruling group to the political and economic status quo can be, for most purposes, assumed, the educational processes of the private schools can be permitted a fair degree of latitude and independence from the bureaucratic intervention which is constantly required to align the products of the public schools with the purposes of the State.

The years since the end of the post-war economic boom have seen an inexorable loss of economic power and autonomy for countries like Australia. Ingested into a global economy at the mercy of the transnational corporations, Australia has become what Crough and Wheelwright (1982) call a client state. Australian commerce and industry are increasingly in a position of having to react, often helplessly, to the vagaries of a global market over which they have little control. Such economic debility is paralleled by a loss of political and cultural autonomy (see J. Kapferer 1987) which has important ramifications for the forms and processes of schooling. As the Australian State is deprived of a role in the international marketplace, it turns in upon itself, tightening its control of the people in both economic and cultural affairs. Given the moral centrality of education in democratic societies, it is not surprising that the increasing lack of economic and political self-determination by the State (and its constituent citizens) results in an increasing pressure for hegemonic ideological control. The development of the non-determining state can be marked by an enormous increase in the number of experts who daily exhort citizens to 'improve' everything from their household budgeting techniques to their interpersonal relations, and a corresponding increase in the numbers of bureaucratic planners and controllers of everyday life.

The bureaucratic experts and planners are nowhere more active than in regulating the schools and, especially, the families of the nation, a phenomenon which has been the subject of much academic interest in the last decade (see e.g. Lasch 1977; Donzelot 1980; Barrett and McIntosh 1982; Reiger 1985). While much of the concern about the policing of families stems from feminist research centred upon family relations and psychoanalytic theory (see e.g. Chodorow 1978), research into the relationship between school and family has largely remained separate from analyses of the ideological functions of schooling. The conception of education as the dominant ideological apparatus of the State (see Althusser 1971) seems to have produced a bifurcation of interest:

the family *or* the school is taken as the primary focus of concern, and little attention has been paid, with the notable exception of the work of Miriam David (1980), to Althusser's characterization of the school–family couple as the foundation of the dominance of the educational apparatus in performing the ideological work of the State.

Yet there is massive evidence to attest to the State's understanding of the importance of the school–family couple in its regulation of the social relations of schooling. The South Australian Education Department (1981), to take only one example, proclaims:

> Both parents and teachers have a vital role in the education of young people. Parents have the prior responsibility; teachers provide expertise and skills to assist them. Each has a role to play, and the partnership is most productive when both contribute.

Parental 'expertise and skills' are, however, confined to that area of child development commonly referred to as socialization; correctly 'productive' attitudes and orientations to society, towards work and leisure and schooling itself are taken to be the central province of parental concern, leaving academic instruction and curriculum design in the hands of the trained experts. But even more significantly, through its monopoly of accreditation, the State retains control over the life chances and career trajectories of young people, thereby regulating and ensuring the reproduction of the structured inequalities which are characteristic of the total social formation.

The problem for the State is to balance the production of competitive individualism, as crucial to the maintenance of the capitalist economic order, with the rhetoric of egalitarianism and democracy vital to the maintenance of the social order. Since the economic, social and political interests of the private school clientele (which includes the dominant fractions of the ruling group) are *already* those of the State, it follows that it is the public schools which are the prime targets of ideological intervention. In this, both curricular arrangements and selection processes require the constant surveillance and control of the agents of the State to secure the reproduction and legitimation of the social order.

My focus in this chapter is upon the ordering of relations between family and school in the service of the State. Specifically I propose to discuss educational practices in which parents and teachers may be seen to be complicit in the maintenance of a social order which depends upon the popular legitimation of the structured social inequalities of the Australian State. The first of these is those parts of the curriculum – often 'hidden' – which seek to instil attitudes towards and understandings of work and leisure, success and failure, employment and unemployment, competition and co-operation, which promote support for the industrial and commercial practices of corporate capitalism. Upon the variable inculcation of such an *habitus* depends the social selection of young people into different positions in the production process. Parallel to, and underpinning, social selection, is the practice of formally measured academic selection. This forms the second area of concern to be addressed later in this chapter.

Character training: technocratic morality and social selection

Preparation for the adult world requires more than intellectual development; it requires social, physical emotional and moral development. Character development is at least as important as intellectual development. Schools should encourage and assist young people in the development of many kinds of knowledge, skills and attitudes to enable them to grow into responsible adults capable of understanding and contributing to their society.

So proclaims the Education Department of South Australia (1981) in its document *Our Schools and Their Purposes: into the 80s*. While it has long been the practice of elite private schools to include a passage expressing similar sentiments in their prospectuses for intending clients, it is only in the last decade or so that public schools, through the state education departments, have sought to advertise their wares in this way. Phrases like 'the building of character'; 'development of individual talents and qualities'; 'development of each child as an individual'; 'vital importance of the individual'; and 'pastoral care' (from private school prospectuses) are now balanced in the public sector by phrases like 'the greatest possible development of each student' (from the South Australian Education Department). Indeed, private schools have even taken over some of the discourse of the public schools – references to 'the full potential of each child', and equality of opportunity, for example.

But the emphasis on character building in the public schools is a relatively new phenomenon, and suggests a major re-orientation of those schools, away from the 'narrowly academic' training of classroom-based schooling, to a much broader concern for 'social training' – social, physical, emotional and moral 'development' which is no longer to be confined to the classroom but to reach out into 'the wider community'.

This movement of the public schools away from the intellectual realm to what might be called the affective realm is a response to a number of pressures which have been steadily building over the last decade. These pressures come from disparate sources: from students and teachers themselves, with their complaints about irrelevant curricula and patronizing pedagogies; from parents concerned for what they see as a lack of purposes and direction in their children's schooling and anxious for their children's employment prospects; from the general public and the mass media, alternatively bemused and outraged by anarchic music and anti-social behaviour premised upon the slogan 'No Future'; and from business and industry, fearful of falling profits and social instability.

It is no coincidence that, during this period, a drift to the private schools has been discerned. In the period between 1976 and 1982, for example, secondary school enrolments in Catholic schools increased by 2.2 per cent to 18.8 per cent of the total; enrolments in non-Catholic private schools increased by 1.4 per cent to 8.9 per cent of the total. Public secondary school enrolments, on the other hand, fell by 3.6 per cent to 72.3 per cent of the total (Hogan 1984; p. 57). The rate of transition of South Australian students to higher education in 1985 has been calculated by Power and Robinson (1986) as 28 per cent of Year 12 students, 25 per cent of these are drawn from public schools, 32 per cent from Catholic schools, and 45 per cent from other private schools.[4]

Beyond a belief, common amongst the clients of Catholic schools, but also perceptible among others, that private schooling, especially that which is connected with religious bodies, attends more closely to matters of discipline and morality – character training, in fact – some perhaps baser motives are at play. As one parent said, in justifying her decision to send her child to a private school, 'You never heard of a St X's boy being unemployed, did you?' referring to the most prestigious school in the city.

But another, reflecting the increasingly overt moralism of educational thinking, pleads:

My child is in Year 5 and I can't get them enrolled anywhere in a private school for Year 8 in 1989. What chance is there of a new Christian school in our area? (The local school has no 'values'.)

(McArthur 1986)

The State has not been slow to respond to this perceived dissatisfaction with the public schools, which, in a time of falling birthrates, are frequently seen to be in competition with the private schools for clients. Curricula have been pruned and altered and expanded to cater to the interests of erstwhile early leavers, and to equip young people for a more 'constructive' or at least a more amiable approach to the labour market and what will be for many, inevitable periods of unemployment. Senior secondary school timetables, especially those which are designed to be attractive to the less academic student, have become replete with employment-related courses including the now ubiquitous Work Experience.

Since neither the schools nor the community can guarantee paid employment for school leavers, the State has provided a number of training schemes under the aegis of the Department of Labour and the Department of Technical and Further Education in order to ease the transition into the labour market. But the provision of such schemes and school-based training does not of itself produce a mobile, willing and docile pool of casual or temporary workers, which is largely what employers of unskilled young people require. Nor does it produce a contented voting population.

What has to be added to the straightforwardly instructional processes of school's processes which anyway do not vary significantly between the public and private domains is a massive ideological onslaught in the public schools. The classroom mode of educational production, characteristic of these schools, has a centrifugal effect upon pupils and parents, while the schoolwide mode of the private schools draws pupils, parents and teachers into a close-knit association deeply committed to the project of the school (see J. Kapferer 1986). The elaborate extracurricular programmes, the ritual and tradition (often validated by religious practice), and the frequently intimate relations between teachers and parents all go towards producing a centripetal effect in the private schools, and it is this goal to which the public education system now aspires.

This is why the State has decided that 'character training is at least as important as intellectual training'. The means it has chosen to this end, constrained as it is within a bureaucratic framework, have been focused upon the enculturation process within the classroom. Special courses and classes for girls and non-English speaking students are now common, for example. There is much talk, but little action, about decentralization. The formal curriculum has been expanded to include many of the 'subjects' which form part of the extra-curriculum or family-related activities of private school students: drama, crafts, dance, sex education, photography, driver education, religion studies, social education. Exercises in 'values clarification' seem to have fallen into disfavour, but there is no shortage of substitutes. Currently, the South Australian Education Department is investigating (with the help of teachers, academics and a representative of the Catholic Education Office) the possibilities for 'moral education' within its secular ambit.

'Character training' and 'moral education' assume the kind of homogeneity of class interest which characterizes the private schools, particularly those of the non-Catholic sector. The conjunction of faith and morality in Catholic schools (and in the small fundamentalist schools) is less easily discernible in the daily practice of the elite Protestant schools, despite their rhetoric of providing 'an education based on Christian principles'. In general, religious practice is perfunctory, and references to Christianity are brief and somewhat shy:

> Added to the Education Department syllabuses...are the personal touches of the social graces, moral standards and Christian principles.

> [The school] is open to students of all denominations. Education in a Christian environment has always been its strength.

> The Minister of X Church is the visiting Chaplain of the College and boarders attend Sunday services at X Church.

> [The school] is an Anglican foundation and seeks to maintain, within the framework of the Christian religion, the highest possible academic standards and to provide the discipline of a well-ordered yet motivated life...

The primary concern of the elite schools whose prospectuses are cited above is not faith and morals, but rather the satisfaction of a clientele knowledgeable about and deeply concerned for their children's employment futures. 'Character training' is assumed to permeate all classroom activities, but the enculturation practices of these schools are most clearly focused within the extracurriculum, which includes charitable community service and wide-ranging sporting activities. As one elite school puts it,

> In the parliaments, in local governments, on boards and committees, old boys... willingly have allowed themselves to be nominated for the common good. In part, this active recognition of such responsibilities is a measure of the product of the school itself which would prefer to produce character and worthwhile citizenship in distinction to an unbalanced intelligentsia.

In the past, public schools have concentrated almost entirely upon academic activities in the final years of schooling – indeed, it was customary for the 'non-academic' child to finish formal schooling at the age of fifteen – and one can assume that this concentration is what leads to the production of 'an unbalanced intelligentsia'. The elite private schools, in their concern to provide 'an all-round' education, have maintained their less able pupils for the full length of secondary schooling, thereby enabling all pupils to accumulate the kinds of cultural capital including the 'character training' which will serve them well in parliaments, local governments, boards and committees. Faith in the circulation of elites, a central tenet of the meritocracy, is perhaps more correctly to be analysed in terms of the *maintenance* of the privately educated in positions of power and prestige, or at least comfort, with the addition of revivifying new blood from the ranks of the academically successful students of the public schools.

Where public schools have stressed, in the past, their straightforwardly instructional processes, and have only recently (in the last ten years) fully developed an officially stated concern for 'pastoral care' and 'skills for social living', the elite private schools and their clients have long taken for granted the equal priority of their academic instructional functions and their enculturating roles.

The schoolwide mode of educational production allows for greater overall amounts of time to be allocated to activities which are *mainly* academic, or *mainly* social-cultural. The public schools have not this leeway, and are thereby constrained to combine both enculturating and instructional processes within classroom or classroom-related activity. Their enculturating functions can be neither as penetrating nor as effective as those of the private schools.

Such a differential allocation of teacher effort and pupil participation is one of the major distinctions to be drawn between public and private schools. Furthermore, the schoolwide mode allows for the inclusion and participation of parents in their children's social development, while leaving academic instruction firmly in the hands of the professionals, the 'experts'. The classroom mode of the public schools ignores, even denies, parental involvement in both curricular *and* extracurricular matters. This observation brings us to a consideration of the area of pedagogical practice, in which parents have the greatest interest, but, generally, the least expertise, that of the selection of students for their future situations in the adult world of the marketplace.

Gatekeeping: academic selection and assessment

The following comparison of selection and assessment procedures in two schools highlights a number of aspects of the gatekeeping function of all schools. The first of these is the way in which assessment procedures are centred upon the school-work nexus; the second is the way in which such procedures serve the 'needs' of capitalist relations of production through contributing to and legitimating the circulation of elites.

It is to be noted that, while much discussion on the part of teachers is concerned with what are perceived to be the 'needs' of the individual (in line with the rhetoric of both public and private schools which stresses the catering for individual differences in ability and motivation and interest), the end products of assessment and reporting are organized to fit with the interests and perceived needs of two groups of clients — parents, in the case of the private school, and 'the community' in the case of the public school. The definition of community in public schools is an ongoing problem. Depending on circumstances, the community which is to be addressed may be (a) the amorphous and heterogeneous group of parents; (b) the local geographically defined neighbourhood; or (c) the wider 'society' of potential employers of the school's product. On occasion, all of these may be implied.

For private schools, on the other hand, the community may be that of either an ideologically cohesive group of parents, often attached to a religious sect and not bounded by a discrete neighbourhood or locality, or again, the wider world of the marketplace. In private schools, references to 'the community of the school' are abundant, evincing a belief in the common interests of parents, teachers and pupils in the production of an end result of schooling which is carefully aligned with the insertion of the school's product into those sectors of the economy and polity which confer power, prestige and/or wealth upon the inhabitants of those sectors. It will not escape notice that in this situation, there is often great overlap between the parental group and the group of employers and managers towards which assessment procedures are ultimately oriented.

Assessment and grading are vitally important features of the work of all schools. In a culture which is firmly attached to notions of individual difference, and one in which differential financial and psychic rewards are distributed on the basis of perceived merit, this is hardly surprising. The ultimate goal of academic assessment is the legitimation of the competitive ranking of students in line with achievement in those areas — social and cultural as well as intellectual – which are assumed to be the basis of success in later life. But the competitive ranking of students presents the gatekeepers with a dilemma. For it is not only measured achievement in schoolwork which is to be addressed, for that is clearly not all there is to success in the marketplace. As well, qualities of character and personality which are thought to be fundamental in the attainment of such success must also be judged, even if they cannot be accurately measured.

Schools go to much trouble to apprise outsiders of their judgements of the worth of individuals. They provide written reports and references attesting to character traits which may be thought admirable and useful in the economic sphere and in the workplace. In effect, the schools endeavour to provide guidelines regarding the exchange value of traits of character and personality which are not amenable to statistical measurement.

The following transcripts of staff discussions illustrate the kinds of conflict which arise from this situation, and the ways in which resolution is reached.[5] The first set deals with discussions about mid-year examinations held by the middle school staff at a private co-educational school which, given the social situations of its clients, must qualify as what Connell *et al.* (1982) call a ruling class school.

Headmaster: The marks will be scaled. We will be looking to pass at least 75 per cent. Much discussion and thought has gone into this, and I have made enquiries of other schools and even interstate. We have looked back over the past results and found the distribution of them. It seems that a failure of 25 per cent is far too high. Because, firstly, at years nine and ten we have culled out the pupils with the greatest difficulty and put them in a separate streamed group. The tail is taken off. Second, the range of abilities is not typical. We do have a skew towards the top end of the normal curve. Thirdly we are not in the business of squashing people, especially at this age. So: how about 10 per cent fail; 20 per cent get a D (a weak pass); 40 per cent a C (a sound pass); 20 per cent a B (credit) and 10 per cent an A (distinction)? In a class of thirty then, three would fail, six would get a D, twelve a C, six a B, and three an A. Do you feel this distribution is about right, or is it hopeless?

There followed a lengthy silence. Finally, a French teacher pointed out that only mathematics and science were 'creamed off' so that maybe 10 per cent was too few to fail. A history teacher, Mrs Wheelwright, added that the examination in English was for the whole year group (what is generally known as a core test) and not tailored to any individual class.

Mrs Wheelwright: I teach 823 in history. I could give them an exam that they'd all pass, or I could tailor it.
Headmaster: You mustn't expect a particular class to get this distribution.
Mrs Wise (Science): About a third of the double science class [i.e. the high ability group] can't cope, so 10 per cent failing is unrealistically low.

At this point another Science teacher, Mr Evans, nodded in agreement, and Mrs Wheelwright added that this was also the case in English. Mrs Wise suggested that they might, by this means, be inflating parents' opinions of their children's capabilities, and that a percentile ranking might be more appropriate. The headmaster said that this exercise would have the same effect, and Mrs Wise countered with the opinion that though a 75 per cent pass rate sounded good, it was not a true representation of the current state of affairs; Mr Evans opined that the distribution of ability in the school was much more normal than the headmaster thought. The seventh grade teacher, Mrs Tower, brought the discussion to a broader plane by saying:

Mrs Tower: So when we get down to it we're really running this school as a grammar school rather than a comprehensive.

Headmaster: Yes.

Mrs Tower: So it doesn't matter about hurting the kids in pushing them to matric [the public school leaving examination].

Headmaster: We are concerned with academic standards but we try to provide assistance for those who are struggling, as a back-up. But we also have a range of other activities to provide a comprehensive education. We don't lower our sights to academic achievement *as you very well know*.

Mrs Tower: I agree that parents want it, but we can't really say we aren't going to harm those who get E's all the way through school.

Headmaster: They've got to get an appreciation of their strengths and weaknesses – we can pursue these here as an independent school. Also, we don't ridicule them and put a dunce's cap on their head. I honestly feel we do support them.

Two weeks later, when the examination results were available, another stormy staff meeting took place. The headmaster stipulated that all the result sheets presented by teachers must contain the rank order of students in the particular subject for the whole year group, and that adjustments might need to be made in accordance with the modal distribution previously discussed. Mr Adams, a Social Studies teacher, expressed his disappointment that the result sheets called for a percentage especially in the light of that percentage being adjusted, rather than its being a percentage of marks actually gained in the examination. The headmaster replied soothingly that he had not yet seen any sheets which required adjustment, so that Mr Adams's problem might not exist. Mrs Wheelwright asserted that if it did, she would go along with Mr Adams in preferring a letter grade rather than a change in the percentage. The headmaster explained the rationale for the scaling of marks:

Headmaster: Some exams are too hard, and progress in each subject needs to be gauged.

Mrs Wheelwright: Wouldn't a letter grade do the same thing?

Headmaster: Yes, but we're committed to a percentage [on the report card] and you yourself worked on the new report format.

Mrs Wheelwright: I might have agreed to a percentage, but not to an adjusted percentage.

Headmaster: Look, this isn't dishonest, I haven't dreamed it up: the staff did.

Mr Grainger (Mathematics) to Mrs Wheelwright: There's nothing specific about a D. We want to know what it means and the parents do too.

Mrs Richardson (German): Most teachers don't set exams that are too difficult. If there are low marks it's because the child hasn't got the ability.

Headmaster: Or the child has been poorly taught. Take maths. Say only 30 per cent of children get 50 per cent. There is something wrong here. If the exam is at fault the marks should be adjusted so that the subject is not out of phase with all the others. Let's leave it there.

However, the matter was not allowed to rest. In the following week, the Physics teacher from the senior school, Dr Braithwaite, came to discuss the mechanics of scaling with the middle school staff. She pointed out that almost half of the tenth year group had scored 35 per cent or less in the recent mathematics examination, and that the school would 'have to bash through a heavy remedial programme'. She reported that the Headmistress, who taught Mathematics in the senior school, had suggested that no marks for Mathematics be awarded for the current assessment period, and that there had also been 'too many' failures in tenth year Science – about 16 per cent of the year group. (One of the History teachers pointed out that 36 per cent of the year group had gained less than 50 per cent in the History examination, but this was ignored.) The general, somewhat grudging conclusion of the meeting was that all pupils would have to work harder in Mathematics and Science, and that a further examination would be held in these two subjects at a later date.

A number of issues, two of which are of particular interest here, are raised by an analysis of the content of these discussions. The first is the care with which the school authorities, in the persons of the Headmaster and the Headmistress's delegate, considered the way in which parents might be expected to react to their children's progress reports. As in the public schools, Mathematics and Science are taken to be the clearest indicator of academic achievement. It is taken for granted that children, and their parents, need to be given an assessment of the individual child's *academic* strengths and weaknesses, but unlike the public school practice, such an assessment must be couched in terms of competitive ranking – hence the percentage marks. The choice of subjects for senior school study and eventual public examination and matriculation chances is dependent upon the possession of this measured ability to perform. Thus entry into tertiary education, and particularly into its most prestigious faculties, ultimately requires the achievement of high grades in a competitive and public examination. It is the headmaster's job to cool out those children whose parents have too great an idea ('unrealistic') of the capabilities of their offspring, but at the same time the school must be seen to be doing everything within its power to enable children to reach high standards of academic performance.

Secondly, while the school did, as the headmaster pointed out, offer a wide range of non-academic activities in which less able children could achieve status and recognition, parents were vitally concerned that their children should perform as well as possible in the academic stakes. This was one of their most frequently stated reasons for sending their children to the school – something of which both the headmaster and the staff were very much aware. But the staff were aware, too, that their pupils were drawn from a wide range of ability ('following a normal curve'), and they were resentful of the headmaster's suggestion that failure in examinations might reflect poor teaching. There were mutterings about making silk purses out of sows' ears, and turning ducklings into swans.

Consideration for parental sensibilities was markedly absent from discussions about grading and reporting at a nearby public high school. Here discussion turned on the use of the state-endorsed school-leaver statement, a document of particular concern to the numerous pupils who were planning to leave school before the end of year 12, or before undertaking public examinations.[6] These pupils would be required to use this statement as a report, but also as a standard reference for employment. Throughout the school, annual reports had been traditionally presented with letter grades which corresponded to the scheme suggested by the private school headmaster, i.e. with A meaning distinction and so on. The new scheme involved a range of marks from one to five, representing, it was believed, the teachers' judgements of effort as well as achievement. This confusion, and teachers' anxiety about the rationale for the statement, is evident in the following staff meeting discussion.

> *Headmaster:* Say that putting a 'two' is equal to 'is achieving well'. Does this mean 'is achieving well for her'?
>
> *Mr Fraser* (Mathematics): I don't see my role as sorting out employers' problems in this way.
>
> *Headmaster:* What about our credibility [as a school]? Is it being fair by the student in his approach to an employer?
>
> *Mr Fraser:* I'm not here to serve the employer.
>
> *Mrs March* (Counsellor): But we do.
>
> *Mr Saunders* (Social Science): We do this [report-writing] when a student changes schools.
>
> *Mr Fraser:* But [that] is confidential.
>
> *Headmaster:* Some universities are admitting students on [that basis of] school reports.
>
> *Mr Fraser:* That's quite different. It's easy to do, and it's got nothing to do with employment.
>
> *Miss Moffatt* (Craft, deputy principal): It's a step to it.
>
> *Mr Saunders:* Don't we have a responsibility to those kids?
>
> *Mr Fraser:* I'm trying to do this. Not do the employer's job for him. An employer said to me that it's the reference bit that's most important, not the grades. Punctuality, reliability, things like that.
>
> *Headmaster:* I would still want to know what his quality is. Is he accurate? Can he do seventy words per minute?
>
> *Mr Fraser:* It's easy enough to do a test for this.
>
> *Headmaster:* I have been an employer. Say you've got fifty-six applicants for a job. You can't interview them all.
>
> *Mr Fraser:* That's their [the employers'] problem.
>
> *Mr Glyn* (unknown): You're only an intermediary, to help make a short list [of applicants for interviews].
>
> *Mr Fraser:* I can't see it as legitimate on any educational grounds.
>
> *Mr Sorenson* (English): How can we handle the kids' needs

and the employers' at the same time?

Mr Glyn: You just have the written reference for the employer [not the report card].

Headmaster: In [the old] days we had the [tenth and eleventh year public] exams. To meet the employers' requirements our kids will be disadvantaged, because there will be schools which will do it [i.e. provide reports as well as references] and not all schools are within the state system. Even here, there won't be uniformity. Already the reports of some schools are more readily accepted than those of others . . . some are considered more accurate than others. Employers do talk to each other, you know.

Mr Fraser: Surely this is an argument to do away with the whole [school-leaver's] statement?

Headmaster: But we will still have the school references, with grades on them.

Mr Fraser: Why were the [old] exams phased out? Because they only tested a few qualities. Too many things were left out.

Mrs March: The conditions were unnatural. You should give a school the chance to assess its own.

Mr Fraser: Employers don't just use grades. But you [Mr Glyn] would give them a reference. I can't see the difference.

Mr Fraser's antagonism to what he took to be the employers' expectations of his gatekeeping role is evident here, though the general consensus amongst the staff appeared to be that this was in fact one of their proper functions as teachers. None the less, his comments point to a general concern of teachers about report-writing and grading. This is related to their recognition of a conflict between protecting and advancing the employment interests of their students, and writing a 'responsible' reference which will not undermine the credibility of the school in the marketplace. It is this conflict which leads to public school teachers' acceptance of letter or number grades rather than percentage marks, and writing general comments which are relatively denuded of specific information about individual students and their competitive ranking. Indeed, the similarity – even interchangeability – between grades and written comments was commented upon by Mr Saunders.

To summarize: public school teachers present generalized comments and grades; private school teachers present individua- lized percentage marks and teacher comment. This outcome is created by the particular location of a school within the overall binary education system, as in a situation of state mediation or of consumer patronage. Private school teachers are no less concerned for their pupils' employment prospects than are their counterparts in the public school. But this is not their primary interest. They are equally oriented towards the requirements of parents, and the reputation of the school amongst those parents. Paradoxically, public school teachers' concerns to protect the employment interests of the child operate to place their students at a competitive disadvantage in the labour market, while the individualized reporting and grading of private school teachers places their students at an advantage.

Grading in terms of percentage marks has the effect of appearing to present an individualized result, discriminating as it does between one student and another in a way not possible with letter grades. A letter grade categorizes a student as one of a number of roughly similar performers, a percentage mark discriminates among students and becomes their personal property. Further- more, a percentage mark has implicit within it the idea that it has been competed for, and thereby represents the individual's capacity on a ranked scale. It is this competitive aspect of percentage marks which often causes teachers to object to their use, as 'testing only a few qualities' in 'unnatural' conditions.

In general, a percentage mark has a high degree of taken-for- grantedness; the meaning of a letter grade is much more ambiguous: 'There's nothing specific about a D'. Armed with his or her school percentages, the private school student can meet a prospective employer as an already discriminate individual with variously proven abilities to perform competitively, abilities highly relevant to working in an economic order which values competition and properties ('hard work', 'conscientiousness') which are associated with the successful competitor. Percentage marks, like money, have a generalized value, a currency, beyond the specific situation in which they were originally produced. Letter grades and written comments on the other hand, are dependent for their value upon the (variable) reputation of the school and the teacher. Moreover, the student with letter grades and comments confronts a potential employer as relatively indistinguishable from a number of other applicants. This gives the student less leverage in the employer's selection processes, a disadvantage which is compounded by the greater scope for interpretation which attaches to letter grades and generalized written comments.

The foregoing discussion has relevance for the argument advanced here that both public and private schools function in the service of the capitalist state. The point is that the different types of school serve complementary ends, rather than competing ones. The products of the public schools are being trained to fill those jobs for which minimal educational qualifications are required, and competition is grounded in the principle of first-come-first served and last-on-first-off. In contrast, the products of the private schools are being prepared for careers which do demand competitively achieved academic qualifications, if not for entry, then for legitimation. The contrasting modes of certification characteristic of the public and private schools reflect not only a stratified school system, but also a stratified labour market.

The promulgation of what are usually called 'relevant' curricula, and new methods of assessment adopted in South Australia in the last two years, may be seen as a response to the Federal Ministry of Education's call to institute greater 'participation and equity' in the senior secondary school. But such a response has the effect of further mystifying the value of school-based credentials. In an effort to achieve parity of esteem, the Senior Secondary Assessment Board of South Australia accredits a wide range of subjects at the senior secondary level, 44 of which are currently classified as Publicly Examined Subjects required for matriculation, and 140 of which are classified as School Assessed Subjects which do not qualify for matriculation. The former group includes twenty modern languages and those subjects traditionally thought of as 'academic' in the schools. The SAS subjects, on the other hand, range from Environmental Science and Technical Drawing and Home Economics through Outdoor Education, 'Lifestyle' and Small Business Management to Furniture Construction, 'the Individual and the Group' and Farm Mechanics. A number of SAS subjects such as Garment Design and Construction, Word Processing, Digital Electronics are half-year subjects, thereby offering students a wider range of studies than is possible with full year courses. Grading for each full year subject will be on a scale of 1 to 20, giving students a total school leaving mark out of 100. However, subjects in the SAS group, which are not externally examined, are worth, for entry into tertiary

education other than university, three points less than those in the
PES group. The highest possible score in PES is thus 100, in SAS,
85. (See SSABSA, 1986.)

The Assessment Board points out that almost all students ask for
higher education entrance scores to be calculated, and results for
this purpose are currently reported on a tear-off attachment to the
certificate, to an even decimal point – e.g. 19.4, 18.6. By these
means, percentage scores are available: 19.4 becomes 97 per cent,
18.6, 93 per cent, thus enabling universities to establish cutoff
points in different faculties. Subject committees for PES have
university representation, those for SAS generally do not. While it
remains to be seen whether schools will adopt more than a fraction
of the SAS group, and whether employers will continue to prefer to
hire school leavers with low marks in the Publicly Examined
Subjects, it is clear that the traditional manual–mental distinction
still applies.

The inclusion of School Assessed Subjects in the official Year 12
curriculum represents something of a victory for teachers who, like
Miss Moffatt, believe that 'schools should assess their own' and for
those like Mr Fraser who believe that the old matriculation
syllabus tested too narrow a range of abilities and achievements.
Many of the SAS group are thought to be more 'relevant' to the
needs and interests of young people, and indeed of potential
employers. The promulgation of this new scheme, therefore, does
little to loosen the school-work nexus. On the contrary, it tightens
it further.

The State and egalitarian individualism

As with curriculum design and implementation, so with
assessment and evaluation practices. As the curriculum is altered to
take into account the perceived wishes of parents and the local
community, so evaluation of students must take into account not
only the results of the instructional process, but also traits of
character and personality thought to be conducive to the
furtherance of the careers of individuals and the economic ends of
the State.

The State, through its universities and other higher education
institutions, and through its interlocking examining and accredi-
ting instrumentalities, has long controlled entry into the
professions and semi-professions; it is also now deeply involved in

the accreditation (through school reports and other credential-granting schemes) of students entering the skilled trades and clerical work. Because of this, it exercises vast power over the life chances of almost all its citizens.

The co-operation of school and family in attaining entry qualifications for young people has always been a feature of the consumer patronage world of the private schools with their equal emphasis upon academic instruction and enculturation within the schoolwide mode of educational production. Today, the public schools are also being realigned with the economic and career interests of families and individuals through a concerted effort to broaden the curriculum and to pay closer and more overtly organized attention to 'character-training' and 'moral education' – to enculturation, in fact – than heretofore. The school–family couple is being utilized to serve the economic ends of the ruling group, and to support the social stability of the State which promotes and orchestrates those ends.

While the existence of a dual education system based largely upon social class might be expected to create or at least exacerbate dangerous social and cultural divisions within the populace, there is actually only sporadic objection to the system as such.[7] Few Australians perceive a contradiction between the egalitarian rhetoric of the State and the individualist thrust of its dominant ideological apparatus, the system of formal, State-regulated education. The 'equal' expenditures on schools and the perceived commonality of the core curriculum, the ideology of the nuclear family and the rhetoric of private choice and equal competition, all serve to maintain the ideal of a democratic society as an aggregate of individuals free to choose their destinies.

The educational apparatus has become more and more involved in the shaping of individual 'character' and motivation, more and more deeply implicated in the life of families and the community, more and more in control of the selection of workers and higher echelon employees. As the school-work nexus tightens, as the school–family couple dominates both individual and collective educational decision making, and as increasing numbers depend upon government assistance for their very survival, neither family nor community remains to stand between the individual and the State.

The worst excesses of rampant dog-eat-dog individualism in Australian society are masked and defused by the egalitarianism of a people who believe strongly in a 'fair go', luck, mateship, the rewards of hard work allied with natural talent and an abhorrence of 'artifically created' difference (see B. Kapferer 1987). Thus does the dual education system serve the State, and through it, the dominant fraction of the ruling group; both public and private schools work to establish the hegemony of capital. Thus is the labour market regulated, and meritocratically achieved worldly success legitimated. Humphrey McQueen's dictum, 'Capitalism does not have a party, it has the state' (cited in Crough and Wheelwright 1982, p.195) resonates with nothing more loudly and clearly than with the enculturating and selecting projects of the public and private schools of Australia.

Notes

1. For the purpose of this paper I define 'State' as the sum of those structures, processes and agencies which maintain and underpin the social order of capitalist production.
2. Australian education is taken here as a specific case of a more widely observed western phenomenon. While the substantive details presented here are perhaps peculiarly Australian, even South Australian, the general argument from them is, I think, widely applicable beyond national boundaries.
3. They are also massively supported by the communications apparatus of the State. Local television programmes, radio programmes and the daily and weekly press include regular items on the desirability of the freedom to choose particular types of school, value for money invested, laudable examination results, high levels of discipline, and the superiority of private schooling in terms of autonomy, lack of bureaucratic intervention, and – the preferred term of the private schools themselves –independence.
4. While (non-Catholic) private school students constitute 6 per cent of all Year 8 students in South Australia, the private schools produced 14 per cent of Year 12 students in 1984, and 21 per cent of those entering higher education in 1985. Furthermore, 28 per cent of those entering South Australia's most prestigious institute of higher learning, the University of Adelaide, have come from private non-Catholic schools, with a further 16 per cent drawn from Catholic schools which enrol 11 per cent of Year 8 students (see Power and Robinson 1986, pp.50, 56).
5. These transcripts were collected in the later 1970s. Despite changes in the public examination procedures in South Australia since then, the overall concerns expressed by teachers remain identical, as later observations and interviews have revealed.
6. Although this scheme has been largely superseded, it is still in use for those (apparently around 57 per cent, though probably about 45 per cent) who do not remain in school to the end of Year 12.

7. The abolition of private schools has seemed a lost cause since the interest group Defence of Government Schools brought, and lost, a case against state aid in the Supreme Court of Victoria in the early 1980s.

References

Althusser, L. (1971) 'Ideology and ideological state apparatuses' in *Lenin and philosophy and other essays*. London, New Left Books.

Barrett, M. and McIntosh, M. (1982) *The Anti-social Family*. London, Verso.

Chodorow, N. (1978) *The Reproduction of Mothering*. Berkeley, Univ. California.

Connell, R.W., Ashenden, D., Kessler, S. and Dowsett, G. (1982) *Making the Difference*. Sydney, Allen and Unwin.

Crough, G. and Wheelwright, T. (1982) *Australia: a Client State*. Harmondsworth, Penguin.

David, M.E. (1980) *The State, the Family and Education*. London, Routledge & Kegan Paul.

Donzelot, J. (1980) *The Policing of Families*. London, Hutchinson.

Education Department of South Australia (1981) *Our Schools and Their Purposes: into the 80s*. Adelaide, Government Printer.

Hogan, M. (1984) *Public Versus Private Schools*. Harmondsworth, Penguin.

Hyams, B. and Bessant, B. (1972) *Schools for the People?* Camberwell, Longman.

Kapferer, B. (1987) *Legends of People, Myths of State*. Washington, Smithsonian.

Kapferer, J. (1986) 'Curricula and the reproduction of structured social inequalities', *Curriculum Inquiry*. 16, 1: 5–31.

Kapferer, J. (1987) 'Youth policy and the state: Australia, Britain and Sweden', *Discourse*. 8, 1.

Karmel, P. (chairman) (1971) *Education in South Australia*. Adelaide, Government Printer.

Lasch, C. (1977) *Haven in a Heartless World*. New York, Basic Books.

McArthur, M. (1986) 'Fair go! A values base for floundering public schools?' S.A. Education Department: unpublished paper.

Marginson, S. (1986) 'Selection into higher education', *Australian Universities' Review*. 29, 1: 21–24.

Power, C. and Robinson, F. (1986) *Access to Higher Education*, Canberra, CTEC.

Reiger, K. (1985) *The Disenchantment of the Home*. Melbourne, Oxford U.P.

Senior Secondary Assessment Board of South Australia (1986) *Annual Report 1985*. Adelaide, Government Printer.

CHAPTER 6

The 1980s: De-Industrialization and Change in White Working Class Male and Female Youth Cultural Forms[1]

Lois Weis

The field of cultural studies has exerted increased impact on research in education during the past ten years. A number of studies have been conducted on youth cultural forms in school, and we now possess a great deal of information regarding cultural forms of males and females of varying social class and racial backgrounds in Canada, the United States, Britain, Australia, and elsewhere.[2] There is a danger, however, that such snapshots, including my own work, become reified, denying the ever-changing quality of culture. Thus, there is a danger that Willis's description in 1977 becomes 'the' culture of working class boys, or my own analysis of black students in an urban community college in the United States, 'the' culture of underclass blacks. Culture is ever changing and it is important to monitor such change by engaging in field studies.[3]

My research in Freeway was designed with this end in mind: to focus on the process of cultural formation during a period of intense de-industrialization. I focus specifically on white males and females in a secondary school in the United States in order to compare and contrast their identity formation with that described in earlier studies. It is my intent to examine the dynamic quality of culture so that *our* constructions of culture do not become reified.[3] This is an ever-present danger, of course, since we become invested in the cultures we construct. It is all too easy to encourage reification of black underclass culture, for example, since I did the work, even though the data were gathered eight years ago. This is perhaps, 'natural', but ought to be guarded against. We should continually check our social constructions against the real world.

The purpose of this chapter is to compare and contrast the culture of white working class males and females in one secondary school in the United States as well as compare these cultures with those noted by previous investigators. The possible relationship between the economy and cultural form will be speculated upon.

De-industrialization

At the end of the Second World War, American corporations dominated world markets. The American steel industry, for example, was virtually the only major producer in the world. By the 1960s, Germany, Italy, France, Japan and Britain had rebuilt their steel industry, using the most advanced technology, and they became highly competitive with American industry. By the 1970s the American steel industry was in decline relative to other countries. For whatever reasons (and many have been offered), the industry continues to decline and its effects are being widely felt in the United States.

Factory closings are not restricted to the steel industry, and, while more common to the north-eastern United States, are not confined to this area. Gone are many of the jobs in basic production–jobs in heavy industry, automobiles and manufacturing. The largest growth sector in the economy is now service, not production. Jobs in the service sector demand retraining, pay less, provide less security, and often demand relocation. De-industrialization means a less secure, generally lower, standard of living for working class Americans.

Bluestone and Harrison argue that 'when the employment lost as a direct result of plant, store, and office *shutdowns* during the 1970s is added to the job loss associated with runaway shops, *it appears that more than 32 million jobs were destroyed* [my emphasis]. Together, runaways, shutdowns, and permanent physical cutbacks short of complete closure may have cost the country as many as 38 million jobs.'[4] Many displaced workers remain unemployed today; others obtained jobs in the lower paying service sector. From all indications, de-industrialization is not temporary. It represents a radical shift in the nature of the American economy and the way in which workers intersect with this economy.

Capital is more mobile than ever before. Investment is taking place but in ways that signal a radical departure from previous decades. Basic production is occurring with the help of American finance, but American labour is being used less and less in this capacity. Jobs available in the United States are simply different than those available even a decade ago. Bluestone and Harrison are worth quoting in full here:

> U.S. Steel has billions to spend, but instead of rebuilding steel capacity, it paid $6 billion to acquire Marathon Oil of Ohio. General Electric is expanding its capital stock, but not in the United States. During the 1970s, GE expanded its worldwide payroll by 5,000, but did so by adding 30,000 foreign jobs and reducing its U.S. employment by 25,000. RCA Corporation followed the same strategy, cutting its U.S. employment by 14,000 and increasing its foreign work force by 19,000. It is the same in the depressed automobile industry. Ford Motor Company reports that more than 40 per cent of its capital budget will be spent outside the United States, while General Motors has given up its plans to build a new multibillion-dollar plant in Kansas City, Missouri, and instead has shifted its capital spending to one of its facilities in Spain.[5]

Given that working class subjectivities as noted by previous investigators have taken their shape and form historically in an economic context that is undergoing radical change, what is happening to cultural forms? In particular, for present purposes, what is happening to white working class male and female youth cultural forms given that the forms noted in previous investigations are linked to patterns of male employment, in particular, which are being eroded? Data reported here are not to be construed as a strict empirical test of a 'hypothesis' regarding the primacy of the economy in any sense. However, data were gathered on youth cultural forms in school in an area which is undergoing intense de-industrialization. The question is, are white youth cultural forms different from those noted in previous investigations? There is no apparent evidence that Freeway – the community in which data were gathered – is any different from other working class communities in which previous investigators did their work except that de-industrialization and associated job loss are current. In other words, the speculated upon long-term trend of the American economy is being enacted right before the eyes of today's youth.

Freeway

Data were gathered as part of a larger ethnographic investigation of Freeway High. I spent the academic year 1985–6 in the high school, acting as a participant-observer for three days a week for the entire year. Data were gathered in classrooms, study halls, the cafeteria, extra-curricular activities and through intense interviews with over sixty juniors, all teachers of juniors, the vice principals, social worker, guidance counsellors, and others. Data collection centred on the junior class since this is a key point of decision when PSATs, SATs and so forth must be considered.[6] In addition, this is, in the state where Freeway is located, the time when the bulk of a series of state tests must be taken if entrance to a four-year college is being considered.[7] I focus on the high school both as a way of gaining access to adolescents and to discuss, at a later point, the relationships between within-school processes and cultural production.

Freeway is an ideal site in which to conduct this investigation. Examination of data gathered for the Standard Metropolitan Statistical Area (of which Freeway is a part; data for Freeway *per se* are not available) confirms a number of trends which are reflective of Bluestone and Harrison's argument. Occupational data for 1960–80 (see Appendix) suggest that the most striking decreases in the area are found in the categories of 'Precision; Craft and Repair' and 'Operators, Fabricators and Laborers'. These two categories constitute virtually all of the so-called 'blue-collar jobs'. When combined, data suggest a relative decline of 22.3 per cent in the 'blue collar' category from 1960 to 1980. A look at some of the more detailed sub-categories reveals more striking decline. Manufacturers, for example, have experienced an overall decline in the area of 35 per cent between 1958 and 1982.

Data also suggest an increase in the 'Technical, Sales and Administrative Support' category. These occupations constituted 22.8 per cent of the total in 1960 as compared with close to 31 per cent in 1980, representing an increase of over one-third. Increases in 'Service' and 'Managerial and Professional Specialty' categories also reflect a shift away from industries and toward service occupations.

Although data on occupational trends in Freeway *per se* are not available, the 35 per cent loss in manufacturing noted above is due in part to the closing of the Freeway steel plant. The plant payroll in 1969 was at a record high of $168 million dollars, topping 1968 by \$14 million. The average daily employment was 18,500. Production of basic oxygen furnace and open hearth was at a near record of 6,580,000 tons.[8]

In the first seven months of 1971, layoffs at the Freeway plant numbered 4000 and decline continued into the 1980s. From 18,500 jobs in 1970, there were only 3700 production and 600 supervisory workers left in 1983, and 3600 on layoff.[9] At the end of 1983, the plant closed. All that remains of close to 20,000 are 370 bar mill workers.

Here I will explore one piece of the larger project in which data were gathered. I focus specifically on male and female cultural form and the extent to which youth in a de-industrializing area construct a culture similar to that noted in previous studies. Data presented here are based on in-depth interviews with twenty white working class girls and twenty boys. All students are in their junior year of high school.

Males

Previous studies of white working class boys suggest that opposition to authority and school meanings is deeply embedded within the cultural formation. The most obvious dimension of the lads' culture in Paul Willis's *Learning to Labour,* for example, is a generalized opposition towards authority and school meanings. The lads engage in behaviour designed to show resentment while stopping just short of outright confrontation. They also exhibit extensive absenteeism, signalling their generally oppositional stance; their 'struggle to win symbolic and physical space from the institution and its rules, and to defeat its main perceived purpose: to make you "work" '.[10] The core skill here is being able to get out of any given class, thus preserving personal mobility within the school. Personal mobility encourages the preservation of the collective – cutting class means meeting friends elsewhere. This can be seen as a limited defeat of individualism.

In important ways Willis's analysis goes further, and it has become a model, in a sense, for the 'reading' of cultural form. By rejecting the world of the school and the compliance of the 'ear 'oles', the lads reject mental labour, cross-valorizing patriarchy and the distinction between mental and manual labour. Thus, for the lads, manual labour is associated with the social superiority of masculinity, and mental labour with the social inferiority of femininity. Since, as Harry Braverman, Michael Buroway, and others have argued, hierarchical capitalist social relations demand the progressive divorce of mental from manual labour, and certainly profit from (if not demand), gender-based distinctions, the lads' rejection of the world of the school, and the way in which this rejection is linked to masculinity, reproduces at an even deeper level the social relations of production necessary for the maintenance of a capitalist economy.[11] Although the lads live their rejection of the school as a form of cultural autonomy and freedom, they help, at the level of their own culture, to reproduce existing social structure.

While it is tempting to relate these behaviours to adolescence rather than social class *per se*, it is important to note that white working class males in the community college exhibit similar attitudes toward authority and engage in comparable behaviour.[12] About a month or so after school opened, students in Howard London's study began injecting *sotto-voce* taunts into classroom lectures and discussions. This opposition took a distinctively class form in that, for the most part, it was done by students in manual training programs and aimed at liberal arts teachers or vocational training teachers who were considered too abstract. Law enforcement students did not harass teachers who were ex-detectives, for example, but they did harass the lawyer who taught legal aspects of police work. Students reacted negatively only in those classes that were 'too intellectual', that is, too centred on mental labour.[13]

A third example of white working class male cultural forms comes from Robert Everhart's ethnography of a junior high school in the United States.[14] Unlike Willis, Everhart does not focus on those students who create *overtly* opposition forms in the school, but the disengagement from mental labour is, nevertheless, clear. He focuses on those who more or less strike a compromise with school culture, giving the bare minimum, taking care to complete necessary assignments without causing undue trouble.

That Everhart's students complete assignments and do not engage in the *overt* rejection of school content or form does not mean that they are involved in the process of schooling, nor that their valuation of achievement *qua* achievement is any different from that of the lads. All it means is that they do not value the specific and overt negation of school meanings in the same way the lads do. Students view school as a place to meet friends, 'goof off', smoke a joint, and pursue other activities that are not related to the official learning process. To students at Harold Spencer Junior High School, it was important that one should conform to the requirements of the school in sufficient detail so as to 'get by', all the while creating a separate culture that permitted the maximum element of self-determination.

A common thread runs through these studies: that being the often overt and sometimes covert rejection of school meanings and culture. There is an attempt on the part of the working class youth to carve out their own space within the institution – space which can then be filled with *their* fundamentally, anti-school meanings rather than institutional meanings.

A second and third element of culture noted by previous investigators is that of racism and sexism. The most articulate on these points is Willis, but other investigators have noted these themes as well. Willis argues that male white working class youth culture is formed in reaction to that of females and racial minorities. For example, mental labour is not only less valued than manual labour, but it is less valued than *because* it is feminine. This encourages patriarchal relations in the sense of separate spheres for males and females, the male being superior. The lads also impose upon girlfriends an ideology of domesticity, 'the patterns of homely and subcultural capacity and incapacity', all of which stress the restricted role of women.[15] The very cultural affirmation of the male self, and the particular form of the female 'other' affirms patriarchal relations.

The lads, too, emphasize racial division and, in so doing, help to fracture a potentially non-fractured working class.[16] In suggesting that racial minorities are different than themselves, white working class youth encourage the fractured nature of the working class which ultimately benefits capitalists more than anyone.[17] The living out of racism and sexism, then, sets white working class males apart from 'others'.

The question of the extent to which the Freeway youth are the same or different must be raised. Unlike the girls (who I will discuss later), the boys in Freeway are remarkably similar to boys in previous studies, although there are some elements of beginning departure. The racism and encouragement of patriarchy are indeed there. So, too, is the negative attitude towards authority and school meanings. There are differences, however; there is a more contradictory attitude toward education among Freeway boys than previous investigators have uncovered. This contradictory attitude is more reminiscent of the black underclass in the United States than the white working class. This may be due to the changing social structure.

Male attitudes towards institutional authority and school meanings

The same resentment towards authority characterizes the Freeway boys as boys in earlier studies. Basically, resentment surrounds institutional control over student use of time, space and dress. As with Willis's lads, resentment tends to be caged in practice, and stops just short, on most occasions, of outright confrontation. Their expressed attitudes tell the story. It is noteworthy that this is unique to male cultural form, although females in Freeway exhibit some of the same sort of resentment. It must be pointed out that ideas expressed here were in response to probe questions regarding what they like and did not like about school. Many statements reflect attitudes toward control over space – where students should be and when, and what they should be doing there. Students particularly resent the lack of a place to smoke. This must be seen as more symbolic than anything else. Students resent the control institutional authorities have over their lives, and it is expressed most forcefully in the case of smoking.

Tom: I don't like the principals. Most of the teachers are assholes.

LW: Why?

Tom: They have a controlling power over the kids, or at least they try to. Me, I won't take shit from no one. That's the way I am.

[...] Whatever they do, they can't bother me, cuz when I get my diploma I can say what I want to them.

[...] The kids should have some rights. Like, let me say for one example, I know there's smokers in this school. Alot of kids smoke. To solve all smoking problems with kids going outside and skipping classes, give the kids at least once a day a place to go to – a room – and have one cigarette or something. Five minutes a day.

[...] They [school authorities] play head games with kids... They think they can push you any which way they want.

LW: If they're pushing you around, why stay for your diploma?

Tom: Cuz it helps for, like, a job or whatever. It's like a reference for this, this, this. It's like a key that opens many doors.

***

Bob: I think _____ is an asshole. He's an assistant principal. I know he's in an authority position, but he just seems to think he has control over anything that happens in this school at any time.
[...] The way the control is handled [is what I resent]. Mr _____, that man has no sense of humour. He's like, blah, and he just starts acting like God or something. [...] They have to have control somehow. It's their job. It's jus the way they're going about it [that is bad]. The way_____is going about it bothers me.

***

Rob: It's like a dictatorship here [school].
LW: Who dictates?
Rob: Mr_____ , Mr_____ , Mr _____ is the worst. He'd take me out of school for being late to class. You woke up late or something, and he comes and kicks you out. He suspended us for two days for skipping class.
[...] That just makes you more mad and you wait to get even with him. Next time you come in, you come in late again. Put a stink bomb in his office. Walk by and throw it in.[18]
LW: So, who wins in the end?
Rob: Probably he will. Or we do when we graduate.

***

Jim: I'd like to see the teachers give the students a chance to become a mature adult. I'll give you an example. The smoking. About 50/60 kids get caught a year and get butt duty. You got to pick up paper. Do you think that is going to stop the kids? No way, that doesn't make any sense.
I'd like to see them give the kids a chance ... The seniors ... What they should do is just try it – a lounge, seniors only. Have it supervised every period by the teachers, like a hall duty, but only seniors would go in there.
[...] I'd like to see the students pick what they want to wear. In the summer it gets extremely hot. You got to wear jeans; you can't wear shorts.

And I think that administration is a little too harsh on
students. A kid skips a class. Three days' detention. School
policy. They're going out of their way to look for what's
wrong. They're going out of their way. Like they go to
[the local donut shop] to find the kids.

***

Joe: There should be a smoking lounge. Because why should
kids get in trouble for smoking. Other schools have
smoking lounges. It sounds reasonable.
[. . .] [Also] the detention. The reasons why kids get
detention are stupid.
LW: Like, give me an example.
Joe: Like being late a certain amount of times. You get a
detention. That should be changed.
LW: Why?
Joe: Because why should somebody get detention for something that might not have been their fault? A locker that
won't open. Reasons like that. Go to the lavatory. If you
have to go to the lavatory, you're gonna be late. Teachers
don't let you go during the period.

Generally speaking, students follow school rules and anyone
walking into the high school would gain the impression of 'order'.
Students do, however, skip out to go to the local donut shop and
stink bombs are thrown occasionally into the vice principal's
office. There is a grumbling over authority, and occasional
struggle, but the school obviously wins since there is no
breakdown of order.[19]

Students resent the institutional authority and the way in which
it plays itself out in the form of detentions, administrators walking
to the donut shop, the continual patrolling of parking lots and
school exits to look for smokers, and the existence of even a
minimal dress code. In this sense, students parallel earlier studies.

At the same time, students express a more positive attitude
towards schooling per se and accompanying mental labour than is
the case in earlier studies. There is, at Freeway, a group of about
thirty juniors who were pulled out in grade nine and given an
accelerated curriculum. This is known as the 'advanced group'.
Although, as will be seen below, students in the advanced class
tend to want to pursue college more than others, virtually all the
students express *some* value for education, even though it is in
highly utilitarian terms. It is not the wholesale rejection
articulated by Willis, for example.

John: College prep [is my major]. It's the only thing to do.

LW: What do you mean?

John: Well, around here cuz there's nothing else. Everything's going down south. Like any kind of good jobs, a better education's what you're gonna hafta need. Unless you plan to sweep the floors someplace the rest of your life. And that ain't really gonna be my style.

[...] Like, I work at the Aud Club [private club] now, and he'll [dad] pick me up and I'll be complaining and he'll say, 'See, get a good education, get a good job.'

[...] I'm a bus boy. I wait on people. Serve 'em shrimp cocktail. Pick up their dirty dishes, things like that. You're there and you do nothin' but runnin' around. Do this and do that for this person. Get their dishes and bring these people soup. It's a bitch.

[...] He [dad] says, 'Wouldn't you rather have these people waiting on you? Go to school and get an education.' My father never get a high school education. He got a GED [high school equivalency diploma]. He wants me to keep going.

***

Bob: Well, I want to go to college. I don't know what for yet. I was thinking of something like Biology, something like that. Probably [City Community College] or [Suburban Community College]. Probably transfer [to a four year school].

[...] My mother wants me to [go to college]. So does my father. My mother has post-education [at a local hospital]. She was a worker there. But my father quit school in the middle of 12th grade.   (an advanced student)

***

LW: What do you think you want to do when you graduate?

Sam: I want to go to college for two years. And, then, hopefully get into computers. If not that, the business field.

***

LW: What do you hope to do when you leave high school?

Jerry: College, but I'm still not certain which one, I'm looking around here, but if I get a scholarship, I'll go away. Right now it looks pretty good, whether it be sports or educational. (an advanced student)

***

Jim: I've got a couple of colleges I've been looking at. University of Maryland or University of Seattle. And I was thinking of pursuing the Commercial Art field and becoming, eventually, a comic book artist or an illustrator. I'll probably take out student loans. Working part time. I'm a stock boy. I have a bit of money put aside. I've been doing it six months.

***

Seth: I'm going to go to college; hopefully an aeronautical school in Chicago. I been thinking to myself, I'm really going to do well in college.
LW: What made you decide to do that?
Seth: The greediness. The money. I want a well-paying job.

***

LW: What do you plan to do when you graduate?
Steve: Go to college.
LW: For what?
Steve: I haven't decided. I just wanna go. Can't get a job without going to college. You got to be educated to get a job, a good job: you don't want to live off burgers when you're old.

***

LW: What do you plan to do when you leave school?
Larry: Go straight to college.
LW: Where do you want to go? What do you want to do?
Larry: You know, I can't tell you specifically, but I want to make money. I don't want to end up like my parents. Nothing against them.
LW: What do you mean?
Larry: Well, I want to own a house. I don't want to use the term 'made ends meet'. I don't ever want to have that in my vocabulary. (an advanced student)

***

> *Bill:* My dad is a machinist. He needs one more day in the plant to get his twenty years. He's fighting now to get one more day.
> [...] [I want to get to college] cuz I see what happened to him. He's working for like 7/8 dollars an hour. Like [what] he used to get in the plant, compared to that, it's nothing. To get a better chance, you got to go to college.

I do not mean to imply here that all white working class youth intend to go to college, or that they have turned their back on manual labouring jobs totally. But it is noteworthy that of the boys interviewed, 40 per cent expressed the desire to go to a two- or four-year college, and there is far less celebration of manual labouring jobs than earlier studies suggest. If students celebrate traditionally working class jobs, they are skilled or craft jobs, such as motorcycle mechanic, machinist, tool and dye maker, and so forth. Such jobs require further training as well. Not one boy interviewed discussed the possibility of being a generalized wage labourer.

The boys tend to look at schooling in highly utilitarian terms. The school will allow them to make a lot of money, get a 'good' job, and so forth. They are explicit about the fact that they expect the school to keep them 'off burgers', and buy a house. They may resent institutional authority and school meanings, but many intend to go on simply because they feel they 'have to'. It is not the flavour of Willis's lads at all; indeed, even those most negative about school concede the importance of the 'credential', and are willing to put in their time, and even go to college. As Rob puts it when discussing the guerrilla warfare between students and school officials: 'I guess we [win] when we graduate', thus suggesting the usefulness of the credential.

Patriarchal relations

There is emerging a more contradictory attitude towards education than previous studies suggest; students resent institutional authority but affirm the process of schooling in other ways. In terms of affirmation of patriarchal relations, basically, students exhibit the same attitudes as in previous studies. One or two boys seem to exist slightly outside of these boundaries, but basically white working class males affirm patriarchy. Discussions with males indicate that the vast majority speak of future wives and families in highly patriarchal terms. This, as I will suggest in the next section, contrasts sharply with the current sentiments of females.

LW: You say you want more kids than your parents have. How many kids do you want?

Bob: Five.

LW: Who's going to take care of these kids?

Bob: My wife, hopefully. Unless she's working too. If she wants to work, we'd figure something out. Day care centre, something like that. I'd prefer if she didn't want to. I'd like to have her at home.

LW: Why?

Bob: I think it's up to the mother to do it. I wouldn't want to have a babysitter raising my kids. Like, I think the principles should be taught by the parents, not by some babysitter.

***

LW: How about your life ten years from now; what do you think you'll be doing?

Rob: Probably be married. Couple of kids.

LW: Do you think your wife will work?

Rob: Hopefully she won't have to cuz I'll make enough money.

LW: Would you rather she didn't work?

Rob: Naw [Yes, I'd rather she didn't work].

LW: Women shouldn't work?

Rob: Housework.

***

Jim: Yes, I'd like to get married, like to get myself a nice house, with kids.

LW: Who is going to be taking care of those kids?

Jim: Depends how rich I am. If I'm making a good salary, I assume that the wife, if she wanted to, would stay home and tend to the kids. If there was ever a chance when she wanted to go someplace, fine, I'd watch the kids. Nothing wrong with that. Equal responsibility because when you were consummating the marriage it was equal responsibility.

LW: So, you're willing to assume it?

Jim: Up to a certain point ... Like if she says I'm going to go out and get a job and you take care of the kids 'You draw all day' [he wants to be a commercial artist]. 'So, I draw; that's what's been supporting us for so many years.' I mean, if she starts dictating to me, there has to be a good discussion about the responsibilities.

[...] When both parents work, it's been proven that the amount of education they learn, it goes down the tubes, or they get involved in drugs. Half the kids who have drug problems, both of their parents work. If they are doing terribly in school, their parents work.

***

LW: When you get married, what will your wife be doing?
Lanny: Well, before we had any kids, she'd be working, but if we had kids, she wouldn't work, she'd be staying home, taking care of the kids.

***

Seth: I wouldn't mind my wife working as far as secretarial work or something like that. Whatever she wanted to do and she pursued as a career. If there was children around, I'd like her to be at home, so I'd like my job to compensate for just me working and my wife being at home.

***

LW: Do you think your wife would want to work?
Sam: I wouldn't want her to work.

***

LW: Let's say you did get married and have children, and your wife wanted to work.
Bill: It all depends on if I had a good job. If the financial situation is bad and she had to go to work, she had to go to work.
LW: And if you got a good job?
Bill: She'd probably be a regular woman.
LW: Staying at home? Why is that a good thing?
Bill: I don't know if it's a good thing, but it'd probably be the normal thing. But in today's society most women are working, so...

Without question, most of the boys are envisioning family life in highly patriarchal terms. They see the possibility that their wives might work, but only out of 'necessity', or before children are born. They wish to see their own income sufficient to 'support' a family, enabling their wives to take care of their children. Of course, the vast majority of their own mothers work, so their vision is not necessarily grounded in their own lived reality. They would 'help when they could', but they see children as basically *her* responsibility and they intend for their wives to be at home in a 'regular' fashion.

Only a handful of boys constructed a future other than that above. Significantly, only one boy constructed a future in which his wife *should* work, although he does not talk about children. A few boys reflect the sentiment that marriage is a 'ball and chain', and one boy said the high divorce rate makes marriage less attractive. Both these latter themes are elaborated by the girls, as I will indicate later.

> *LW:* What kind of person do you want to marry?
>
> *Vern:* Someone who is fairly good looking, but not too good looking so she'd be out, with other people screwing her up. Someone who don't mind what I'm doing, let me go out with the guys. I won't mind if she goes out with the girls either. I want her to have a job so she ain't home all the time. Cuz a woman goes bonkers if she's at home all day. Give her a job and let her get out of the house.
>
> [...] People tended to get married as soon as they got out of school, not as soon as, but a couple of years after. I think people nowadays don't want to get married until 20, 30.
>
> *LW:* And that's because of what?
>
> *Vern:* They've seen too many divorces.

It is noteworthy that Vern is the only boy that discusses divorce as an impediment to marriage. Almost every girl interviewed discussed divorce.

The boy below expresses the sentiment that marriage is a 'ball and chain', and that he wants no part of it. Only a couple of the boys expressed a similar sentiment or elaborated a theme of 'freedom' associated with being single. Again, this is unlike the girls.

> *Tom:* I don't want to get married; I don't want to have children. I want to be pretty much free. If I settle down with someone, it won't be through marriage.
>
> *LW:* Why not?
>
> *Tom:* Marriage is a ball and chain. Then marital problems come up, financial problems, whatever. I don't really want to get involved in them intense kind of problems between you and a spouse... To me it's a joke.
>
> *LW:* Tell me why you think that.
>
> *Tom:* Well, I see alot of people. I look at my father and mother. They don't get along, really.

Drawing on their own experience the vast majority of boys at Freeway High hope to set up patriarchal homes. Only a few question the basis of marriage, and only one even begins to question a fundamental premise of patriarchy – that women's place is in the home and men's place is in the public sphere.

Racism

Among the boys there is evidence of racism within the school, as was the case in earlier studies. Freeway is a divided town, even though it is small, and blacks and Hispanics tend to live on one side of the 'tracks', and whites on the other, although there are whites who live in a certain section of the largely minority side. Virtually no minorities live in the white area, which is not true of larger American cities. Most of the blacks live in a large public housing project, located near the old steel plant. Most project residents receive welfare and have done so for a number of years. Much of the racism seems to play itself out around girls, and to some extent drug use, as the examples below suggest.

> *Jim:* The minorities are really bad into drugs. You're talking everything. Anything you want, you get from them. A prime example, the _____ward of Freeway, about twenty years ago the _____ ward was predominantly white, my grandfather used to live there. Then Italians, Polish, the Irish people, everything was fine. The houses were maintained; there was a good standard of living.
>
> [...] The blacks brought drugs. I'm not saying white people didn't have drugs, they had drugs, but to a certain extent. But drugs were like a social thing. But now you go down to the _____ ward, it's amazing, it's a ghetto. Some of the houses are ok. They try to keep them up. Most of the homes are really, really terrible. They throw garbage on the front lawn; it's sickening. You talk to people from [surrounding suburbs]. Anywhere you talk to people, they tend to think the majority of our school is black. They think you hang with black people; listen to black music.
>
> [...] A few of them [blacks] are starting to go into the _____ ward now, so they're moving around. My parents will be around there when that happens, but I'd like to be out of there.

* * *

LW: There's no fighting and stuff here [school], is there?
Clint: Yeah, alot between blacks and whites.
LW: Who starts them?
Clint: Blacks.
LW: Do blacks and whites hang out in the same place?
Clint: Some do; [the blacks] live on the other side of town.
   [...] Alot of it [fights] starts with blacks messing with white
   girls. That's how alot of them start. Even if they [white
   guys] don't know the white girl, they don't like to see ...
LW: How do you feel about that yourself?
Clint: I don't like it. If I catch them [blacks] near my sister,
   they'll get it. I don't like to see it like that. Most of them
   [my friends] see it that way.
LW: Do you think the girls encourage the attentions of these
   black guys?
Clint: Naw. I think the blacks just make themselves at home.
   They welcome themselves in.
LW: How about the other way around? White guys and
   black girls?
Clint: There's a few that do. There's people that I know of,
   but no one I hang around with. I don't know many white
   kids that date black girls.

***

Bill: Like my brother, he's in ninth grade. He's in trouble all
   the time. Last year he got jumped in school ... About his
   girlfriend. He don't like blacks. They come up to her and
   go, 'Nice ass', and all that shit. My brother don't like that
   when they call her 'nice ass' and stuff like that. He got
   suspended for saying 'fucking nigger'; but it's alright for a
   black guy to go up to whites and say stuff like that.
   [...] Sometimes the principals aren't doing their job. Like
   when my brother told [the assistant principal] that something is going to happen, _____ just said, 'Leave
   it alone, just turn your head.'
   [...] Like they don't know when fights start in this school.
   Like there's this one guy's kid sister, a nigger [correction]
   – a black guy – grabbed her ass. He hit him a couple of
   times. Did the principal know about it? No!
LW: What if a white guy did that?
Bill: He'd probably have punched him. But alot of it's cuz
   they're black.

Racial tension does exist within the school and it reflects tension within the community and the society as a whole. It is clear that such tension exists and that white boys attribute much of it to blacks hustling white girls. This is a male perception, but I heard no such comment from any female in the school. White males view white females as their property and resent black males speaking to them in, at times, crude terms. However, it must be noted that white boys themselves say 'nice ass' to white girls, and so forth. It is the fact that *black males* do it, not that males do it, that is offensive to white males. I never saw a white male go to the defence of a white female if she were being harassed by another white male. It is only when the male is black that their protectionist tendencies surface, indicating a deep racism which comes out over girls, in particular. White girls are considered the property of white boys, as the above section on patriarchy suggests, and they resent black intrusion onto *their* property. It is not the crude interaction *per se* that these males resent, but the fact that it comes from blacks. The thought is that they should properly address such crudeness toward their 'own' women – not 'ours'. Not one girl voiced a complaint in this area. This is not to say that females are not racist, but it is not a central cultural element in the same way as it is for boys.

Thus males tend to reflect the same patriarchal and racist attitudes and resentment toward institutional authority as expressed in earlier studies. The only obvious difference between Freeway boys and boys in earlier studies is that these boys are willing to place a more positive value on schooling in the abstract.

Females

Previous studies of working class high school females suggest that girls elaborate, at the level of their own culture, a private/public dichotomy which emphasizes the centrality of the private and marginalizes the public.[20] Home/family life is central for adolescent girls, and wage labour secondary. As many studies have shown, working class girls elaborate what Angela McRobbie has called an 'ideology of romance', constructing a gender identity which serves to encourage women's second class status in both the home and workplace. The centrality of the private is as key to girls' culture in high school as opposition to authority is to boys' culture. It is also noteworthy that studies of working class girls in school do not uncover the opposition to authority noted for boys. There is some opposition, to be sure, but it is expressed in uniquely female terms, according to McRobbie, and is not central as it is for boys. I will treat three themes below: work outside the home, marriage and family, and attitude toward institutional authority.

Work outside the home

In light of data from previous studies which suggest a marginalized wage labour identity, the most striking point about female culture at Freeway High is that there is little evidence of such an identity.

In fact, these girls have made the obtaining of wage labour a *primary* rather than secondary goal. Almost without exception the girls desire to continue their education and they are clear that they intend to do so in order that they can get their own life in order. The girls below exemplify this point. It is noteworthy that only *one* girl interviewed mentioned marriage and a family first when talking about what they wish to do after high school. All the rest of the students stressed jobs or 'careers', with college or some form of further education being specifically discussed. It is only when I actually enquired about a family did most of the girls mention this at all. I will return to this point in the next section.

The first set of interviews below details the responses of girls in what is known as the 'advanced' curriculum. I divide the girls into advanced and non-advanced for present purposes, since, unlike the boys, their overall responses do tend to differ somewhat. Advanced students were selected in ninth grade for accelerated work. Only thirty out of a class of approximately 300 are so accelerated. Students in this group generally want to attend a four-year college and girls talk in terms of actual careers, often non-traditional ones. Girls in the 'regular classes' also talk about continuing their education after high school, but generally focus on the two-year college, business institutions, or schools for hairdressing. Both groups of girls, however, stress job or 'career' ahead of family, although the form of work desired tends to differ.

Judy, Rhonda, Jennifer, Jessica and Liz are members of the advanced class. With the exception of Rhonda, who wants to become a medical technician, all intend to pursue careers which demand at least a four-year college degree. Some, like Jennifer, intend to go to graduate school. It must be clear that these are responses to a question about post-high-school plans.

Judy: I'm thinking of [State University] for Electrical Engineering. I know I'm going to go into that.

LW: How did you pick Electrical Engineering?

Judy: Cuz my brother is an electrical engineer... He works for General Electric. He has a BA.

***

Rhonda: [I'll] probably go into Medicine.
LW: Any particular area?
Rhonda: Medical technician, maybe.
LW: Would you consider being a nurse or doctor?
Rhonda: I considered being a nurse. But with all the strikes and them saying they're underpaid. I read alot about the job.

***

Jennifer: [I want] to go to college but I'm not sure where. And I want to go into Psychology, I think.
[...] I'd love to be a psychiatrist but I don't think I'll ever make it through medical school. So I was talking with a guidance counselor and she said you could get a Ph.D. in Psychology and there are alot of good jobs that go along with that.
[...] I think I'm forced [to go to college]. I don't think I have a choice.

***

Jessica: My mother wants me to be in engineering like my brother cuz he's so successful. I have an interest with the the behavior of marine animals. Which is kind of stupid cuz we don't live anywhere near an ocean so I was thinking of going to Florida State. My parents don't want me to go to any other school but [State University] so I haven't brought this up yet. I figure we can wait awhile.

***

LW: What are you going to do when you leave high school?
Liz: College.
LW: Do you know which college?
Liz: I'm thinking of [State University] in Physical Therapy.

Aside from Jennifer, whose father is head of the Chemistry lab at a local hospital, these girls are not from professional families. On the contrary, they are the daughters mainly of industrial labourers and they are thinking of obtaining a four-year college education and gaining some type of career. It is noteworthy that two of these girls are being encouraged by their families to go into engineering, one of the most non-traditional fields for women.[21] It might be hypothesized that as working class individuals do obtain professional positions, they are disproportionately in areas such as engineering, which are seen as having a direct relation with hands-on labouring processes. Obviously, I cannot prove this, but it is noteworthy that two girls are being encouraged by their families to pursue this end.[22]

The excerpts below are statements of girls in the regular classes. They, too, are, without exception, planning to pursue jobs, although most are those associated with two-year colleges or business institutes. They also tend to be jobs in sex-segregated ghettos.

Lorna: Well I go to [a cooperative vocational education programme] for food service and I think I want to be a caterer.

I don't want to be sitting down all the time. I like to be on my feet moving [she does not wish to go into business even though her shorthand teacher says she has 'potential'.] I like to cook and stuff [but] you get to do everything, not just stay in the kitchen.

[...] [Suburban Community College] has got a two-year course, and then if I want to, I can transfer my credits and stuff and go to a four-year college. My mother's got a friend, she teaches Food Service in a college and she was telling me about it. Like what to do and stuff.

***

Loretta: [I want to go to] [State University].

LW: When you get out of [State University], what do you hope to do?

Loretta: Become a lawyer, have a family, I guess, but not until I graduate from college. A lot of my friends want to go to college.

***

Susan: I'll go to [the community college]. I don't want to go four years to school. I can just go two years and become a registered nurse and get a job. I volunteeer at [the local hospital] so I'm hoping to have a foot in the door when it comes time for a job.

***

LW: When you leave high school, what do you want to do?
Carol: Alot of things. I do want to go to college for Fashion Design. I don't know how good I'll do.
LW: Where do you want to go?
Carol: I haven't thought about it. But as soon as I graduate [from high school] I want to get my New York State license [for hairdressing] and get a job and then save money so that I have money when I want it. I want to have my own salon but first of all I want to start off in somebody else's salon so I get the experience.

***

Valerie: I didn't really think I was going to go to college, unless business courses. I'm going to try for a job [after high school], and if I can get a good job out of it then I won't go to college. If it requires college training, then I'm going to go.
LW: What kind of job?
Valerie: Something with word processing.

***

Avis: I want to [go to] college around here ... They [business institute] have medical secretary; they have a lot of business stuff and that will help out. And they could get you a job.
LW: What do you think you'll be doing five years from now?
Avis: Hopefully working. A medical secretary or something.

***

Gloria: [I'll probably] go to [State University or [State College]. Become a registered nurse specializing in pediatrics.

With the exception of Loretta and Gloria, all the girls in the non-advanced curriculum wish to attend two-year colleges, business institutes or schools for hairdressing. In addition, most are thinking in terms of sex-segregated occupations. Avis and Valerie are thinking of being secretaries; Carol wants to be a hairdresser; Lorna, a food service worker; and Susan and Gloria, nurses. This is in contrast with the girls in the advanced curriculum, where there appears to be some desire to break out of these ghettos.

Unlike previous studies the students think first of continuing their education and a career or job. Students in the advanced curriculum tend to think more in terms of four-year colleges and training leading out of a sex-segregated occupational ghetto, whereas the students in the non-advanced class tend to think largely in terms of two-year colleges, business institutes, cosmetology and so forth, leading ultimately to sex-segregated jobs. This relationship is not perfect, however, and there are students in the advanced class who are intending to prepare themselves for jobs that can be obtained with two-year college degrees. Not all students in the advanced classes are thinking outside the sex-segregated labour market and not all within the other classes think within its boundaries. The relationship does exist, however, even though it is far from perfect.

Two important points should be noted here. One is the lack of primacy for a home/family identity. These girls are thinking first and foremost of obtaining jobs and the further education necessary to get these jobs. Second, it must be noted that some of these girls are, in fact, thinking of non-traditional jobs: marine biologist, engineer, psychologist, and so forth.

Given the primacy of a wage earning identity, the question must be raised, do they envision a home/family identity at all? If so, what shape does it take? I will now turn to this point.

Marriage and family

The fact that students do not marginalize a wage labour identity contrasts sharply with data collected by Valli, McRobbie, Gaskell and others[23] who argue for the creation of a *core* collective identity along these lines. Wolpe, for example, argues:

> By the time teenage girls reach school leaving age, they articulate their future in terms of family responsibilities. They reject, often realistically, advice about pursuing school subjects which could open up new avenues; the jobs they anticipate are not only within their scope, but more importantly, are easily accessible to them and in fact in conformity with their future familial responsibilities.[24]

The girls in Valli's study similarly had notions of the primacy of family responsibilities; raising children and possibly working part-time. As Valli notes:

> Experiencing office work as either secondary to or synony-mous with a sexual/home/family identity further margin-alized these students' work identities. The culture of femininity associated with office work made it easier for them to be less attached to their work and their workplace than men, who stay in paid employment because they must live up

to masculine ideology of male-as-provider. Women's identities tend to be much less intrinsically linked to wage labour than are men's.[25]

By denying wage labor primacy over domestic labor they inadvertently consented to and confirmed their own subordination, preparing themselves for both unskilled, low-paid work and unpaid domestic service.[26]

Angela McRobbie's research on working class girls in England also examines the role of gender as it intersects with class in the production of culture and ideologies. In spite of the fact that the girls in McRobbie's study know that marriage and housework are far from glamorous simply by virtue of the lives of female relatives and friends, they construct fantasy futures and elaborate an 'ideology of romance'. They create a specifically female anti-school culture which consists of interjecting sexuality into the classroom, talking loudly about boyfriends, and wearing makeup. McRobbie casts the culture in social control terms as follows:

Marriage, family life, fashion and beauty all contribute massively to this feminine anti-school culture and, in doing so, nicely illustrate the contradictions inherent in so called oppositional activities. Are the girls in the end not doing exactly what is required of them – and if this *is* the case, then could it not be convincingly argued that it is their own culture which itself is the most effective agent of social control of the girls, pushing them into compliance with that role which a whole range of institutions in capitalist society also, but less effectively, directs them towards? At the same time, they are experiencing a class relation in albeit traditionally feminine terms.[27]

The Freeway youth are markedly different. Although some assert that they wish to have some form of home/family identity, it is never asserted first, and generally only as a possibility 'later on', when their own job or career is 'settled'. Some of the girls reject totally the possibility of marriage and children; many others wish to wait 'until they are at least thirty'. The primary point, however, is that they wish to settle *themselves,* first, go to school, get a job and so forth before entering into family responsibilities. Only one of the twenty girls elaborates a romance ideology, and this girl is severely criticized by others. Significantly, they do not construct fantasy futures as a means of escape.

It is important to point out that few of the girls discuss the possibility of marriage without considering divorce. The attitude towards marriage and children does not differ between the advanced and non-advanced students. Although these students tend to differ in terms of type of envisioned relationship to wage labour and future schooling, they do not differ at all with respect to the fact that they assert the primacy of a wage labour identity over that of the home and family. The language of wanting to be 'independent' is often used in discussions about home/family and the wage labour force. It must be noted here that the initial probe questions revolved around what they wanted to do after high school, what they wished to do in five years, and in ten years. Many times the issue of family was never even mentioned. It is only at that point that I asked the girls, *specifically*, whether they wished to get married and/or have a family. Again, I quote at length here in order to give the full flavor of the girls' perspectives. The perspectives of the advanced students are presented first.

LW: Why not just get a man to support you and then you can stay home?

Penny: Cuz you can't fall back on that.

LW: Why do you say that?

Penny: Cuz what if I get a divorce and you have nothing to fall back on.

LW: Does your mother encourage you to get a job because, 'What if I get a divorce'? [her father is no longer alive]

Penny: No.

LW: So, where did you get that?

Penny: Just my own ideas. Just how things are today.

***

LW: Do you want to get married?

Jessica: Gee, I don't know. After I see all the problems that go on now, I just don't know. All the divorce. Just how can you live with somebody for forty years? I don't know, possibly... You see it [divorce] all over. I'm not living to get married.

***

Judy: I want to go to college for four years, get my job, work for a few years, and then get married... I like supporting myself. I don't want my husband supporting me. I like being independent.

LW: You're doing something very different from your

mother. Why? [mother was married at nineteen; went back
to work when Judy was in grade 3].

Judy: I think I have to. What happens if I marry a husband
who is not making good money? My dad works at Freeway
Steel. He's switching jobs all the time (although the plant is
closed, there is still piece work going on and workers are
called back according to seniority rules). He used to work
at the strip mill; now he's not. Now everything is gone,
benefits and everything.

***

LW: Do you want to get married?

Pam: I want to and I don't. I'd like to have a child but not
get married. I would like to have a child just to say it's
mine. Just to be able to raise it. If you get married, like my
mother and father are two different people. I would be
afraid that my kids would come out like me and my sister.
Like I can't talk to my father . . . And if I did get married I'd
want to be sure it would last if I had kids cuz I wouldn't be
able to get a divorce. They say that it's 'ok' if you get a
divorce and have children, but the kids change. I wouldn't
want kids to go through that, cuz I, like, see the people
around me.

***

LW: Do you think you'll get married?

Rhonda: I always thought that if I get married it would be
after college.

***

LW: Do you hope to get married; do you hope to have
children?

Liz: After college and everything's settled.

LW: What do you mean by 'everything's settled'?

Liz: I know where I'm going to live. I know what I'm going
to be doing; my job is secure, the whole thing. Nothing's
open. Everything's going to be secure.

***

Carla: Oh, I'm going to do that later [get married; have
children]. I'm going to school to get everything over with.
I wouldn't want to get married or have kids before that.

LW: Why not?

Carla: It'd be too hard. I just want to get my school work over with, get my life together, get a job. I want to be independent. I don't want to be dependent on him [my husband] for money. Then what would I do if I got divorced fifteen years, twenty years, you know how people are and marriages. Twenty years down the line you have kids, the husband has an affair or just you have problems, you get divorced, then where is that going to leave me? I want to get my life in order first, with my career and everything. Maybe it has something to do with the high divorce rates. Or the stories you hear about men losing their jobs and not having any job skills, and you see poverty, and I just don't want that. I want to be financially secure on my own.

All the above girls in the advanced class express the desire to get their 'own lives in order before marrying'. They all say that they will get married eventually, however. Only Suzanne, below, says she will never get married.

LW: Tell me a little bit about whether you want to get married?

Suzanne: [interrupts me] No. No marriage, no kids!

LW: Why not?

Suzanne: I don't like that.

LW: Why?

Suzanne: I don't think you can stay with somebody your whole life. It's dumb. Like this one kid says, 'Marriage was invented by somebody who was lucky if they lived to twenty without being bit by a dinosaur.' It's true. It started so far back and it's, like, people didn't live long. Now people live to be 80 years old. You don't stay with one person for 80 years. It's, like, impossible.

LW: [...] What makes you say that?

Suzanne: A lot of divorce. A lot of parents who fight and stuff. I couldn't handle the yelling at somebody constantly cuz I wanted to get out. I just don't want to be trapped. Back when they [parents] were kids, like, girls grew up, got married, worked for a couple of years after graduation, had two or three kids, had a white picket fence, two cars. Things are different now.

LW: How so?

Suzanne: Girls don't grow up just to be married. They grow up to be people too.

LW: And that means they don't want these other things?

Suzanne: Not that they don't want them. A lot of girls in school, they're like, 'Hey, you're [Suzanne] crazy'. I want to be married sometime, I want to have kids [but] they all want to wait. They all want to get into a career first; wait until they're thirty. It's [marriage] only 'if' though, and it's going to be late.

[...] You've got to do it [make a good life] for yourself. I don't want to be Mrs John Smith. I want to be able to do something.

[...] I mean just from what I've seen a lot of people cheat and that. I don't want that. You can't rely on them [men]. You just can't rely on them. [Also] drinking a lot. It's like, I know a lot of older guys, they drink all the time.

The girls in the advanced class all suggest that they have to get themselves together first before entering into home/family esponsibilities. Only Suzanne says she does *not* want to get married, but the rest of the girls clearly want the economic power to negotiate terms within the marriage. It is very clear from these excerpts that the conditions of their *own* lives mediate their response to family and paid work. Numerous students note the high divorce rate. Penny, for example, says, 'What if I get a divorce and you have nothing to fall back on?' Jessica states, 'After I see all the problems that go on now, I just don't know. All the divorce.' Carla also states, 'Then what if I get divorced fifteen years, twenty years, you know how people are and marriages. Twenty years down the line you have kids, the husband has an affair or you just have problems, you get divorced, then where is that going to leave me?' The lack of male jobs is also brought out by the students. Judy, for example, says 'What happens if I marry a husband who is not making good money? My dad works at Freeway Steel. He used to work at the strip mill, now he's not. Now everything is gone, benefits and everything.'

The students assert that men cannot be counted on for a *variety* of reasons – high divorce rate, drinking, lack of jobs, lack of skills, affairs and so forth. They respond to this aspect of their lived experience by establishing the primacy of wage labour in their own lives in order to hedge their chances. They are attempting to control the conditions of their *own* lives in a way that previous generations of women did not, thus articulating a challenge to the domestic code.

This same challenge is exhibited by the girls who are not in the advanced curriculum. Although they are preparing themselves for jobs in largely sex-segregated ghettos, they nevertheless challenge the Domestic Code as strongly as the others. *None* of the girls place home/family responsibilities before wage labour.

LW: Do you want to get married?
Chris: Yeah, eventually. Once I'm settled down with myself and I know I can handle myself.

***

LW: Do you want to see yourself getting married; do you think you'll have children?
Valerie: Yeah, but not right away. I'll wait until I'm about twenty-four. I just feel that I want to accomplish my own thing, like getting a job and stuff.
LW: Why not find a guy and let him support you?
Valerie: Feels like I have a purpose in life. Like I can do what I want.
LW: As opposed to?
Valerie: Feeling like *he* [emphasis hers] has to support me, and *he* has to give me money.
LW: Is that bad?
Valerie: I don't know.

***

Carol: Well I know I'm not going to get married until I'm at least 30 and have kids when I'm around 31, 32.
LW: Why?
Carol: Cuz I want to have my own freedom to experience life, everything, to travel, to go out places without having to have a babysitter or worry about kids. Plus with a beauty salon [her envisioned job] it would be hard to have kids to take care of and do that at the same time.

***

LW: Do you want to get married?
Susan: Yes.
LW: When do you think you'll get married?
Susan: I want to prove to myself that I can be on my own. I don't want no man to have to take care of me.
LW: Why?
Susan: Because my mother told me that, I don't know what the statistics are anymore, but for every marriage that lasts, every marriage doesn't, so...

Women, when they go into a marriage, they have to be thinking, 'Can I support myself?'

***

LW: When you think about your life five years from now, what do you think you'll be doing? Do you think you'll be married?

Lorna: I'm trying to get all my education so I can support myself. Why put effort and then let somebody support you? [. . .] I saw my friends getting pregnant so young. If you get married young, you're going to get pregnant young and it's going to ruin the rest of your life. That's the way I see it.

[. . .] Five years from now I'll just be able to go out to a bar. I'll be 21. And I don't want to ruin my life in just five years. Cuz as soon as you get married you're going to start having kids; then you're going to have to stay home and raise them and stuff. I don't want to have to do that.

LW: Why not?

Lorna: I like to do things. I don't want to have to sit around all the time. I just don't want to stay home all the time.

LW: Does marriage mean you're going to have to stay home all the time?

Lorna: Well, that's what I think of. You get married; you got to stay home. You can't just go out with other people. I like to go out with my friends when I want to. I like to be able to make my own decisions and if you're married, you have to sort of ask the other person, 'Can I spend the money here, can I do that?' It's, like, you got to ask permission. Well I been asking permission from my parents all my life, you know. I don't want to just get out of high school and get married, and then have to keep asking permission for the rest of my life.

LW: Will you ever get married?

Lorna: I was just talking about that today. Probably when I'm thirty. Then I'll take a couple of years to have kids.

Although the girls in the non-advanced class tend to exhibit the same themes as the advanced class girls, there is some tendency on their part to elaborate the theme of 'freedom' and, in contrast, the restrictions imposed by marriage. This is true for the earlier set of interviews as well in that a number of girls stressed 'independence'. Non-advanced girls, however, seem a bit more strident about it. Lorna, for example, states that, 'As soon as you get married, you're going to start having kids; then you're going to *have* (my emphasis) to stay home and raise them and stuff.' She then states, 'You get married; you got to stay home. You can't just go out and go out with other people. I like to make my own decisions and if you're married, you have to sort of ask the other person, "Can I spend the money here; can I do that?" It's like you got to ask permission.' Valerie, too, notes that she doesn't want to feel that '*he* (emphasis hers) has to support me, and *he* has to give me money'. Carol states that she wants 'to have [her] own freedom to experience life', implying that marriage means that she forsakes such freedom. This point cannot be pushed too strongly since both groups stress the importance of their own independence. The non-advanced students tend to stress the possibly oppressive conditions of marriage in that you have to 'ask permission', whereas the advanced students tend to stress the high divorce rate and the possibility that their husbands may leave them or not be able to get a good job. This is, however, not an overwhelming difference.

I have argued here that the girls' culture exhibits a challenge in many ways to the Domestic Code and its current manifestation in women's 'double bind'. They are definitely envisioning their lives very differently from girls in previous studies, and very differently than investigators such as Lillian Breslow Rubin and Glen Elder suggest that their mothers and grandmothers did.[28] At the end of the chapter I will speculate as to the meaning of this challenge and the way in which patriarchal forms may be challenged and reinforced at one and the same time.

Attitude towards authority

I mentioned earlier the nature of the lived contradiction emerging regarding schooling for white working class males. There is a greater acceptance of schooling than previous studies suggest, but white working class males resent institutional authority in Freeway in similar ways to that noted in earlier studies. It is interesting that this is *not* the case for girls. Basically the girls do not, as in previous studies, articulate a resentment towards institutional authority, although they are more critical than in earlier studies. Only three girls expressed resentment toward institutional authority, as follows:

Pam: They got the stupidest rules. The guys can't wear long earrings. The clothes, you have to watch it. You have to watch how you do your hair. The dress code is really stupid.

***

Chris: I want to wear shorts [in school]. The guys have to
wear pants. No halters [for girls]. If you have something
that shows your shoulders, you have to put a jacket on.
They complain about the hair, the spiked hair, they said
it was disruptive to the school.

***

LW: If you could change anything at Freeway High, what
would you change?

Carol: A lot of things. The principals, I think. I don't think
they're fair. Mr _____ [the assistant principal]. Like, if
you're late for school. Me and my sister were late two
minutes for school and we have to sit in his office the whole
period. You miss a whole class.

[. . .] At lunch, he [the assistant principal] treats us like we're
stupid or we don't know what we're doing, or we're just, I
don't know how to put it. He doesn't give anybody a fair
chance. This one table of boys all has to sit and face the
window.

He comes up every day to our table and calls us pigs.
There might be garbage on the floor, not just from us, but
he still calls us that name. And we're all sitting there going
'oink, oink, oink'. One day the whole table was sitting
there going like that and he didn't know what to do. He
acts like we're in prison.

Lunch is a free period and everyone goes in there to talk
to each other. It's like a social hour. He split our whole
table up. He told us we couldn't sit at that table anymore.
We went to a different table and he'd come to our table
every day and say there's too many people at our table.

[. . .] Like, if you're standing by a door with your jacket on,
he'll say, 'get out of here'. Or he'll give you a choice
between going home or detention for two days.

The girls do not resent authority in the same way that the boys
do. Few express any sort of resentment at all, but it is noteworthy
that a few do. Female culture in Freeway is not quite as overtly
passive as it has been portrayed in the past.

We have a very interesting situation in terms of what has
changed and what appears to have remained the same. The girls do
not marginalize a wage labour identity in the same way as earlier
studies suggest, but rather elaborate it. In line with previous
studies, however, they do not resent institutional authority either.

They are, in other words, moving closer to a convergence on this dimension.

The boys, on the other hand, celebrate patriarchy and resentment towards institutional authority. They have, however, moved to a more positive *perception* of the usefulness of education than earlier studies suggest. Interestingly enough, they appear to be moving more in line with what I called a 'lived contradiction' towards education among the American black underclass. The underclass affirms and denies education at one and the same time. This may be what is happening among white working class males as the economic base shifts.

Cultural form, patriarchy and attitudes towards school

In this section, I will briefly sketch the possible meaning of the forms described above. The formulation of female collective identity exhibits a possible challenge to patriarchal structures. They are, at least in terms of the ways in which they envision their lives, breaking down the Domestic Code. For them, the domestic is *not* primary; wage labour is. If patriarchy rests on a fundamental distinction between men's and women's labour, and currently the domination of women in both the home/family sphere and the workplace, these girls partly challenge that. They understand, to the point of being able to articulate, the fact that too many negative consequences result if you depend on men to the exclusion of depending on yourself, and that this means you must engage in long-term wage labour. They do not suggest the 'part-time' work solution and flights into fantasy futures offered by girls in previous studies.

In this sense, then, they challenge a fundamental premise of patriarchy – that women's primary place is in the home/family sphere and that men will, in turn, 'take care' of them. The boys do not challenge this at all; indeed, they affirm it.

In another sense, however, the girls only partially challenge patriarchy, and it is the partial nature of their challenge which may result in so many girls ending up exactly as their mothers, and in the boys' collective patriarchal vision having more power than it might otherwise have. Many of the girls express the desire to obtain jobs in the sex-segregated ghettos. This is not to denigrate such jobs in any way, but simply to acknowledge, along with Heidi Hartmann, that such jobs do not usually pay enough to allow women to exist outside the bounds of marriage.[29] In other words, one reason why the girls want to have a job/career is the high divorce rate. They suggest the fact that they do not want to be in a bad marriage simply because of money. In fact, as they point out, the husband might drink, have an affair, or simply leave, in which case the wife needs to have a source of her own support. Yet the jobs many of the girls envision for themselves will not give them that level of support. A secretary cannot, for the most part, support herself and her children should anything happen to her marriage. In this sense, then, the 'selection' of traditionally female jobs limits their own chance to escape patriarchal structures despite their intentions.

This may be too simple an analysis, however. Given that girls selecting these jobs do so in order to escape patriarchy in some sense, it is likely that they will organize at some point to ensure that such jobs pay them a living wage. At least part of the reason why females in occupational ghettos are not as organized as males in labouring jobs is precisely because women have lived out a marginalized wage labour identity – thus making organization within the workplace less likely. This is not to deny sheer male power in the workplace and in the home, but to suggest that women's own marginalized wage labour identity has encouraged oppressive conditions to persist. The girls in Freeway do not marginalize their wage labour identity and it is the very centrality of this identity that may encourage greater organization and political activity among female workers, most of whom are in the occupational ghettos. If Hartmann is right, that it is the sex-segregated labour force which encourages male dominance in both the workplace and the home, then the sex-segregated workplace must be dismantled before patriarchy is seriously challenged. This may well be. It is also the case, however, that female workers who have a central wage labour identity may move to organize traditionally female occupational ghettos in a way not yet imagined. I tend to agree with Hartmann and, therefore, see the overwhelming selection of jobs in the ghetto as ultimately serving patriarchy even though the girls intend otherwise. It may not, in fact, work that way, however, and the time may soon be ripe for this form of political activity given the nature of gender culture described here.[30]

The girls who select careers outside of the occupational ghetto have a better chance at actually controlling the conditions of their own lives in that they may earn enough money to do so. In other words, if they do as they intend, they might actually be able to determine the conditions under which they marry, stay married, and so forth because the economic constraints will not be the same for them as for the others. My point here is not that middle class women are traditionally more 'free' than working class women. They are not, in fact, necessarily less constrained than their working class sisters as Ferree, Stephen Bahr and others point out.[31] The girls in Freeway, however, elaborate a primary wage labour identity and the question then becomes, to what extent will they be able to enact this identity and what power will it give them over their own family life? Those opting out of the sex-segregated ghettos and actually working in relatively high paying positions have a better chance, I would argue, simply because they control greater personal/financial resources.

One last point needs to be made here. The girls' culture represents a partial challenge to patriarchy in the sense that emphasizing paid labour may allow women to negotiate the conditions of family life. Ferree points out that husbands in working class families base their claims for family consideration and special treatment on the fact that they work hard at often dangerous, tiring and certainly alienating jobs. Women will often say, 'He works hard, he's earned it', in order to justify consideration of his needs for quiet, 'time with the boys', and so forth.[32]

When women enter the wage labour market they also have a claim potentially to special consideration because the family also needs *her* paid labour. As Ferree notes, 'When an employed woman demands consideration for her needs – quiet, escape, leisure and the like – for the family to respond to these demands will mean a shift in responsibilities greater than introduced by her simply taking a job.'[33] If and when these working class girls enter into marriage, they do so with some potential bargaining power. They may have the leverage to attempt to negotiate some of the conditions of family life, division of domestic tasks, financial arrangements and so forth. If the family needs her paid labour in the same way as the family needs male labour, the *conditions* are there for readjustment in family authority and responsibilities. This is likely to be even more the case since traditionally well paid male working class jobs are being eroded. Although the girls do not articulate this directly, their insistence on not wanting to be 'supported', on being independent, and maintaining paid work even after marriage and children, indicates that this may, at least, be in the back of their minds. The concern among some of the girls for not having to 'ask permission', not being told where to go and so forth, suggests that they wish a more equitable arrangement in the home than their own lived experiences suggest is the case.

   The collective identity of the girls challenges directly that of the
boys. Boys still envision a patriarchal future – one in which they
are the breadwinner and their wives stay at home taking care of the
children. They envision patriarchy in its rather strict sense of
separate spheres. Given economic realities, this is unlikely to
happen, of course, and a separate sphere construction does not
exist in its pure form even today. In reality, therefore, what the
boys' collective identity may win is 'women's double bind'. The
girls are attempting, through the construction of an alternative
identity, to break the bounds of the double bind – to break the
present-day manifestation of patriarchy. The boys are affirming it,
and, depending on how collective identities are actually lived out,
we may see a change of some importance in the next decade.
   Patriarchy is thus being challenged and affirmed by males and
females within the white working class. Racism, however, is
affirmed by males and not apparently central to females. It is
noteworthy that the males are creating a collective identity along
far more fractionalized lines than are the females. It is female
culture which shows the greatest promise of challenge to the
traditional place and social construction of the working class – it is
less fractured along a variety of dimensions.
   In terms of institutional resentment, males, once again, exhibit
the resentment as in earlier studies, and, interestingly enough,
females appear to be moving a bit more in this direction, denying
the largely passive nature of their own confrontation with the
institution. Schooling is being affirmed more than in earlier
studies by both males and females. Given institutional resentment
as expressed by males, it is my prediction that white working class
males are moving toward a more contradictory relationship with
education such as that uncovered in studies of the black underclass.
Given economic realities for this class fraction in the sense that
they are not so terribly different from that of the underclass, this
may make 'sense'.
   I have, in this chapter, sketched gleanings from research on
white working class youth culture. I have argued here that there are
departures from previous studies and that these departures may be
of some importance. These data will be subject to further analysis
as *Working Class Without Work* takes shape. Questions yet to be
addressed include: the extent to which the interview data is
corroborated by school-based field notes, and the degrees to which
both school and family encourages or impedes the formation of
collective identities. These will be the subject of future discussion.

Notes

1. These data will be reported in full in *Working Class Without Work* (New York: Methuen, 1988). Thanks to Ava Shillan and Craig Centrie who conducted some of the interviews upon which this chapter is based.
2. See, for example, Paul Willis, *Learning to Labour* (Westmead, England: Saxon House Press, 1977); Lois Weis, *Between Two Worlds: Black Students in an Urban Community College* (Boston: Routledge and Kegan Paul, 1985); and R.W. Connel *et al.*, 'Class and gender dynamics in a ruling-class school', *Interchange* Vol. 12 (1981): 102–117.
3. Philip Wexler raises this point in 'Symbolic economy of identity and denial of labor: studies in high school No. 1', in Lois Weis, ed., *Class, Race and Gender in American Schools* (Albany: State University of New York at Buffalo, 1988, pp. 302–16).
4. Barry Bluestone and Bennett Harrison, *The De-Industrialization of America* (New York: Basic Books, 1982), p. 26.
5. Bluestone and Harrison, pp. 6–7.
6. The Preliminary Scholastic Aptitude Test (PSAT) and Scholastic Aptitude Test (SAT) are tests administered by Education Testing Service in Princeton. Most four-year colleges require the SAT for entrance.
7. The governing body of the state administers a series of tests which must be taken if entrance to a four-year school is desired. Not all students take these tests, however, and track placement often determines whether the tests are taken.
8. *Freeway Evening News*, Magazine Section, June 5, 1983.
9. *Freeway Evening News*, Magazine Section, June 5, 1983.
10. Willis, p. 26.
11. Harry Braverman, *Labor and Monopoly Capital* (New York: Monthly Review Press, 1974). Michael Buroway, 'Toward a Marxist theory of the labor process: Braverman and beyond', *Politics and Society*, Vol. 8 (1978): 247–312.
12. See Howard London, *The Culture of a Community College* (New York: Praeger, 1978).
13. See chapter 3 of London's book.
14. Robert Everhart, *Reading, Writing and Resistance* (Boston: Routledge and Kegan Paul, 1983).
15. Willis, p. 49.
16. Capitalists have encouraged this directly, however. It is not *simply* 'produced' at the lived cultural level.
17. This is historically contradictory, however. Capitalism demands erosion of such divisions as much as it has encouraged them. See my discussion of this in *Between Two Worlds*.
18. This happened on a number of occasions.

19. Philip Cusick has a very insightful analysis of the way in which the potential for the 'breakdown of order' shapes school policy. See Philip Cusick, *American High School and the Egalitarian Idea!* (New York: Longman Press, 1983).

20. See Angela McRobbie, 'Working class girls and the culture of femininity', in Women's Study Group, ed., *Women Take Issue* (London, Hutchinson, 1978), pp. 96–108 and Linda Valli, *Becoming Clerical Workers* (Boston: Routledge and Kegan Paul, 1986).

21. See Lois Weis, 'Progress but no parity', *Academe* (November/December 1985): 29–33.

22. One of the machine shop teachers also had a daughter in engineering. He was the person who initially pointed out to me that a number of students from manual labouring families who do become professionals go into engineering.

23. See Valli, McRobbie, and work by Jane Gaskell. See, for example, Jane Gaskell, 'Gender and class in clerical training'. Paper prepared for session on 'Work and unemployment as alienating experiences' at World Congress of Sociology in New Delhi, August 1986. Jane Gaskell 'Gender and course choice', *Journal of Education* (March 1984) 166, 1: 89–102.

24. Ann Marie Wolpe, 'Education and the sexual division of labour', in *Feminism and Materialism: Women and Modes of Production*, eds Annette Kuhn and Ann Marie Wolpe (London: Routledge and Kegan Paul, 1978), pp. 290–328, as cited in Valli, p. 77.

25. Linda Valli, 'Becoming clerical workers: business education and the culture of femininity', in Michael Apple and Lois Weis, eds. *Ideology and Practice in Schooling* (Philadelphia: Temple University Press, 1983), p. 232.

26. See Madeleine MacDonald, 'Cultural reproduction: the pedagogy of sexuality', *Screen Education* 32/33 (Autumn/Winter 1978/80): 152, as cited in Linda Valli, p. 232.

27. Angela McRobbie, p. 104.

28. Lillian Breslow Rubin, *Worlds of Pain* (New York: Basic Books, 1976); and Glen Elder, *Children of the Great Depression* (Chicago: University of Chicago Press, 1974).

29. Heidi Hartmann, 'Capitalism Patriarchy and Job Segregation by Sex', *Signs* 1, 3 (Part II): 137–74.

30. Linda Valli argues in *Class, Race and Gender in American Schools* (1988) that it is the experience of office work itself that encourages women to marginalize a wage labour identity since such work is repetitive and alienating. This may be the case but the ideology of the primacy of a home§family identity for women enables this to occur, I would argue. If such an ideology is attacked to begin with, the chance of this happening on the job is lessened. In other words, the Domestic Code enables this to occur for women and not for men.

31. Myra Marx Ferree, 'Sacrifice, satisfaction, and social change: employment and the family', in Karen Brodkin Sacks, ed., *My Troubles Are Going to Have Trouble With Me* (New Brunswick: Rutgers University Press, pp. 61–79). See also Myra Marx Ferree and Stephen Bahr, 'Effects on Power and Division of Labor in the Family', in Lois Wladis Hoffman and F. Ian Nye, eds, *Working Mothers. An Evaluative Review of the Consequences for Wife, Husband, and Child* (San Francisco: Jossey-Bass, 1975).
32. Ferree, p. 69.
33. Ferree, p. 70.

Appendix Occupations by year for Freeway area SMSA*, all persons

Occupation	% of all occupations			Absolute Change	Net %change
	1960	1970	1980		
Managerial and Professional Specialty Occupations	19.2	21.9	21.7	+2.5	+13.0
Technical, Sales and Adm. Support Occupations	22.8	25.4	30.7	+7.9	+34.6
Service Occupations	10.1	12.9	13.9	+2.8	+37.6
Farming, Forestry and Fishing Occupations	1.0	0.6	0.9	−0.1	−10.0
Precision Production, Craft and Repair Occupations	16.8	15.4	12.5	−4.3	−25.6
Operators, Fabricators, and Labourers	25.3	23.6	20.2	−5.1	−20.2
Occupations Not Reported	5.1				

*Standard Metropolitan Statistical Area

CHAPTER 7

Women in Education in the State of Victoria

*Marg Malloch**

Women are like the dregs of good wine:
they sink to the bottom.
(adapted from Rose Laub Coser, 1981)

Introduction

I have called my chapter, 'Women in Education in the State of Victoria'. It could equally have been entitled 'Women and Victorian Education'. The Victorian Ministry of Education has turned its attention to the position of women in education administration and realized that women are located in the lower echelons of the hierarchy. Very few have 'made it to the top'. In July 1977, the Victorian Committee on Equal Opportunity in Schools reported to the Premier, Rupert Hamer, stressing the absence of women from all the top levels of policy- and decision-making. It recommended that the Department take positive steps to encourage women to take up positions of responsibility and authority in schools and the professional sector. Formal and informal barriers were going to have to be removed. It was also recommended that inequalities in education of girls be addressed, particularly by the appointment of a consultant. This led to the establishment of the Education Department's Equal Opportunity Unit in 1978.

The subsequent policies which have been initiated fall into two major categories. Equal Opportunity in Education (1978) for both women and girls concentrates on curriculum and programme development in schools. The Affirmative Action Plan for Women in the Teaching Service (1984) focuses on women and promotion.

---

*The views expressed in this chapter are personal and do not necessarily reflect the views of the Victorian Ministry of Education.

The approach of this policy is to introduce women into the male pattern of career structures using promotion as an indicator of success, of obtaining equality. Neither of these policies, in the short term, is sufficient to bring about widespread changes to the quality of working experiences for women or girls in education.

Equality of educational opportunities for women and girls has been an unpopular issue with many in the education community and school administrator's being somewhat slow in following stated government policies. It must be recognized that much of the power and control exerted by the school administrators over classroom practice issues from and is legitimated by educational policy. Many educational structures and procedures are manifestations of policy and much of the school administrator's work has to do with ensuring policy is followed (Prunty 1985). Furthermore, these policies appear to clash with the sex-role stereotyping of Western society. Socialization into specific sex roles and stereotypes is extensively documented. People learn what is acceptable and sanctions and socialization are directed to preserving that approved behaviour (Sampson 1986). Women's lower occupational achievements and status is explained as a result of stereotype beliefs bringing about the undervaluing of female occupations and achievements (Archer and Lloyd 1982). Women and men learn there are three different rewards for the same behaviour (Lips and Colwill 1978) and the role of women is diminished in order to uphold the position of men (Miller and Swift 1976). It is legitimate for a man to exercise authority over adults; women should be in charge of children.

These sex-role stereotypes are reflected in the organization of the teaching service. Women form a majority at the assistant level of teaching, in emergency teaching (supply) and in part-time work. There is a distinct and different work experience for women in the teaching service. The overall position of women in teaching was summarized by Acker.

If we consider the model location of men and women teachers, we observe that men and women typically teach different subjects to different groups of children, hold responsibilities for different functions within schools, and generally have different chances for rewards within the system. Women are more likely to teach younger children, men older; women to teach girls, men boys; women to teach domestic subjects and humanities, men technological subjects and physical sciences; women to have pastoral responsibilities, men administrative and curricular ones. As Stober and Tyack put it, women teach and men manage. The divisions are not of caste-like rigidity, but the probabilities that the sexes will experience differential career lines and typical locations in school are striking enough to allow us to speak confidentially of a sexual division of labour in teaching. (Acker 1983, in Riseborough 1986)

Research in Australia reinforces this stated division of labour based on gender differences. A 1984 nationwide survey indicated that more women expect to remain as class teachers (42 per cent compared to 15 per cent of men), and that fewer women seek promotion outside the school. Women named after-school and domestic responsibilities and their partners' careers as reasons for not applying for promotion (Sampson 1985). Women are as qualified as men, if not more so, upon entering teaching. Men however, go on to further higher studies at a significantly greater percentage than women (Sampson 1985). Men undertake a significantly greater amount of in-service training on administration and computers. Women are more involved in curriculum and pastoral care. Women teachers experience less administrative training on the job (57 per cent compared with 73 per cent males), especially in the first five years of their work. Males are asked to organize camps, to convene committees and draw up timetables. Men are therefore encouraged to aspire to promotion. Men run the schools and women are not perceived as having administrative potential. Family related factors have been found to be important handicaps to women who would seek promotion. There is a need for action on this (Sampson 1985).

Teachers in Victoria are seen as traditional role models for students. Sampson maintains that teachers hold stereotyped notions of gender differences in ability and in their own private role choices are quite conservative (Sampson 1986). Women are not applying as often as men for promotion, (in the last five years 24 per cent of women applied compared, with 46 per cent of men). Women are encouraged less than men to apply for promotion (for primary schools, 50 per cent men compared with 23 per cent women) (Sampson 1986). Students see women much less in authority than men. This is a traditional message about hierarchies, unlikely to encourage young women to use their talents or young men to question their prejudices. Women show a highly professional commitment to the classroom but by their own role choices are reinforcing current stereotypes and prejudices (Sampson 1986).

This chapter outlines current government policies and programmes aimed at increasing the percentage of administrative positions held by women in the Ministry of Education, in Victoria, Australia. The Victorian Government has introduced a range of policies aimed at improving the working conditions of women in Victorian schools, and in particular, getting more women to promotion and administration positions. These policies appear to have had minimal success. Women in teaching service are seen as traditional role models, and are not rushing to be promoted, and are not encouraged to apply for promotion, so where exactly are 'the dregs of the wine'?

A history of discrimination

During the 1970s, research in Australia and overseas drew attention to the fact that the situation for women within education was grim with a history of limited industrial rights. Within the Victorian Teaching Service systematic discrimination because of personal characteristics irrelevant to the job has brought about denial of opportunities.

Examples of direct discrimination include:

until 1956   if a woman teacher got married she had to resign as a permanent teacher and be employed as a temporary teacher at two-thirds of her previous full time salary.

until 1970   in secondary and technical schools, women teachers could only be principals of girl's schools, schools for the disabled or one-teacher schools.

until 1971   women teachers did not receive equal pay.

until 1972   in primary schools, women teachers could not be principals of schools, with the exception of schools for the disabled or one-teacher schools (Ministry of Education 1986a).

Examples of indirect discrimination include:

until 1956   no confinement leave was available.

from 1974	18 months' confinement leave without maternity pay was available.
until July 1975	married women were unable to join the State Superannuation fund.
until 1984	permanent part-time work was not available (now available only at Assistant Class/Band 1 level).
until November 1984	18 months' confinement leave with 12 weeks' maternity pay was available.
from November 1985	7 years' family leave became available to both men and women teachers. This policy is not discriminatory in its view that either parent may choose to take responsibility for child-rearing (Ministry of Education 1986a).

The promotion system in the Victorian Teaching Service is further evidence of discrimination against women. Promotion was often gained by being prepared to be geographically mobile. Such mobility tended to be the prerogative of men teachers rather than married women teachers. Thus, a promotion system which involves this mobility as a significant factor, indirectly discriminates against married women (Ministry of Education 1986a). Suitability for promotion is also an issue in discrimination. Primary and secondary teachers are promoted on seniority and assessments performed by male-dominated interviewing panels. Men are considerably more likely to gain *suitable as principal* gradings (Victorian Committee on Equal Opportunity in Schools 1977). Technical teachers apply for senior teacher promotion by making an application, supported by references, to the Appointments Board. The teachers' seniority is considered. This process is criticized as one allowing schools to provide favourable references to be rid of specific teachers (Interview 1986).

Breaks in service for child bearing and rearing also affected seniority and opportunities for promotion because upon resuming their careers, women had to re-enter at a lower level (Victorian Committee on Equal Opportunity in Schools 1977).

In 1972, primary teachers were placed on a common roll, a combined seniority listing of all staff. The qualification most commonly held by women, the Infant Teachers Certificate, was down graded. Women were therefore further disadvantaged in applying for promotion (Victorian Committee on Equal Opportunity in Schools 1977). Discriminatory conditions enshrined in the Public Service regulations, government wage policies and social attitudes, have for many years adversely affected women's employment, working conditions and promotion opportunities in the Victorian Teaching Service. By 1972, women technically had equal opportunity to enter any field for which they were qualified and to reach the highest level they might aim for (Schwarz 1984). However, the realities were different.

The numbers debate – school administration

Despite the focus of the International Women's Year (1975), the Decade for Women and ensuing reports, statistics gathered indicate a decline in the percentage of senior positions held by women. In secondary schools, between 1976 and 1981, the percentage of women principals went from 16 to 13 per cent and for technical schools from 3 to 2 per cent (Sampson 1983). More recent statistics show variations. They indicate that senior positions in secondary schools have shown a continuing decrease for women in administration (see Table 1). However, the corresponding positions in technical schools show a steady increase. Technical schools no longer belong to a separate Division within the Ministry and are now post-primary schools with curricula steadily becoming more general. Does this mean they are no longer of interest to men with technical education backgrounds, or is it that a smaller group of schools with a one-third female workforce encourages talent for administration more readily? (Malloch 1984). Primary positions also have shown slight increases at some senior levels (see Table 2). One category, the Band 4 level, has shown a significant increase, however it should be noted that there are only eight people in this category and the position is similar to that of a Senior Teacher in a larger school.

Overall these statistics do not indicate a surge in the number of women occupying senior positions. The interpretation of these statistics requires further investigation. Statistical analysis is made

Table 1: Women as a percentage of the total category of secondary and technical school teachers: A comparison. (*Source:* Analysis of Teaching Service Personnel Employed. Pay Period 8603. Computer Services. Ministry of Education, 1986.)

Class	Year	Secondary	Technical
Principal	1981	11.8	2.3
	1983	10.3	3.1
	1984	12.0	6.0
	1986	7.8	9.7
Vice Principal	1981	16.9	16.2
	1983	13.4	15.4
	1984	12.0	15.0
	1986	13.0	17.4
Senior Teacher	1981	22.7	10.8
	1983	24.3	12.6
	1984	25.0	13.0
	1986	24.7	17.0
Assistant with Responsibility	1981	33.3	9.5
	1983	33.5	8.5
	1984	34.0	8.0
	1986	36.1	8.3
Assistant	1981	57.7	26.9
	1983	58.0	22.6
	1984	59.0	28.0
	1986	59.8	32.0
Total Classified Teachers	1981	51.1	23.7
	1983	52.0	24.7
	1984	52.0	25.0
	1986	53.4	28.9
Grand Total	1981	n/a	n/a
	1983	n/a	n/a
	1984	55.0	29.0
	1986	57.3	34.3

more difficult because there are some women who have been promoted to principal class who are based in administrative offices yet are included in school-based statistics (Schwarz 1986).

Table 2: Women as a percentage of the total category of primary school teachers: A comparison. August 2, 1986, with March 2, 1984. (*Source:* Analysis of Teaching Service Personnel Employed. Pay Period 8605. Computer Services, Ministry of Education, 1986.)

Class	1984	1986
Principal Grade A	23	25
Principal Grade B	12	11
Principal Grade 1	17	*
Band 4		
Interim Principal	57	75
Interim Special	78	80
Band 4	17	16
Band 3		
Interim Senior Teacher	25	*
Head Teacher	1	19
Band 3	40	43
Band 2 Head Teacher	23	23
Band 1 Head Teacher	53	52
Band 1	84	85
Total Classified Teachers	71	72

*No people in this category.

Trends indicate that women are being appointed to technical principal positions in inner suburban *tougher* schools, and to newly established post-primary schools. In the primary sector women appear to be appointed to both the challenging inner suburban schools and to *well-established, well-disciplined middle class* suburban schools. These are trends to be investigated.

The increase in senior teacher positions (head of faculty/department) held by women provides a potential pool of women for principal and vice-principal positions. These numbers reflect the population bulge of the post-war baby boomers (*Times Educational Supplement*, 10 October 1986). However, the ongoing restructure of Victorian education, the current decline in student enrolments and the decrease in the availability of senior positions raise the question as to whether the baby boomers, now in their late thirties and forties, will mark time in these senior teacher positions.

Table 3: Women in Senior Levels of Administration. (*Source*: Analysis of Teaching Personnel Employed. Pay Periods August 1983, August 1986. Ministry of Education, 1986.)

Position	1983		1986	
	Men	Women	Men	Women
Government Appointments	24	0	17	0
Senior Administration	17	0	7	0
Senior Education Officers	101	11	89	13
Others	358	239	204	175
Total	500	250	317	188

The numbers debate continued – middle and senior level management

Superficially, at middle and senior management levels, there appears to be a small positive change in the percentage of women occupying such positions (see Table 3).

Statistical analyses of these non-school based senior management personnel are made difficult by the broad categories used by the government. Lobbying for the past three years to have the categories updated has been to no avail (Interview 1986). This 4 per cent increase in the number of women holding these positions appears to be due to an attrition in overall staffing rather than any increase in the actual numbers of women employed.

Equal Opportunity Programmes

When inequality of the sexes was discussed in education in the 1970s, the focus was on girls and the curriculum. A government enquiry was instituted in 1974 with the Federal Minister for Education Mr Kim Beazley announcing that:

> For far too long girls have been under-achieving in school and ending their formal education early. This has restricted the career and life chances open to them.

The report arising from that enquiry highlighted the inequalities and difficulties experienced by women and girls in education (Committee on Social Change and the Education of Women 1975).

In Victoria the Committee on Equal Opportunity in Schools, 1977, recommended that an Equal Opportunity Unit be set up within the Education Department. The philosophy of the Equal Opportunity Unit, as outlined by the initial Co-ordinator, involved taking note of what is happening, and what is wanted, and taking it a little further, like ripples spreading from a stone thrown into the water (Interview, October 1986). The EO Unit focuses on research, in-service, non-sexist curriculum materials production, inclusive curriculum and development of policy guidelines relating to girls in the education system. An Equal Opportunity Resource Centre was established as a consequence. Committees, such as the Ministerial Advisory Committee for Women and Girls and the Curriculum Committee for the Education for Women and Girls, were established. However, although included in the titles of these Committees, women as distinct from girls tended to be left out of the policy objectives. The Equal Opportunity Unit was initially funded by the Australian Government in 1978, paying for a consultant and for the establishment of a resource centre. By 1985, the Victorian Government had financial responsibility. By that time seventeen staff were employed and three resource centres were operating.

Other programmes

Additional national funding was allocated to establish the Transition Education Advisory Committee (TEAC), 1980-4, which was replaced by the Participation and Equity Programme (PEP), 1985 onwards. These programmes aim at encouraging equality of education for disadvantaged students. They operate as an additional programme administered outside the ordinary operations of the Ministry of Education with no formal liaison with the state-based Equal Opportunity Unit. Each of these programmes had, as part of their guidelines, an insistence on equality of education for girls. In 1984, TEAC was funding programmes in 230 secondary schools, over half in the state. TEAC programmes were evaluated at local, regional and state levels, and funding, provided on an annual basis, could be withdrawn if guidelines were not followed (Gippsland TEAC Committee 1984).

In 1985, PEP provided funding for 177 schools and in 1986, 183. Its programmes tend to be evaluated at the workplace level. PEP is also funded on a yearly basis, dependent upon continued national funds and priority ratings from the State PEP Committee. Programmes tend therefore to spend the greater part of the year lobbying for continued existence (PEP Secretariat 1985).

Since 1981, TEAC and PEP have funded five specific equal opportunity programmes providing officers and budgets to work on a variety of projects, such as curriculum options for girls, single-sex science and mathematics classes and computer usage for girls. A network of schools and a regional network for women teachers and students have also been established. The original intentions had been that such programmes were to be initially funded by the Commonwealth and then by the State Treasury. The Minister for Education has instructed the PEP Secretariat to continue to fund, to a limited extent, the Equal Opportunity Programmes (Interview, PEP 1985).

Introduction of Affirmative Action

In Victoria, the Ministry of Education recognized that women were not utilized in leadership positions and began to develop policies to rectify this imbalance (Schwarz 1984). Given the backdrop of the 1984 Federal Discrimination Act and the national pilot programme for the Affirmative Action policy, the Victorian Government passed the Equal Opportunities Act making discrimination in employment illegal. Following the establishment of a Public Service Affirmative Action Plan, the Director-General of Education, Dr Norman Curry, in May 1985 formed a committee to prepare an affirmative action plan for the Teaching Service. The Public Service plan served as a model. The Committee consisted of representatives from Personnel and Industrial Relations, Staffing, Manpower Planning, School Administrators, the Equal Opportunity Unit, Regional Administration, the Ministerial Advisory Committee on Women and Girls and the Teacher Unions.

The Affirmative Action plan is described as a systematic means, determined by the employer, in consultation with the Unions, of achieving equal employment opportunity. It is stressed that it is not positive discrimination nor a quota system. It is presented as a way of providing equal access to promotion on the basis of merit, skills and appropriate qualifications. The Affirmative Action Plan is seen as a result-oriented management programme involving:

- commitment of senior management,
- full consultation with the union,
- analysis of the current position of women,
- review of all employment practices to ensure they do not directly or indirectly discriminate against women,
- develop programmes to respond to collected data and
- monitor and audit equal employment opportunities.

The overall aim of the Teaching Service Action Plan is to increase the numbers of women in administrative and promotion positions as well as in non-traditional female teaching areas. This will be achieved through the achievement of the specific objectives of the Action Plan:

- *Awareness, commitment and implementation.*
  To develop awareness of, and commitment to, the need for and the implementation of the Action Plan for Women in the Teaching Service.
- *Recruitment, selection and promotion.*
  To ensure that fields for recruitment into the Teaching Service contain representative numbers of eligible women. To ensure that selection and promotion processes within the Teaching Service are not gender biased.
  The overall objective is to increase the numbers of women in administrative and promotion positions and in non-traditional female teaching areas.
- *Training and development*
  To ensure that eligible women have access to training places, that specialized training needs of women are recognized and that training courses conducted within the Teaching Service are free from discrimination and contain relevant EEO material where appropriate.
- *Career structures and opportunities*
  To ensure that career structures and opportunities are designed in such a way that they do not disadvantage women and that women are encouraged to develop their careers.
- *Working conditions*
  To improve working conditions for all staff members, paying particular attention to the working conditions of women.

(Ministry of Education 1986a)

This plan, officially launched in July 1986, potentially affects some 80,000 personnel and 585,000 students. The Action Plan is an example of a *top down* policy initiated by senior personnel and adapted by a representative committee of management and teacher union representatives.

Effects on schools

The Equal Opportunity Unit issued through the Office of the Director-General of Education an official memorandum recommending that each school establish a committee 'to determine the extent and nature of sex bias in the school and to make recommendations for its elimination'. This 1980 memorandum was followed up with a survey three years later, to determine the extent of implementation of these recommendations. Only 149 out of a possible 400 secondary schools responded to the survey: 9 had established School Committees, 25 had conducted in-service activities to examine sexism in education, 56 had conducted reviews of school curricula to remove sex bias, 101 had encouraged selection of non-sexist resource materials and 120 had made subjects equally available to both sexes (Wells 1983).

The memorandum then had a very limited success rate even three years after its publication! Schools tended to put the policy in the bin or give it to the token feminist on the staff to implement (Interview, Clayton Technical School 1980). The memorandum was couched in terms of 'recommended' and 'desirable', without sanctions or positive clauses. This could explain its overall ineffectiveness. It was found that schools with funded equal opportunity programmes operating in either their school or region had a significantly higher success rate in encouraging students to take non-traditionally sex-typed subjects (Wells 1983). *Lighthouse* models of school change have been provided by these schools.

TEAC and PEP equal opportunity projects have certainly raised the level of debate and have encouraged extensive work on equal opportunity in education for girls. Improvements in the quality of schooling for girls have been made including greater subject choice, support, broad ranging career advice and attention to non-traditional subject training (Gippsland Regional Education Office 1985). In PEP publications, schools were viewed as functioning to reinforce social inequality with girls, the non-

English speaking and working class missing out. The movement from central prescription of curriculum to joint responsibility of ministry, teachers, parents and students reflecting aspects of school population and local community was regarded positively (PEP Secretariat 1985).

The Affirmative Action plan has been in operation for only a very short period of time and so it is difficult to assess its effect on schools. Regional contact people have been nominated and have attended two briefing sessions. Three copies have been issued to each school. A Women's Register has been established to enable women in the Teaching Service to list their experiences and interests for consideration for other employment and for committee work (Interview 1986.) This has not been utilized as yet by the Personnel sector. Negotiations are in progress to appoint and train teachers to be sexual harassment contact people for school networks. Legal implications and difficulties in obtaining time release from schools have lengthened negotiations (*Teacher Federation of Victoria* October 1986).

Recent developments

From the beginning of the Labour Government's second term of office in 1984, and under the new Minister for Education, Ian Cathie, the Equal Opportunity Unit underwent some changes. Previously, the co-ordinator had direct and unlimited access to the Director-General and the Minister. Now the EO Unit was, for budgetary purposes, placed within another unit, Equal Opportunities in Education, along with education for the disabled and migrants. Consequently the autonomy and status of the EO Unit were severely diminished. Programme Budgeting was introduced. While this exercise provided a needed built-in form of annual assessment, it had the added effect of restricting a previous unlimited budget.

Other difficulties were experienced by the EO Unit. Staffing fell from seventeen to seven and there was no secretarial support. Access to the new Chief Executive, Schools Division, was limited and attendance at top level decision making committees was gained only after extensive teacher union lobbying. The Co-ordinator took leave of absence and then resigned in May 1986 (Interview 1986). The EO Unit was eventually informed of this six months later. The Co-ordinator's position was then advertised at a substantially reduced salary. The management style chosen by the unit staff was a shared, democratic representation by three staff members. The bureaucracy found this difficult to cope with (*Teachers Federation of Victoria* November 1986). Finally, plans to increase the number of resource centres and staff have been delayed.

Operation of Affirmative Action

> What is certain is that hitherto women's possibilities have been suppressed and lost to humanity, and that it is high time she be permitted to take her chances in her own interest and in the interest of all.
>
> (de Beauvoir 1972)

These sentiments have been echoed in the Affirmative Action Plan, as a proposed maximum usage of national human resources.

The Prime Minister, Robert Hawke, when he tabled the Green Paper in Parliament on 5 June, 1984, said of the Affirmative Action Pilot Programme:

> The approach we now propose should ensure that women are no longer excluded from many occupations and concentrated at the bottom end of the labour market. Women should now assume the place of their choice in our society. I should emphasise that this, we appreciate and recognise, will see many choosing a traditional role in the home. Affirmative Action of the kind now proposed by the Government is a means of improving women's position in the work force by ensuring that discriminatory practices or traditions are reviewed and removed. We aim to see that women are enabled to compete equally with men for jobs at all levels. Our approach is not one which relies on the experience of other countries. We have explicitly rejected the American model with its system of court-imposed employment quotas. Rather, we have developed a set of proposals which are appropriate for the Australian environment. They are the product of our unique industrial relations and business practice traditions.
>
> Put quite simply, equal employment opportunity is our objective and Affirmative Action is the way to achieve it.
>
> (Department of the Prime Minister and Cabinet 1985)

The Policy Discussion Paper on Affirmative Action for Women (Green Paper) published in 1984 states:.

> The Government defines Affirmative Action as a systematic means determined by the employer in consultation with senior management, employees and unions, of achieving equal employment opportunity for women. Affirmative Action is compatible with appointment and promotion of the principle of merit, skills and qualifications.

Senator Susan Ryan, in moving the introduction of the Affirmative Action (Equal Employment Opportunity for Women) Bill, 1986, stated that this legislation is necessary to ensure that all large employers take seriously their obligations to their female employees. The changing role of women in our society is reflected, to a large extent, in the changing patterns in the workforce. The Government is determined that women should be able to enter and compete in the labour market on an equal footing with men, and that outdated prejudices or conventions should not prevent them from fully participating.

The emphasis is very much left with the meritorious individual woman to obtain equality within a structure organized by the employer after consultation with appropriate unions and associations. The concept of merit, which is difficult to define, and the constant stress that quotas are not to be used, appears less threatening to male machismos. The male career structure is still the model for operation.

It can be argued that the Affirmative Action Plan is an equal outcome policy with comprehensive statistical studies demonstrating under-representation and under-utilization of women and other groups in the workforce. This statistical under-representation and the extent of occupational segregation are seen as evidence of the inherent discriminatory nature of our society. Statistics indicate the existence of discrimination and progress made by equal opportunity management plans. The ideal of equality of opportunity is being replaced by equality of outcomes and result, and there is confusion over this (Moens 1985). The objective of increasing the numbers of women in administrative positions implies a target setting. Measurement is to be in quantitative terms; attitudinal changes, other than an awareness, are not demanded.

The policy development of the Teaching Service Action Plan

involved careful negotiation between the teacher unions and management. A policy of graduated stages outlining what appears to be clear objectives, an established timetable and evaluation steps is the result.

The Affirmative Action Plan has initially focused on areas of transaction and operations which are easy to carry out, for example, removal of sexist language, monitoring operations, training of recruitment panels, interviewing of exit students and secondary teacher assessment panels, development courses and in-service training (Interview 1986).

The Merit Studies and Programmes team has operated since May of 1984. In that time, the policy has been written and published, and three copies sent to each school. The three team officers, who have now been promoted to other areas, were intensely involved in serving on committees and speaking at in-service activities. A cadre model is employed, of going out, speaking and helping to activate others to take up or to continue the strategies for equal employment opportunities. *Permeation* rather than *imposition* is the preferred mode of operation (Interview, 1986). One residential training activity for twenty-five women at senior teacher level and above, has been held.

There have been operational problems. The Affirmative Action Plan for the Victorian Teaching Service was originally called the Equal Employment Opportunities section of the Human Resources section within the Ministry of Education. EEO was, it was claimed, too easily confused with the Equal Opportunity Unit, and the name was changed to Merit Studies and Programmes. Is this a diffusion, a weakening of the task of the unit? The focus seems to have shifted from equality of opportunity in employment to endorsement of merit. There is even more confusion now! Staffing has appeared piecemeal, with a series of short-term appointments and the use of *soft option* people, staff with no avowed commitment to equal opportunity for women, and who are not radical or hard line (Ellis 1986). Staff consisted of one administrative assistant for two months. There is no budget allocation and funding for printing has to come from the Chief Executive's Discretionary Fund. Conference and training activities compete for funds along with all other State activities. No statistics are available on in-service funding (Interviews 1986). Contact people have been named for each region to be responsible for policy implementation, and to answer enquiries and provide support. This group at their first training session exhibited confusion and uncertainty as to their roles and functions. Initial information had been misleading. While contact people are according to the policy meant to be of middle management level and above, this is not the case (April 1986, AA training day).

The context in which the Affirmative Action Plan is operating is in a situation of large-scale unemployment, allied to a world competitive economy, governments face a crisis, and have to try to socialize and occupy the potential unemployed so they do not threaten the State. Education is a prime instrument for this. In the interests of economic competitiveness, governments have to restrict spending on education, making it more efficient and more instrumental in producing appropriate skills and attitudes. The rhetoric is about standards, basic skills, vocational training and accountability replacing previous concerns such as child centred progressivism and equal opportunity (Rachel Sharp 1984 in Yates 1986). Within this context of education, the Victorian Education System (once a department, now restyled as a ministry) has in the past decade structured and restructured its mode of operation under both Liberal and Labour governments. Centralized bureaucracy is being devolved to schools and school councils. The number of regional administrations has been halved. Staffing numbers and expenditure are therefore to be decreased. The line of communication and authority between the Minister and the Schools will be more direct. What happens to equal opportunity in education in times like these? The most recent federal budget wiped out funding for multicultural programmes. Victorian Equal Opportunity programmes for women and girls received smaller budgets than in previous years. Schools inundated with demands to write policies and programmes have not had to place Affirmative Action as a high priority (*Teachers Federation of Victoria* September 1986).

Does the organizational structure of the education ministry reinforce stereotypes of women in the workforce? The more restrictive practices may have been changed, but is the stereotype still there? The research referred to earlier indicates that it does (Sampson 1986). The predominance of women in primary education and the lack in technical, mathematics and science education reinforce stereotypes. Real opportunities might have increased but perceived opportunities are still seen as few. The role of the principal is still defined in terms of the way men typically do it. Women are still seen in terms of limited stereotypes and these are being reinforced by current employment patterns.

The Teaching Service Affirmative Action Plan concentrates on the promotion positions of women. Aborigines, migrants and the disabled will be planned for in the future. The concentration of the plan on women and promotion has been labelled elitist (Interview, 1986). It deals with women who have already put their feet on the rungs of the hierarchy ladder. Does the government hope to increase the proportion of women in administrative positions to such an extent that this is no longer remarkable? Whether they want to at all is not questioned.

Related operations

Local selection of principals and deputy principals was introduced into technical schools a decade ago, and for primary and secondary schools two years ago. Representatives of the School Council, teaching staff, parent and principal organizations and the Ministry interview applicants. The Appointments Board, in charge of overseeing all promotions within the system, conduct training sessions for local selection interviewing panels for administration positions. Very neatly equal opportunity is discussed with the Freedom of Information Act. The dire consequences of aborting the interview process are outlined. Appropriate women are to be interviewed and sexist questioning avoided. Sex role stereotypes are not challenged to any great extent (Interview panel training, May 1986). Of those women who applied for principal positions in August 1986, the success rate was better than that of the male applicants; for secondary, 14.2 per cent of women compared with 12.6 per cent of men. In primary, 24.3 per cent of women and 15.1 per cent of men were successful. However, the Board representatives bemoan that women just do not apply for jobs (Interview 1986). This appears as a 'blame the victim' approach rather than looking at why women do not apply and what strategies might encourage them to do so. Mobility is less important as a factor in promotion now, especially with local selection for principal and administration positions.

In December 1985 the State Minister for Education sent a memorandum to Regional Directors of Education stating that women who applied for senior positions and who were fully qualified with relevant experiences for these jobs were to be interviewed. This memorandum created a negative reaction, established procedures had not been followed, the action plan had been ignored, and women being interviewed felt tokenistic (*Teachers Federation of Victoria Sexism Committee* 1986). Four regional networks have been established independently and prior to the Affirmative Action Plan. These have focused on developing women in education: self-esteem, confidence, assertiveness, skills in management and committees, applications for promotion, and changes to the school structure. Efforts have been made to get women on to school councils, on to Regional Boards of Education, on interview panels and to apply for jobs but as yet such efforts have been conducted by committed individuals and by elements of the teacher unions.

In Victoria there have been two main paths of equal opportunity in education for women and girls. The equal opportunity unit focuses on counter-sexist education, the development of curricula, resources and attitudinal change for girls' education. The Affirmative Action Plan concentrates on an 'equal outcome' approach. The emphasis is on women and promotion and statistical analysis. The former introduced by a Liberal (conservative) government, the latter by a Labour government. An overlap of these has occurred in that both advocate a study of positions held by men and women in schools. The teacher unions have had *two bob each way* in that they have been party to all negotiations and formations of policy with the Ministry of Education. At the same time, the unions are working on the development of an alternative style of management in education.

Concluding comments

To try to be positive, the policy of the Affirmative Action Plan has assisted with some advances towards equal employment opportunities. Selection panels will have to include a woman and women applicants with sufficient experience and qualifications for positions will have to be interviewed. The field of applicants for positions is to be supplemented if few or no women have applied for the job. There are to be more personal approaches in informing people of the interview results through a written report. Verbal feedback is sometimes possible. Counselling for interviews and career developments are yet to be developed. A pamphlet has been published to raise women's awareness of the action plan and promotion possibilities. Another is planned for the women of the 'lower ranks' of the public service. A bridging course has been conducted for women in the public service without the Higher School Certificate (O/A levels) to make them more eligible for promotion and to raise their self-esteem. Higher Duties allowances are made available for acting in more senior positions. These are regarded as very useful for obtaining experience for promotion. Women are to be encouraged to apply. Expressions of interest are called for six months on a temporary basis, after which the position is reviewed. This is seen as a training process. A monitoring device has also been established in that all applications for positions and records of process go to the EEO branch to be checked for correct following of procedures. A contact person for each region is required for both the public and teaching services. The sexual harassment policy for both services has also been printed.

School level action

The Equal Opportunity Unit has made a series of recommendations for schools for the implementation of the Affirmative Action Plan. Schools are expected to collect and document the facts of the relative power positions of men and women in the workplace. Staff meetings should be held to discuss findings and develop strategies such as job rotation, balance of the sexes on committees or the taking on of jobs often assigned to men by women. As well as this, a women's network and supportive strategies in staff meetings could be developed. Female teachers are encouraged to apply for promotion and to encourage other women to apply. The involvement of the school council could be helpful. All school practices and structures, it is recommended, should be examined for gender bias, for example, do the males make decisions in areas where they are often away from women, such as the pub or on the sport's field? (Schwarz 1986).

The policy of the Affirmative Action Plan has raised the level of debate about equality of employment opportunities. Resources, both human and material, are more readily available. It is difficult, however, to remain positive about such policy initiatives. The Affirmative Action Plan has been introduced by male leaders to satisfy the demands of some feminist lobbyists, to utilize human capital, to appear more concerned about equality and to thereby encourage some women to be absorbed into male career paths. It is of interest to ask whether the changes can be absorbed into the existing system or will the entry of women into a system concerned with success and recognition lead to demands which threaten the workings of the system? (Eisenstein in Yates 1986). Female members of the teaching service encouraging each other to apply for promotion and forming networks for professional development and support are informal and dependent upon individual effort with few systemic contributions.

Unions in seeking alternative 'non-capitalist', 'non-patriarchal' forms of organization have proposed a replacement of the dominance of hierarchy and seniority with dominance of meritocracy and contractual employment for administrative positions. An expert teacher class is also to be created. Work practices instead of ignoring child bearing and rearing patterns are to be more sensitive to them.

Schools are expected to carry out government policies. In a time of a decade of curriculum frameworks, of greater responsibilities of school councils and communities, of changed assessment procedures, of the creation of middle level and senior secondary schools and a severe cutback to support staff, consultancy services and school staffing, it can be expected that policies requiring a change to the hierarchy will be approached slowly. School councils are not renowned for positive encouragement of women.

While the Affirmative Action Plan has raised the issue of equal employment opportunity, the focus is very much on the meritorious individual and individual effort to obtain promotion. 'With individual successes and social mobility, no great change to society is achieved.' Traditional, hierarchical structures are still being reinforced with women working double and triple shifts (Yates 1986). There needs to be more than approaches to fair hiring and promotion and admitting of women into the ranks of male career patterns. The policy's reinforcement of the male career path and method of organization helps to support differences in gender stereotypes. There appears to be an uncertainty about interfering with Australian male machismo. Schools in general only nominally carry out equal opportunity policies and middle level management might understand that the policies are to be encouraged but may choose not to do so. Upper level management are good at speaking on the policies, but words require action.

Affirmative Action in the Teaching Service is described by its designers as a systematic, managerial approach to work against systematic discrimination. However, a budget allocation and the development and implementation of supportive policies, for example, child care and retraining, would create a more serious view of the Action Plan. There has to be a recognition that women tend to be the people who look after children. The 'no budget' government affirmative action policy will move very slowly. The slowness of implementation and the emphasis on meritocracy are peculiarly suited to Victorian conditions. One Committee member concludes that the Affirmative Action Plan is being competently carried out and that positive results will be seen in a few years. Such optimism may be well founded when the government examines the operation of its policies more carefully, and ensures that supplementary policies are in place. Then the Victorian Education Ministry may be able to achieve a more equitable equality of employment opportunities in education for women.

References

Archer, J. and Lloyd, B. (1982) *Sex and Gender*. Harmondsworth, Penguin.

Arnot, Madeleine (1985) 'Current developments in the sociology of women's education', *British Journal of Sociology of Education*. 6, 1.

de Beauvoir, S. (1972) *The Second Sex*. New York, Knopf. (translated by H.M. Parshley)

Chapman, Judith D. (1984) 'The selection and appointment of Australian school principals', *Commonwealth Schools Commission*. October, Canberra.

Chapman, Judith D. (1986) 'Improving the principal selection process to enhance opportunities for women', *Unicorn*. 12, 1.

Committee on Social Change and the Education of Women (1975) *Girls, School and Society: report by a study group to the Schools Commission*. Australia, Commonwealth Schools Commission.

Deem, R. (1981) 'State policy and ideology in the education of women, 1944–80', *British Journal of Education*. 2, 2.

Department of the Prime Minister and Cabinet (1984) *Affirmative Action for Women, 2*. Canberra, Australian Government Publishing Service.

Department of the Prime Minister and Cabinet (1985) *Affirmative Action for Women. A Progress Report on the Pilot Program*. Affirmative Action Resource Unit, Office of the Status of Women, Dept. of the Prime Minister and Cabinet. Canberra, Australian Government Publishing Service.

Ellis, G. (1986) Doctoral Studies, Monash University.

Gippsland Regional Education Office (1985) *Curriculum Options for Girls in Schools. Project Report*. Gippsland Regional Education Office.

Grant, Rosemary (1986) 'A career in teaching: a survey of teachers' perceptions with particular reference to the careers of women teachers', *BERA Conference*, Bristol.

Karmel, Peter (1985) 'Quality and equality in education', *The Australian Journal of Education.* 29, 3.

Labour Statistics (1985) August 1984. Canberra, ABS.

Lips, H.M. and Colwill, N.L. (1978) *The Psychology of Sex Differences.* Englewood Cliffs, N.J. Prentice-Hall.

Malloch, M. (1984) 'Women in the Technical Teachers' Union of Victoria, a study.' Masters of Educational Studies Thesis, Monash University.

McGrath, Patricia (1976) 'The unfinished assignment, equal education for women', *World Watch Paper,* 7 July.

Miller, C. and Swift, K. (1976) *Words and Women.* Garden City, NY, Anchor Press.

Ministry of Education (1986a) *Action Plan for Women in the Teaching Service.* Victoria, Government Printer.

Ministry of Education (1986b) 'Perspectives on inclusive curriculum: gender, ethnicity and class', *Equal Opportunity Unit In-Service.* Ministry of Education, March.

Moens, Gabriël (1985) *Affirmative Action, The New Discrimination.* The Centre for Independent Studies Limited.

PEP Secretariat (1985) *Inclusive Curriculum.* Melb. Participation and Equity Program.

Prunty, John J. (1985) 'Signposts for a critical educational policy analysis', *The Australian Journal of Education.* 29, 2.

Riddell, Sheila. (1986) 'Teachers' perceptions of the role of the school in the production of a gender differentiated curriculum', *BERA Conference,* Bristol.

Riseborough, George F. (1986) 'Schooling and patriarchy: a study of the lives and careers of women teachers'. *BERA Conference,* Bristol.

Ryan, Senator Susan (1986) 'Affirmative Action Equal Employment Opportunity for Women Bill.' Second Reading Speech, Canberra.

Sampson, S. (1983) 'Women and men in the teaching service.' *Equal Opportunity Forum.* No. 12, March.

Sampson, S. (1985) 'Women Teachers and Promotion: A Search for Some Explanations.' Research Paper. Monash University.

Sampson, S. (1986) 'Teachers are traditional role models.' Paper presented at AARE Conference, November.

Schwarz, Veronica (1984) *Women in the Education Department of Victoria.* Victoria Policy and Planning Unit, Education Department.

Schwarz, Veronica (1986) 'The invisible barriers.' Conference Speech.

Times Educational Supplement (1986) 'What you wanted to know about promotion ... but didn't like to ask.' 10 October.

Victorian Committee on Equal Opportunity in Schools (1977) Report to the Premier, Melbourne, July.

Weiner, Gaby (1986) 'Feminist education and equal opportunities:

unity or discord?', *British Journal of Sociology of Education.* 7, 3.

Wells, Polly (1983) *Equal Opportunity in Victorian Schools Questionnaire Report.* Victoria, Education Department of Victoria.

Wieman, Gabriel (1985) 'Sex differences in dealing with bureaucracy.' *Sex Roles* 12, 7/8.

Women (1985) Social Report, Victoria Australian Bureau of Statistics, July.

Yates, L. (1986) 'Theorising inequality today', *British Journal of Sociology.* Vol. 7, No. 2.

CHAPTER 8

'A School for Men': An Ethnographic Case Study of Routine Violence in Schooling

John Beynon

Introduction

This chapter is in line with the argument that real life acts of violence must be understood in their context of social structures, relationships and interactions. Most research on pupil violence is decontextualized from the school locale in which it occurs, while very little has been written to date on teacher violence. What follows is intended, in small measure, to rectify these shortcomings through a naturalistic examination of violence in Lower School; the purposes it served to further both teacher and pupil tasks-at-hand; and the meanings it held for them. It must be made clear, however, that I did not enter Lower School to study violence *per se*. I undertook fieldwork on a wider project, namely the initial encounters between teachers and pupils at the start of the latter's Secondary School careers and to observe staff induction strategies towards the new intake of eleven to twelve year olds; and to discover how, in turn, pupils reacted to the new regime and its varied academic and disciplinary demands (Beynon 1985a). In this chapter I argue the case for Educational Ethnography in that I seek to show that both *actual* and *symbolic violence* in Lower School could only be understood through the meanings it held for teachers and pupils alike and its functions in the *temporal* (time of year demands); the *historical/institutional* (the Secondary Modern origins of the dominant educational paradigm in Lower School, as propagated by the headmaster, Mr Changeable); the *pedagogical* (highly traditional, transmission teaching); and the *ecological* (the characteristics of site and area) *contexts* of Lower School. Routine violence was, indeed, one of the ways teachers and pupils 'coped' with the process of establishment at the onset of the school year. It was also the vehicle by which definitions of 'acceptable' masculinity was conveyed and confirmed.

Lower School housed the 350-first year boys of Victoria Road, a large 11–18, all-male comprehensive in Seatown, South Wales. During the period of initial encounters (here defined as the first eight weeks of the Autumn term) institutional and teachers' personal demands are announced before becoming settled and taken-for-granted as part of the everyday, negotiated order.

To observe how teachers introduced their subjects and groundrules, and how pupils reacted and established themselves with staff and peers, I collected data through participant observation and followed up with formal and informal interviewing. I sat in the back of classrooms and accompanied one form, 1Y, across the school day. As an outsider I had first to be accepted by teachers and ensure I was regarded by pupils as a trusted adult in whom they could confide, rather than just another authority figure (see Beynon 1983 for a discussion of the difficulties of the fieldwork process). A number of the fourteen Lower School staff I observed employed threats and physical coercion from the outset as part of the institutional 'welcome' (Goffman 1971). Boys were hit, pushed and shaken, even by the apparently docile Mr Piano who, on discovering in the second week that I was a former teacher commented, 'Well, well, fancy that! I can start thumping them now!', erroneously assuming that the experience had naturally led me to accept teacher violence as legitimate. This is surprising in that teachers have good reason to conceal violence: it can, at worst, lead to the courts, humiliation and dismissal; at least, to conflict with parents and the local authority. In Lower School, however, a hardcore of male teachers regarded coercive measures as synonymous with 'good' teaching itself and, therefore, a virtue to be upheld. They were mostly former secondary modern teachers who had lost out in career terms to the grammar school staff when Victoria Road Comprehensive emerged out of an amalgamation a decade earlier. A high degree of uncompromising discipline was a mark of their identity as a group. Not all their colleagues agreed with them, but the rhetoric of tough, disciplinary schoolmastery, reminiscent of Grace's (1978) Elementary teachers, predominated.[1] Therefore, shaking, pushing and cuffing boys (which would have been deemed assaults outside in the street) were widely accepted as part of the Lower School landscape. In observing such violence the research is invariably placed in an ethical dilemma: there were occasions when I clearly disapproved of what was happening and felt like saying so, even intervening. That would have wrecked my stance as a fly-on-the-wall, 'neutral' observer and would probably have had no effect in preventing teacher or pupil violence in the long term. Most violence threatens personal rights, undermines social order and is illegal. However, some violence is traditionally and commonsensically deemed acceptable between teachers and pupils. It takes the form of 'manhandling', a term particularly appropriate to Lower School in that it was male teachers who were the aggressors and women staff (with one exception) rarely threatened or hit boys. The manhandling increased the more accepted I became as a 'temporary' member of staff and, as the weeks passed, I inevitably moved from 'outsider' towards 'insider' status. Violence towards pupils was clearly so deeply embedded in these teachers' practices of crowd control that no apology or explanation was ever offered. Rather, it was flaunted as necessary at this time to establish authority. From the earliest days of the fieldwork I became increasingly interested in the 'routine violence', its forms and occurrences; its meanings for both parties; and the functions it served as part of teacher–pupil induction and coping strategies, as well as its role in pupils' provocative 'sussing' of teachers. Routine, but often spectacular, shows of violence appeared important at the start of the year as the moral climate of Lower School was being negotiated, and was worthy of close attention.

The school as a gendering agency

Before turning to the Lower School data on routine violence I want to say something about research into the role of schools as agencies for gendering pupils. Lower School was, as I have stated, described as 'a school for men ... the ethos is male'. It was a place where 'old fashioned schoolmastery' ruled supreme and where 'cuffing a boy across the head' was acceptable. The accuracy of Mr Changeable's description was amply borne out by my fieldwork: Lower School was the site of much violence and this was linked by both staff and pupils to 'being a man', 'learning to stand up for yourself', and of surviving in a world in which 'the weaklings go under' (Mr

Megaphone). I shall argue that the use of actual and symbolic violence in Lower School delimited what was 'acceptable masculinity', both on behalf of pupils and teachers. Men and boys were expected to behave in a certain kind of way, put up a certain kind of 'manly' performance, if they were to win the accolade of being a 'good teacher' or a 'good lad', whether that was a praiseworthy 'rough diamond' or playground 'hard'. Violence, and the threat of violence, was not only the principal means of speedily laying down the groundrules at the start of the year, but it encoded messages about the nature of masculinity and, by implication, femininity. If women teachers were castigated by (most) male colleagues, then so was 'womanish' behaviour, whether by male teachers or pupils. It is interesting to note that Metcalf and Humphries (1985) conclude that violence is at the very heart of contemporary masculinity: it is not just learnt early as male activity, but actually shapes the contours of adult masculinity. Seidler (1980) goes further and argues that violence becomes so encoded in boys' bodily stances that, as a consequence, they have to be 'constantly on the alert either to confront or avoid physical violence'. Masculinity thus becomes, in their view, something young males in our society have to be ever-ready to prove and defend, both actually and by means of aggressive, macho posturings and threatening stances.

The study of gender politics is at the heart of the emerging field of Cultural Studies. Writers point out that there has been little study of the social-cultural formation of masculinity. Easthope (1986), for example, shows that in spite of twenty years of research into femininity, masculinity has remained relatively concealed. Similarly, Metcalf and Humphries (1985) call for a closer scrutiny of gender differentiated practices and an investigation into how masculinity is actually structured and transmitted in schools. The gendering forces at work there, especially in relation to girls, have led to a blossoming and insightful tradition of Interactionist research in recent times (Griffin 1985; Weiner 1985; Whyte *et al.* 1985).

The Open University course E.813 and its two readers (edited by Arnot and Weiner, 1987) is extending and strengthening this line of enquiry. Amongst the many notable studies to date are those by Measor (1985) on how the curriculum is used to construct and reinforce gender roles; Llewellyn (1980), Sharp (1976) and Byrne (1978) on girls' perceptions of each other; McRobbie and Gerber (1976; 1980) and Meyenn (1980), who look at how girls appropriate and use teenage culture in different ways for different purposes; and Fuller (1978) on black girls in a comprehensive school; and Delamont (1980) and Stanworth (1982), who argue that teachers view and treat boys and girls unequally and thus contribute towards a hierarchial system of gender divisions in classrooms.[2] In reviewing what has been achieved one is led, however, to conclude that gendering processes have been explored more extensively by reference to girls than to boys. Indeed, there is now a need to know a great deal more about masculine gendering in both mixed and all-male schools, as well as the formation of gender identity within the three interpenetrating contexts of family, school and peer group.

Classroom-based research has attempted to explain male pupil behaviour either in terms of the Subcultural or Marxist models. In the former streaming, banding and setting are held to result in differentiation and polarization into pro- and anti-school cultures. This view, particularly associated with the work of Hargreaves (1967), Lacey (1970) and Ball (1984), sits well alongside Cohen's (1955) reaction formation theory. Deviant boys' delinquent subculture is viewed as a response to status problems arising from being male and working class: upward mobility, governed by middle class criteria, leads to status frustration and an inverting of middle class norms. In the Marxist model anti-school culture is viewed as the product of working class culture and not a mere reaction to status frustration. Such a case is compatible with Miller's (1958) thesis regarding male gang delinquency in the USA, whose members were not reacting to middle class culture, but adhering to the behaviour and values defined by their lower class community. 'Style' in this model is not a reaction to school, but an expression of class culture operating through socialization in family and community. This model finds expression in the Willis (1977) study in which working class boys' masculinity is viewed as a kind of 'performance', a front to offset disappointment. More likely to be defined as an academic failure, the working class boy expresses his masculinity through the collectivity of the peer group and makes himself a force through aggressive style, banter and symbolic play. The Willis thesis, too familiar to reiterate at length here, presents 'the lads' as refusing to compete in their oppression: education is seen not as an opportunity to advance through merit, but as an elitist exclusion of mass through a spurious recourse to merit, with the working class having to overcome the handicap of possessing the 'wrong' culture. By penetrating the contradiction at the heart of working class culture the counter-school group helps liberate its members from the burden of conformism and conventional achievement: instead they express and prove their masculinity through disruptive activities, smoking, swearing, sexism and racism. The irony that Willis claims to present is that the lads' counter-culture effectively achieves, in unintended ways, one of the main objectives, namely the directing of working class boys voluntarily into skilled, semi-skilled and unskilled manual work. His explanation for this phenomena is that although conformism to the dominant school norms may hold a certain logic for the individual, it does not for the working class as a whole. Viewed in this light 'the lads'' activities are a logical response, a rebuttal of the ideology of individual success as it operates through schooling.

If Willis concentrates on working class masculine identity, Tolson (1977) focuses more upon the 'obsessive masculinity' into which the archetyphal middle class boy is schooled: 'In his education it means a constant show of competence at the expense of sensitivity and feeling. The aggressive performance and the avoidance of feeling amount to a complex, self-sustaining syndrome.' His oft-repeated argument is that, for both working and middle class men, 'being a man' in our society demands 'a certain inarticulacy or distance towards the complexity of personal experience'. He argues that middle class men are socialized into masculinity through schools which define competence and achievement in terms of academic and sporting success. Such institutions encode traditions to cultivate personality traits such as confidence, competitiveness and ambition. He sees the ethic of the all-male boarding school and its definition of 'manhood' as the ideological reference point for the training of 'gentlemen' (with qualities of personal endurance; unquestioned devotion to duty; and the ability to both give and take orders) still serving middle class interests. Although the day of the classical public school tradition may be over, elements of middle class socialization into the gentleman role endure, with a renewed emphasis on personal ambition, achievement, and social responsibility. Middle class schools still instil notions of privilege tempered by duty and service, for its products are 'bound to lead but also, paradoxically, to serve those they lead'. The experience elicits an emotional commitment to self-discipline and a long-term investment to a ladder of achievement and satisfaction in service to an authority greater than himself. The concept of career dominates the working lives of middle class men because their experiences at school have shaped them to a life of competitive struggle, a struggle which they maintain throughout adulthood, buttressed and supported by the domestic/leisure domain of home and family.

Both Willis (what of the 'earoles'?) and Tolson (where's the field data on schooling?) can be criticized for their generalities and assumptions. We still need to know far more about the shifting connections between schooling and gender; between working and middle class pupil cultures; and between feminine and masculine cultures. To turn to the Lower School data is to examine how the actual and symbolic use of violence was directly associated with definitions of teacher and pupil masculinity. I start with pupils' perceptions of teacher and peer violence and its role in 'sussing' and provisional typing (Beynon 1984a), ending with an examination of the many 'myths of aggression' I recorded. All the time the message is that to fit into this 'school for men' one has to 'act like a man': it is no place for either women or for children!

Pupil perceptions of teacher violence

Pupil perspectives of teacher violence fell into three categories, namely:

1. Aggression that was 'funny' as opposed to genuinely frightening or dangerous;
2. 'Real' violence;
3. Violence on pupils which was deemed either 'deserved and fair' or 'undeserved and unfair'.

1. Funny violence

This often took the form of a pretend fight when teacher and pupils played at violence, or the Physical Education teacher's ritual slippering of offenders:

> When we arrived back in the yard, Mr Megaphone gathered 1Y around him whilst he dressed down Ginger for running on the road and racing across the juction without looking on the way back from Seaview Park. 'It's the dap for you, twit!' he said.

Violence was often enjoyed in retrospect when it was re-interpreted and embellished as was this incident (see 'myths of aggression' later):

> As Miss Floral was taking the afternoon register Ginger was talking loudly and turning around to prod and push the boy in the desk behind. Mr Changeable must have spotted him through the glass panel in the classroom door because it suddenly swung open and he strode in, walked straight up to Ginger, smacked him across the head and shoulders and pulled him out of his chair. 'Don't you realize Miss Floral is marking a legal document, you young ignoramus? Don't you?' he shouted. 'You will sit quiet and behave yourself, do you understand? And that goes for every single one of you!' With that he turned and left, saying nothing to Miss Floral.

Months later Ginger was still recalling what had taken place with considerable pleasure:

> *Ginger:* I got clouted a first time an' all when I was talking when Miss Floral was doing the register and Mr Changeable came in behind me and then gave me a clout. I was sitting down and he clocked me around the shoulder.
>
> *J.B.:* Did that worry you?
>
> *Ginger:* No, 'cos it don't hurt because there's padding in the shoulders in the blazer! [laughter]
>
> *King:* And when I was in the yard in the first couple of days, I was looking around and I got a clout. He chucked me out of the barn [dinner hall], didn't he, Mike? I laughed me head off at him. It didn't hurt . . .
>
> *J.B.:* Do you think a school can operate without physical punishment?
>
> *Ginger:* It wouldn't be any good without physical punishment because you wouldn't be able to have a laugh . . .
>
> *King:* No, you couldn't have a laugh.
>
> *Ginger:* . . . you couldn't have a laugh watching other people getting hit. That's the best fun in school.
>
> *King:* . . . it wouldn't be a laugh unless the teachers hit you, would it?

Funny violence was the boys' principal source of laughter, enjoyment and excitement in Lower School. It was repeatedly talked about by them as humour, as the following excerpts illustrate:

You can't help laughing at it...it's just so funny it creases you up...it's really exciting and funny...it breaks up the day...it's a comedy...it's far better than *Charlie's Angels* ...you come to school and you look forward to it happening...it's like a holiday camp...

Although they subscribed to the view that physical punishment was necessary for school order (it was both proper and expected), they also argued that without it the daily experience of school would be less of a laugh, less enjoyable. What was intended as a deterrent to bad behaviour and mucking around was, paradoxically, transformed by pupils into 'a laugh'. They, therefore, created combative scenes and interludes of aggressive confrontation with teachers as a means of transforming the reality of school. This observation is supported by those writers who argue that for many pupils 'laughing' is the only satisfying part of school life and what makes it tolerable (e.g. Walker *et al.*, 1975; 1977; Woods, 1983). Lower School boys spoke of 'laughing' and 'mucking' as the vehicles for redefining the school experience and creating a 'holiday camp atmosphere'.[5] Teacher violence was repeatedly appropriated and used by boys as they exploited and transformed teacher outbursts to turn the tables on their aggressors. Violence became the principal source of entertainment to neutralize the monotony, as well as used by some to 'bodybuild'[4] that is, impress peers through acts of cheeky bravado against staff. Indeed, the highest peer status was earned by standing up to teachers, negating their physical superiority through cockiness and defiance:

As Mr Changeable lectured and 'drilled' the boys into straight lines in the yard at lunchtime today, King was seen to spit on the back of the boy in front of him. Mr Changeable went berserk and belted King so hard he nearly knocked him over. Absolute silence as he propelled King up to the front by the scruff of the neck. He allowed the others to 'lead on' into the 'barn' [lunch hall] and I left him lecturing King on hygiene and good manners. The amazing thing was how quickly King recovered his cockiness: he stands up to the teachers and doesn't appear to fear being hit, but trades off such assaults and is making his reputation that way:

'If a teacher starts throwing you around or belting you around the head an' that, like Mr Changeable does, well the thing is not to cry like a little girl or cower in the corner covering your head like some of them do! You stand up all cocky-like and laugh at 'em and give your mates a smile and things like that an' cheek 'em an' that! Like Mr Changeable goes to me, 'Did that hurt, King?' and I goes 'No!' all shouted out and he goes wild and goes 'Sir! Sir! You call me Sir!' and I just looks at him. If he hits me again this year I'm going to dead-leg him in the balls!' [Laughter]

'Bodybuilding' (by grinning; waving at friends; retaliating with cheek and gestures; not showing hurt, pain or contrition) was carried out with style and panache to make some teachers look silly, 'soft' and ineffectual. Many of them, on the other hand, admired boys who could take violence in this truculent manner: it was all part of Lower School's machismo culture as a 'school for men', a definition jointly created and supported by the activities of many teachers and many pupils. If boys engaged in 'bodybuilding' based on the ability to 'take violence', then a mirror image was found in the staffroom where some staff consciously publicized themselves through their ability to 'dish it out'. Here, for example, is what one of the rugby teachers said:

The young O'Brien is going the same way as the older one did. He was the only boy whom the staff actually asked me to hurt. 'Get him on the rugby field' they said, 'really hurt him in a tackle!' So I did! He was like an angel after that. This kid looks to be the same – all mouth until he's sorted out. Just give me the word!

2. 'Real' violence, or when the laughter stopped

'Real' violence was when a boy was either hurt; in danger of being hurt; or when events escalated beyond participants' control:

Bright: Mr Megaphone, he just says, 'Right, next one to talk gets the dap', and he just bends you over and goes like that, whack! That's alright, but when teachers hit you around the head and throw you around the hall without warning, well that's all wrong ... Same with Peter Ross in our class, she [Mrs Bear] really lost her temper with him and caught him and sent him flying. She went too far, just lost all control over herself.

J.B.: Was that funny?

Bright: No, it wasn't. Not at all funny.

Real violence was most likely to erupt if pupils were foolhardy enough to stray into the teacher's personal domain:

Martin: Sometimes when someone gets beaten up it isn't funny. Like in Geography Mr Scouse was saying how he had a nice car and a nice wife and a nice house an' that and when he said nice wife somebody started to laugh and wolf-whistle. He thought it was Jason Slow – but it wasn't him – and he just went for him and grabbed him by the neck and lifted him about two feet off the ground. If the window had been open he'd have thrown him through – he was really that mad with him! That wasn't funny 'cos you could see Mr Scouse's expression, the expression on his face, that he was really mad, you know. I couldn't laugh then. If anyone had laughed he'd have gone *really* mad.

The boundary between funny and unamusing, 'real' violence was being explored and settled at the time of the study as boys defined the degree of teacher violence that was acceptable and, also the style in which it was executed. The worst case of real violence I witnessed was when Michael Long (who had misbehaved throughout assembly; was then kept behind; and then adopted a very provocative tone with the Headmaster, Mr Changeable) was pushed backwards over a bench and fell awkwardly. He was clearly hurt and cried, much to the teacher's consternation. At a later date Long commented:

He knew when he'd done wrong because he came to see me at break, then at the end of the afternoon, putting his arm around me and buttering me up. He'd nearly smashed me up and now kept telling me it was my fault! Then the next day he asked me if I'd said anything to my parents, but I hadn't. It would have been his word against mine. I thought he'd broken my back. [See the description of this incident later.]

3. Fair and unfair violence

Boys held that teachers were duty-bound to use physical coercion in order to keep order and scorned 'soft' teachers:

Teachers got a right to hit, mind you, because we're here to learn and they're here to teach us and they get paid for keeping us quiet and learning us and telling us what to do and not be noisy. I think that the only good teachers are the

ones who smash you around because you'll learn in time 'cos
the more they hit you, the more you'll learn to shut up.

They sanctioned 'fair' violence and held that 'good' teachers
followed a protocol of warnings and avoided humiliating or
hurting pupils. They used fair violence, which was held to be a
central element in the teacher–pupil contract:

> A good teacher hits you sometimes when you deserve it, and a
> bad teacher just whacks you for no reason. Like some women.

Mr Stern [a Maths master] was seen as a good teacher because
although 'hard' he warned pupils before punishing them.
Ginger explained: 'I don't dislike Mr Stern even when he hits
me 'cos he's a good teacher . . . he'll give you about three
chances, about three, dun he, Dave?'

> I mess around and gets done a first time and then I starts
> talking and messing around and gets done a second time, I
> ease up then, but you usually take it that a third time you
> have to go to Mr Changeable and get the cane, detention, or
> double detention, or the teacher wallops you. When they lose
> control, it happens all of a sudden, you can't control it.

> *Ginger:* But she's got so much harder and she handles us real
>   good, dun she, Dave?
> *King:* She's got all hard, smacks you around and pulls you
>   around by the hair. Whack! like that, right across the nut.

'Bad' teachers, on the other hand, 'picked-on' or victimized pupils,
either employing illegitimate violence that hurt or was dangerous
(for example, heavy punching or vicious slapping across the head;
the sudden hooking of chairs from under boys, etc.); or they set out
to humiliate (for example, by making a pupil cry in front of the
class):

> *Ginger:* I haven't been made to cry once by the teachers – well
>   only once. It was Mr Changeable, no, it was Mr
>   Megaphone, PE, that was it. I want to forget about it.
> *King:* Being made to cry is worst that can happen. I mean, if
>   you don't cry it's just a laugh. But if you cry . . .
> *Ginger:* Yes, they all made fun of me. They said 'A ya baby!'
>   and all that. It's unfair to make you cry . . .
> *King:* Phil Raymond was made to cry the other day, wun he!
>   Mr New just tapped him on the head! Raymond said he
>   cried because he'd had a bad day, but no one believed him.

Indeed, the most humiliating thing that could happen to a boy was to be physically dominated, hurt or 'showed-up' by a woman teacher (Beynon 1985a). Finally, the two teacher types boys most disliked were either dangerously coercive 'sadists', or 'moody' ones, whose rapidly changing tempers meant they were hard to predict. Mr Changeable was the prime example of the former:

> Long was talking and laughing as boys filed out of the hall into classrooms after assembly. Mr Changeable rushed up, clouted him and threw him across the hall towards his office. Unfortunately he tripped over a gym mat (which was rolled and stored near Mr Changeable's room) and fell awkwardly. For a moment I thought he really was badly injured until he stood up holding his back sobbing. Mr Changeable put his arm round the boy's shoulders and was suddenly very solicitous. There must have been at least a hundred boys left in the hall and yet there was absolute silence.

> The form were queueing up outside the French room. There was a lot of movement between classes and boys were milling around. David King was using his weight to barge other boys out of his way. Suddenly Mr Changeable (the head of the Lower School) shot across the hall . . . and manhandled King, then smacked him loudly over the head with a book. 'I've told you about barging before boy' he shouted, 'Don't fool around with me! I'm more than a little tired of your ignorant behaviour, King!' There was absolute silence throughout the hall, boys quickly disappearing into their classes.

Mr Scouse, on the other hand, was 'moody':

> You get to know what mood a teacher's in. Like Mr Scouse, you've got to know when he's in a laughing, mess-around mood and when he's in a nasty mood. Sometimes he'll have a laugh, other times he'll smash you around the room. It depends what he feels like.

I gathered ample evidence to illustrate how some Lower School boys purposely provoked teachers who were subsequently judged and provisionally typed on the basis of their reactions (whether 'hard', 'soft', 'moody' or 'sadist').[4] The nature of the teacher response provided pupils with valuable evidence far more trustworthy than the claims individuals made for themselves during early meetings. As one boy said, to know what a teacher was really like he had to 'put his fist where his mouth is!' What the pupils termed 'sussing' was composed of a wide variety of hypotheses – testing strategies by a network (what, in my study, I term a 'fraternity') of 1Y pupils as they negotiated with staff the working climates of classrooms. Through it was discovered what could only be found out in this way, namely whether an agitated teacher, who had been placed in a difficult position, would employ violence to keep order; and, if so, whether it was 'soft', acceptable or 'real' violence (Beynon 1984a; 1984b; 1985b):

> At first you don't know the teachers and you have to judge them by their reactions. Some give lines, some whack you or tell you off, and others throw you outside. You just got to see how they act. You got to suss them out – there's no other way.

> *King:* You go for a teacher's weak points, don't you?
> *Blond:* Early in the morning or right at the end of the day, that's the time 'cos you know they're tired after a day's work.

> ... in that first week we were messing around like anything and he took us back behind after a lesson and we knew that if he was soft that he would just tell us off, and if he was hard he'd hit us, and he hit us! He smacked Kingsy against the wall and kicked us both up the backside ... that's how we found out about Mr New!

It was solicited teacher violence to establish the boundaries of tolerance; establish the groundrules for working relationships; and help crystallize identities. If it was to test teachers it was also a means for a boy to 'bodybuild' and adopt a high profile as an adventurous lad, as was pupil–pupil violence in the yard and the environs of Lower School. Violence of this sort was only understandable through the eyes of participants, taking into account the time of year and the urgency for boys to find out about teachers and establish, in this case, an oppositional pupil culture emanating from a small, tight group of 1Y 'muckers' (Beynon and Delamont 1984c).

Pupil violence

Violence was not, of course, solely associated with teachers: in my time in Lower School I observed pupil violence in classrooms, corridors, playground and outside school.[5] Definitions of acceptable and unacceptable pupil violence were being settled at the same time as those relating to teachers. Violence was observed being used to sort out a 'league table' of 'hard' and 'soft' pupils. Battles between boys were discussed and sometimes resulted in the vanquished losing face and having to accept a changed reputation. An extensive typology, based on boys' physical prowess or lack of it, existed, with 'bullies' and 'bigheads' as the most feared and disliked, and 'hards' admired as playground brawlers.

> *Long:* Lawrence Klee could walk into any form in the school and smash up anyone who stood in his way. He could walk through all the desks and just push them out of the way with his legs. He's that hard I'd doubt anyone would stop him. What's he, thirteen stone?

There were widespread attacks on boys regarded as 'queers' or 'poofs', and the same effeminate boys were often also rejected by many teachers:

> You can't describe Mark Mallinder as normal. Look at the way he follows us [the staff] around. I told Bill [Mr Changeable] to give him a clip and send him out to play with the other kids, toughen him up a bit. 'I'm trying to build up Mark's confidence', that was his reply. He's spending more time on that one kid than all the others put together. (Mr Jovial)

> A group of boys was accused at break today of a 'poof-bashing exercise' in which Mark Mallinder was beaten up. He was badly roughed over, given a black eye and cut lip. Mr Changeable was furious and could be heard shouting at them throughout the rest of the morning. They were caned and made to stand silently outside his office throughout the lunch break.

They faced, in effect, an onslaught from both peers and certain teachers and this was another aspect of the creation of a 'school for men'. Indeed, teachers generally were prepared to write-off most pupil violence as normal, healthy, boyish exuberance and horseplay. They distinguished between the acceptable 'boys standing up for themselves' and the 'hard knocks' brand of physicality (as, for example, in rugby) and the 'dirty stuff', namely butting, gouging, kicking and spitting, this being associated with soccer hooliganism. The need for and acceptability of macho posturing and violence was conveyed to boys (and by boys) in the form of what I term 'myths of aggression', to which I now turn.

Myths of aggression[6]

One of the most noticeable features throughout my fieldwork was the extent to which both teachers and pupils talked about spectacular scenes of classroom violence:

Long: Wilde had a fight with Mr Piano next door.
Green: Yes, they were in the hall, I heard that.
Long: He was in front of me and had a pile of pens and he was fooling and kept on taking these pens out and he came to his last pen and he [Mr Piano] came up and took 'em off Wilde and hit him across the head. He ran away to the other side of the class and Mr Piano was just pushing the tables away and when he got him Wilde just ran around to the other side of the room and he pushed him against the cupboard and he was on the floor fighting him. And Mr Changeable came in and he just took him out into the hall and he was just shaking him around and everything. Terrible!

These narratives were, I concluded, not only part of impression management (both teachers and pupils used them), but also

Nature of violence	Teacher on teacher	Pupil on pupil	Teacher on pupil	Pupil on teacher
Actual violence	Non observed or recorded	✓	✓	Non observed or recorded
Symbolic violence	✓	Threats and aggressive postures : 'showing hard' by teachers and pupils		✓

Figure 8.1

functioned to chart out an accepted code of practice (Wilde, it was felt, deserved what he got!). Violence, plus talk about violence, were mutually justifying. Furthermore, these 'myths of aggression' fell into two broad categories: first and second hand accounts of *actual* confrontations; and stories which constituted a form of indirect, *symbolic* violence (in the absence of real violence) by pupils on teachers and teachers on teachers. These can be summarized in Figure 8.1. Taking symbolic violence first, in the examples below incidents are represented in such a manner that the actual loser becomes the winner. In one case a teacher just escapes a boy's revenge for a brutal assault, while in the second another appears as a coward unwilling and unable to counter a pupil's challenge:

> Mark Thompson was messing the Music teacher and he was fooling around at the back of the room in the corner with Christopher O'Mally. They were just thumping each other and laughing. Mr Piano goes all mad and he was throwing Thompson around and then he banged their heads together and O'Mally breaks out crying. He shouldn't have done that so Thompson goes, to the teacher, 'If you don't fucking stop it I'll fucking bullshit your face', he goes. Well Mr Piano is mad and he hit Thompson and kicked him up the aisle and out of the room and smashed his head against the door frame on the way out, really bad! Well, Thompson went down to the Drama room, put his bag in there, and he was punching the wall as hard as he could and then he went down to the cloakroom and then he, he had a drink of water to cool himself off, and then he bought out a knife and he said, 'I'm going to kill that sadist!' He went down through the yard and Mr Piano got into his car and drove off just in time. He saw Thompson coming and he knew he'd gone too far. All the kids were with Thompson, cheering him an' that. He would have used that knife, definite!

> When Mr Dancer first came here to teach French he went around all joking an' that, trying to be friendly. He used to say things like 'Hello horrible!' to kids and 'Watch it, tough guy!', funny things like that. Anyway, one day we were all pushing out of the door breaktime into the yard and he was trying to get into the staffroom and he said to Vidal, 'Stop pushing, skinhead', or 'Watch it, skinhead!', something like that 'cos Vidal had had all his hair cut short and he had his

City red and white scarf on over his blazer and his trousers tucked into his boots, all hard like. Anyway, Vidal didn't like it and he said to Mr Dancer, 'You'd better fucking watch it or I'll stick one on you!' and Mr Dancer he heard, but he was too scared to do anything about it.

J.B.: Are you sure he heard?

He definitely heard. I'm sure of it. He was just too scared to take Vidal on.

Similarly I recorded a form of symbolic violence by teachers against colleagues who were unwilling to employ physical measures against pupils. They were frequently castigated and 'slagged off' behind their backs by the Deputy Head in the staffroom. I recorded many such attacks:

The rough diamonds are alright. We built the Empire with kids like them. A teacher in this school may look okay and sound great, but kids like that show his weaknesses. The test of a good teacher is whether he can deal with kids like that and remain on good terms with them. That's the real test, not being able to manage a crowd of nice, polite middle class kids – anyone can do that! A boy like King responds to a firm hand. The first time I met him he tried me out and got clobbered! From the very start he learned that I wasn't going to take any lip from him. After that we got on like a house on fire. I had to dish out a few gentle reminders now and then, but nothing serious. I had no trouble with him whatsoever. But some colleagues have no idea. They let him run rings around them, the women especially. Unless they can discipline kids, then they shouldn't be teaching. A test of who's a teacher and who's pretending is simple: put them in the hall alone with 300 first years, throw in a few kids like King and mad Freddie Wilde, and close the door! If you went in after half-an-hour with [names four staff] you'd still be able to hear a pin drop. If you left [names another four staff] in there then you'd have to scrape what was left of them off the wall and then you'd have to go out and find the kids! Some of them like [names three staff] are totally dependent on Bill and myself. They can't do damn all for themselves and their classes sound more like football matches than anything else.

In the staffroom teachers often told stories which showed approval of the 'manly' sort of boy:

Darren Stephenson was a very powerful boy. He was one of the biggest kids in the school. He had the body of a man and when he turned nasty, watch out! He was a Youth Club boxer and he was in training. He carried an enormously heavy punch and all the kids knew it. Sometimes when I had to leave the room I'd say, 'Don't misbehave, because Darren is in charge. If I find some of you beaten up when I come back I won't blame Darren!' Of course I was never out of the place for long, but it always worked. There was never any trouble.

He was the biggest, toughest, most foul-mouthed kid this school has ever known. I said to him, 'Talk to me like that and I'll sort you out here and now.' Well, he carried on, so I hit him! I hit him so hard I was off school for two days! I busted my hand on him I hit him so hard! But I had no trouble with him after that. He'd tested me and found he'd get nowhere but into hospital. A boy like that only understands this [shows a clenched fist], but you can work on a kid like that, make him work for you not against you.

If there's anything nasty going on when I'm on duty then I step in – two or more onto one, that kind of thing. But if there's a good, clean scrap, and if no one's getting hurt, then I take my time. These boys have to settle things with their fists – it's the only language some of them understand.

Both teachers and pupils used cautionary tales to warn of the consequences of 'ignoring the rules' or 'not playing the game':

If you swing on that rope the wrong way and it snaps and you go through the window, then you'll fall thirty feet into the yard and get a pile of stitches for being so clever! One boy didn't listen to me one year. I went to visit him in hospital. He was covered from head to foot in plaster with two holes for his eyes and another hole so they could pour soup into his mouth! As far as I know he could be still there, or in a wheelchair somewhere.

I heard about this kid last year who got beaten up in the yard because he was always telling on his mates. Barnsie they called him. Anyway, one lunch hour... [He goes on to relate how the boy was set upon by his fellows and ended up in hospital].

These tales, with their violent catalogue of fights, accidents and brutal confrontations can best be regarded as 'myths' whereby what Measor and Woods (1983) term a 'cultural blueprint' detailing acceptable and unacceptable violence was disseminated. Their view is that during the status passage between schools myths serve a number of functions:

- they reflect in compressed form the principles by which reality should be interpreted;
- organize values and lay down conditions of cultural membership;
- communicate possibilities and help guide actions by offering practical solutions;
- draw attention to key situational features and operate symbolically in providing a social charter;
- encapsulate rules for behaviour and authenticate a set of beliefs and conventions about seeing and knowing in a given setting;
- convey a warning to stay clear of trouble and injury (cf Malinowski 1926; Levi–Strauss 1968; and Barthes 1973);
- present action dramatically, with the degree of accuracy less important than the general truths they contain;
- embody emotional and cognitive messages relating to behaviour and indicate the adjustments to be made in new surroundings.

Conclusion

In this chapter I have argued that we still have much to learn about the school's role in the gendering of boys (witness Walford's study of public school life, 1986) and that this can only be achieved through the Interactionist's close attention to processual detail. We need to know more about where boys derive their notions about masculinity, but also their ideas about girls and women and the role of their experience of schooling in forming attitudes. I have attempted to show how, within the confines of Lower School, there were considerable pressures on both teachers and pupils to display masculinity in rigidly demarcated ways. At the heart of both the acceptable teacher and pupil performance was a machismo based on 'showing hard'. Staff and boys who either could not (or would not) conform were ostracized and castigated as 'soft' (and, by implication, 'feminine', with overtones of incompetence and/or cowardice) and, thereby, a threat to the established order of a 'school for men', a school in which acceptable masculinity was directly linked to the actual or threatened execution of violence. In this environment to be 'a man' was to place violence up front in the presentation of self (and conversely, to be seen to take it without 'cracking up'). Violence in Lower School thus constituted a discourse employed by both teachers and pupils in which both the limits and possibilities of this limited masculinity were encoded. I recorded on tape and in fieldnotes numerous myths on the necessity for 'acceptable' teacher coercion; the desirability of a machismo style for both the delivery and reception of violence; the aggrandizement of 'rough' kids by teachers; the rejection of 'soft' and 'abnormal' kids; the castigation of both female and 'soft' teachers; the rejection of 'bad', 'sadistic' and 'moody' teachers; the consequences of irresponsible behaviour; and revenge stories on all those who had ignored the official and unoffical rules governing violence. These teacher and pupil myths were mirror images and advocated that violence was not only acceptable, but necessary for the well-being of all in Lower School. Acceptable violence rendered life therein manageable and predictable. They vividly reflected and reinforced the socio-economic, historical, cultural and gender backdrop to the place; its staff; its first year cohort; and the geographical area.[8] Moreover, they expressed a great deal about the operating of mass public schooling at a time of falling rolls, low public expenditure, and depressed teacher morale, when there were few new appointments and little opportunity, stimuli or encouragement for ageing (in this case, male) teachers to try new approaches or to retrain. I have shown in this paper how an ethnographic approach to routine violence in the temporal and spatial context of Lower School showed it to be central to the establishment strategies of both teachers and pupils as a working consensus was negotiated. It was the means by which both parties projected themselves; provisionally typed each other; and settled the social charter of Lower School at the start of the year as a 'school for men'. It was supported by symbolic violence in the form of myths of aggression which upheld the ideas of 'old fashioned schoolmastery', firm discipline, and appropriate 'manly' be-haviour. Most violence in Lower School was premeditated and part of start-of-term impression management, yet 'real' (controlled or uncontrolled) violence, whether in classroom or playground, was condemned. Both parties drew on violence as an important strategic resource: it was the means by which pupils provoked and typed teachers, while some of the latter actively sought out and took every advantage of such opportunities to display their 'hardness'. Pupils, too, appropriated teacher violence to bolster their reputations through cocky resilience. Violence was double-edged in yet another sense in that what was meant as a deterrent was simultaneously a source of 'laughs'. Such were the paradoxes that naturalistic enquiry revealed as the Lower School year got under way, both about violence itself and its role in upholding the definition of 'a man' conveyed by (most) male teachers to their new cohort of boys.

Notes

1. I do not propose to dwell on the pedagogical and ecological contexts of Lower School except to say that in the overcrowded and confined space teacher competence was related to the ability to keep classes silent and orderly. Ms Floral, for example, whose Drama lessons were noisy and encouraged pupil involvement, was subjected to a great deal of critical pressure to conform by senior staff, especially Mr Changeable (see below) and to (a) keep her classes quiet; and (b) adopt a more conventional, teacher-controlled mode of instruction. Until she did this she was seen as lacking in both experience and expertise (Beynon 1988). In addition, in common with other female staff in Lower School, she was held to be a liability because she was not prepared to hit pupils and so was dismissed as 'soft' by staff and boys alike. I refer frequently to the temporal context (starting-the-year), and the pedagogical and institutional/historical contexts can best be sketched-in by quoting Mr Changeable, the headmaster. He described himself as a 'secondary modern man' and was distrustful of what he regarded as the 'grammar school types' who held the senior positions in Middle and Upper School. A number of writers have noted how, even within the comprehensive school, earlier divisions between teacher professional groups (for example, that between the university graduate and the B.Ed. holder) are being perpetuated (David Hargreaves 1980 and 1982;
Riseborough 1981; Ball 1984; and Beynon 1985b). Mr Changeable, the head of Lower School, was an advocate of what he termed 'old-fashioned schoolmastery', which included uncompromising (physical) discipline and highly traditional teaching methods. His philosophy; his fears for the future; and the type of school he ensured he presided over are made clear in the statement below:

> I would describe Lower School as *a school for men*. By that I mean quite simply that it is a large boys' school, the majority of the staff are men and the ethos is male. Women often prove to be a liability and that is why they are shunted off down to me in

Lower School. I have to find them jobs because they can't cope with bloody-minded third, fourth and fifth years! In my view a lot of the women – let's be fair! – some of the men, especially some of the younger, more irresponsible ones, let the side down. They're no longer schoolmasters or schoolmistresses, but teachers who couldn't give a damn as long as the cheque is waiting for them at the end of the month. The old skills, the old self-respect, are fast disappearing and the motivation for excellence on all scores just isn't there. They may have better paper qualifications than my generation of teachers, but that doesn't make them better teachers. Many of them would never have survived in the old sec. mods. They're sloppy and some are prepared to let the kids get away with murder. Well, that's not my way: I run this school like clockwork and, as a result, they're either with me or against me, depending on their competence as schoolteachers. I'm a stickler for no-nonsense, old-fashioned schoolmastery and if that means cuffing a boy across the head, so be it!

2. The Open University MA Module E813 [Gender and Education], first presented in 1987, contains reference to most of the texts referred to in this section. [The set books are: Griffin, C. (1985) *Typical Girls?*, Routledge & Kegan Paul. Weiner, G. (ed. 1985) *Just a Bunch of Girls*, Open University Press. Whyte, J. *et al.* (eds, 1985). *Girl Friendly Schooling*, Methuen. Another useful collection is Dean, R. (ed. 1980) *Schooling for Women's Work*, Routledge & Kegan Paul. The two readers for E813 are: Arnot, M. and Weiner, G. (eds, 1986) *Gender and the Politics of Schooling*, Hutchinson/Open University. Weiner, G. and Arnot, M. (eds, 1987) *Gender Under Scrutiny*, Hutchinson/Open University.

3. All terms in inverted commas were used by teachers and/or pupils (for example, 'bodybuild', 'suss', 'laughing', 'show hard', 'old-fashioned schoolmastery' (etc.).

4. There is now a considerable literature on typifications (Schutz 1972) in schools (see, for example, Werthman 1963; Furlong 1977; Nash 1976). In spite of the fact that they researched in different areas at different times a broad consensus emerges of the main attributes of 'good' and 'bad' teachers.

5. This naturally posed a dilemma for me as a 'neutral' researcher as, on occasions, I witnessed considerable violence and petty vandalism on school property (Beynon 1983).

6. I focus on myths relating to violence, but there were others: for example, some stories related to sex. Mr Dancer was repeatedly portrayed as homosexual and Ms Floral as promiscuous; similarly boys were portrayed as 'queers', 'straights', 'screw-ups' and 'perverts'. Sets of myths interacted and the unfortunate Mr Dancer was stigmatized and ostracized on a number of counts.

214   *John Beynon*

7. Seatown was in depressed, post-industrial South Wales with its main
employer, the docks, now lying idle. New jobs in the area were few and
most employment was in Cityton, a dozen miles away. Many of the
boys came from a huge 1960s housing estate noted for its high unemployment rate. There was, in Lower School, a heavy emphasis upon
'teaching basics' and ensuring boys learned how to take orders and
'produce the goods on time'. This, it was argued, would render them
more reliable and employable when they came on to the job market.

References

Ball, S.J. (1981) *Beachside Comprehensive: A Case Study of Secondary Schooling*. Cambridge University Press.
Ball, S.J. (1984) 'School Politics, Teachers' Careers and Educational Change'. Paper to Westhill College Conference, January.
Barthes, R. (1973) *Mythologies*. London, Paladin.
Bernstein, B. (1973) *Class, Codes and Control*, Volumes 1 and 2. London, Routledge & Kegan Paul.
Beynon, J. (1983) 'Ways-in and staying-in: fieldwork as problem solving' in M. Hammersley (ed.), *The Ethnography of Schooling*. Nafferton.
Beynon, J. (1984a) 'Sussing out teachers: pupils as data gatherers' in P. Woods (ed.), *Life in School: The Sociology of Pupil Culture*. Milton Keynes, Open University Press.
Beynon, J. and Atkinson, P. (1984b) 'Pupils as data gatherers: mucking and sussing' in S. Delamont (ed.) *Readings on Interaction in the Classroom*. London, Methuen.
Beynon, J. and Delamont, S. (1984c) 'The hard and the soft' in H. Gault and N. Frude (eds), *School Violence*. New York. Wiley.
Beynon, J. (1985a) *Initial Encounters in the Secondary School: Sussing, Typing and Coping*. Lewes, Falmer Press.
Beynon, J. (1985b) 'Career histories in a comprehensive school' in S.J. Ball and I.F. Goodson (eds), *Teachers' Lives and Careers*. Lewes, Falmer Press.
Beynon, J. (1988) 'The micropolitics of drama teaching' in L. Tickle (ed.), *The Arts in Education*. London, Croom Helm.
Blumer, H. (1969) *Symbolic Interactionism: Perspective and Method*. Englewood Cliffs, NJ, Prentice-Hall.
Byrne, E.M. (1978) *Women and Education*. London, Tavistock Press.
Cohen, A.K. (1955) *Delinquent Boys: the Subculture of the Gang*. New York, Free Press.
Delamont, S. (1973) 'Academic conformity observed: studies in the classroom', unpublished Ph.D thesis, University of Edinburgh.
Delamont, S. (1980) *Sex Roles and the School*. London, Methuen.
Delamont, S. (1983) *Interaction in the Classroom* (2nd edition). London, Methuen.

Easthope, A. (1986) *The Masculine Myth in Popular Culture*. London. Paladin.

Fuller, M. (1980) 'Black girls in a London comprehensive school', in R. Decm (ed.), *Schooling for Women's Work*. London, Routledge & Kegan Paul.

Furlong, V. (1977) 'A nancy goes to school: a case study of pupils' knowledge of their teachers' in P. Woods and M. Hammersley (eds), *School Experience*. London, Croom Helm.

Glaser, B. and Strauss, A. (1967) *The Discovery of Grounded Theory*. London, Aldine.

Goffman, E. (1971) *The Presentation of Self in Everyday Life*. Harmondsworth, Penguin.

Grace, G. (1978) *Teacher, Ideology and Control*. London, Routledge & Kegan Paul.

Hammersley, M. and Atkinson, P. (1983) *Ethnography: Principles in Practice*. London, Tavistock.

Hargreaves, Andy (1978) 'Towards a theory of classroom coping strategies' in L. Barton and R. Meighan (eds), *Sociological Interpretations of Schooling and Classrooms*. Nafferton.

Hargreaves, Andy (1979) 'Strategies, decisions and control: interaction in a middle school classroom' in J. Eggleston (ed.), *Teacher Decision-Making in the Classroom*. London, Routledge & Kegan Paul.

Hargreaves, Andy (1980) 'Synthesis and the study of strategies: a project for the sociological imagination' in P. Woods (ed.), *Pupil Strategies*. London, Croom Helm.

Hargreaves, David (1967) *Social Relations in a Secondary School*, London, Routledge & Kegan Paul.

Hargreaves, David (1972) *Interpersonal Relations and Education*. London, Routledge & Kegan Paul.

Hargreaves, David (1978) 'Whatever happened to symbolic interactionism?' in L. Barton and R. Meighan (eds), *Sociological Interpretations of Schooling and Classrooms*. Nafferton.

Hargreaves, David (1980) 'The occupational culture of teachers' in P. Woods (ed.), *Teacher Strategies*. London, Croom Helm.

Hargreaves, David (1982) *The Challenge for Comprehensive Schools: Culture, Curriculum and Communication*. London, Routledge & Kegan Paul.

Lacey, C. (1970) *Hightown Grammar*. Manchester, Manchester University Press.

Levi-Strauss, C. (1968) *Structural Anthropology*, Harmondsworth, Penguin.

Llewellyn, M. (1980) 'Studying girls at school' in R. Deem (ed.), *Schooling for Women's Work*. London, Routledge & Kegan Paul.

McRobbie, A. (1980) 'Setting accounts with sub-cultures', *Screen Education*. 34, Spring Issue.

McRobbie, A. and Gerber. J. (1976) 'Girls and sub-cultures' in S. Hall and T. Jefferson (eds), *Resistance Through Rituals*. London, Hutchinson.

Malinowski, B. (1926) *Myth in Primitive Psychology*. London, Routledge & Kegan Paul.

Mead, G.H. (1934) *Mind, Self and Society*. Chicago, University of Chicago Press.

Measor, L. and Woods, P. (1983) 'The interpretation of pupil myths' in M. Hammersley (ed.), *The Ethnography of Schooling*. Nafferton.

Metcalf, A. and Humphries, M. (ed. 1985) *Sexuality of Men*. Pluto.

Meyenn, R. (1980) 'School girls' peer groups' in P. Woods (ed.) *Teacher Strategies*. London, Croom Helm.

Miller, W.B. (1958) 'Lower class culture as a generating milieu of gang delinquency', *Journal of Social Issues*. 14, 5–19.

Nash, R. (1976) 'Pupils' expectations of their teachers' in M. Stubbs and S. Delamont (eds), *Explorations in Classroom Observation*. New York, Wiley.

Pollard, A. (1980) 'Teacher interests and changing situations of survival threat' in P. Woods (ed.), *Teacher Strategies*. London, Croom Helm.

Pollard, A. (1982) 'A model of coping strategies', *British Journal of Sociology of Education*. March.

Pollard, A. (1984) 'Coping strategies and the multiplication of differentiation in infant classrooms', *British Educational Research Journal*. 10, 1, 33–48.

Riseborough, G.F. (1981) 'Teacher careers and comprehensive schooling', *Sociology*. 15, 3, 352–80.

Sharpe, S. (1976) *Just Like A Girl*. Harmondsworth, Penguin.

Schatzman and Strauss (1973) *Field Research: Strategies for a Natural Sociology*. Englewood Cliffs, NJ, Prentice-Hall.

Schutz, A. (1964) 'The stranger: an essay in social psychology' in A. Schutz (ed.), *Collected Papers*, Vol. II. The Hague: Nijhoff.

Schutz, A. (1972) *The Phenomenology of the Social World*. London, Heinemann.

Seidler, V. (1980) 'Raging bull', *Achilles Heel*, No. 5.

Stanworth, M. (1982) *Gender and Schooling: a Study of Sexual Divisions in the Classroom*. London, Hutchinson.

Tolson, A. (1977) *The Limits of Masculinity*. Tavistock.

Turner, G. (1983) *The Social World of the Comprehensive School*. London, Croom Helm.

Walford, G. (1986) *Life in Public Schools*, London, Methuen.

Walker, R., Goodson, I.F. and Adelman, C. (1975) *Teaching, That's A Joke*. Centre for Applied Research in Education, University of East Anglia.

Walker, R. and Goodson, I.F. (1977) 'Humour in the classroom' in P. Woods and M. Hammersley (eds), *School Experience*. London, Croom Helm.

Werthman, C. (1963) 'Delinquents in school' in B.R. Cosin *et al.* (eds), *School and Society*. London, Routledge & Kegan Paul.

Willis, P. (1977) *Learning to Labour*. Saxon House.

Woods, P. (1977) 'Teaching for survival' in P. Woods and M. Hammersley (eds), *School Experience*. London, Croom Helm.

Woods, P. (1980a) *Teacher Strategies*. London, Croom Helm.

Woods, P. (1980b) *Pupil Strategies*. London, Croom Helm.

Woods, P. (1983) *Sociology and the School*. London, Routledge & Kegan Paul.

CHAPTER 9

Micro-politics versus Management: Towards a Sociology of School Organization

Stephen J. Ball

Writing in 1984 Ronald King stated: 'I believe we now have a body of theoretical and research studies, concerning substantive matters such as grouping practices, the distribution of authority and school size, which are the makings of a "decent" sociology of school organization' (p. 61). I could not disagree more strongly or more entirely with this view. Indeed I would want to assert that the lack of a theoretically coherent and sociologically viable account of school organization is one of the most serious and inhibiting problems in the current phase of development in the sociology of education. The absence of a sociology of school organization tends to distort and handicap research and theorizing in other specialized areas of the field. And, by default, the area of school organization has been left to be claimed and colonized by the prescriptive ideology of management theory.

I want to attempt three tasks in this chapter. (1) To ask what a theoretically coherent and sociologically viable account of school organization would look like. (2) To consider why no such account has been developed and the untoward results of that omission. And (3) to sketch the outlines of a substantive sociological theory of school organization.

1. What would a sociology of the school look like?

In one sense the first task is a simple one: it is only necessary to look across the specialism boundary into the mainstream field of the sociology of organizations. Salaman (1979) provides a very straightforward set of criteria for what constitutes a sociology of organizations. In general terms these criteria are as relevant to the study of schools as they are to hospitals, factories, offices or prisons, although their specific relevance to school needs to be explored and developed. He derives these criteria from the work of Marx and Weber. He argues that:

> despite their differences, both Marx and Weber in their sociology of organizations isolated and emphasized those key elements in the structure of large-scale organizations which were of most significance to their theoretical interest in processes of control and legitimation within organizations and the relationship between organizational structure and process and societal values and interests. Both stressed that organizational structure – the design of work and control – can only be seen in terms of general processes of organizational control initiated by, and in the interest of, those who ran or dominated the organization. Both saw the purposes of organizations (or those who dominated the organization) and the structures of work and control to which they give rise, as reflecting more general processes, cultures, interests and priorities, in the society at large. They firmly rejected the widely prevalent view that organizational structure follows from the application of neutral, apolitical priorities – such as efficiency, technology, etc. – and insisted that such concepts should be exposed for their political purposes and assumptions, and focus attention on the nature and function of organizational ideologies. These are the ingredients of a genuine sociology of organizations.

(Salaman 1979, p. 23)

I find it impossible to reconcile this with King's list of work on grouping practices, the distribution of authority and school size as constituting the making of a 'decent' sociology of school organizations. Rather what Salaman's outline points to is focus on three key features of the school as an organization, all of which are missing from King's list; first, and most fundamentally, the processes of organizational control, the ways in which the activities of the workers, the employees, that is teachers (for our purposes), are structured, specified and divided; secondly, and concomitantly, the forms of legitimation which underpin and 'naturalize' this control (the essential point here is that organizations *are* structures of control); and thirdly, what interests and purposes are served by the particular forms of control and structure which are employed. And we need to add a fourth point of focus, which is the strategies of contest and resistance used by the workers to challenge or undermine the control exercised or attempted by those sectional interests who dominate the organization. 'Organizational employees actively strive to avoid and divert control; they seek to maximize their own interests which they may or may not see as coincident with the organization's, and they attempt to resist the domination of others while advancing or defending their own area of control and autonomy' (Salaman 1979, p. 144). As Giddens (1984, p. 76) put it, 'we should not conceive of the structures of domination built into social institutions as in some way grinding out "docile bodies" who behave like the automata suggested by objectivist social science'. In effect *control* is frequently directly related to *conflict*. Control is rarely unproblematic. The social relations of the workplace are typically antagonistic and competitive. Control is the subject of and outcome of struggle rather than the natural product of the social authority of the organizational leadership. The workplace is a site of ongoing dialectic interaction between competing groups. But we should note that conflict in the organization is not limited to the vertical relationships between leaders and workers. The complex structure of organizations, certainly schools, also fosters lateral internecine conflicts. These also need to be taken account of in the development of a coherent theory.

On these bases the organization can be viewed appropriately as an arena of political action. The constraints, limitations, deprivations, frustrations and pressures of membership provide the basis for the struggles, manoeuvres, bargains and alliances through which collectivities and interest groups compete for advantage. Organizations, 'as societies' (Albrow 1968) are 'characterized by the same sorts of conflicts and struggles as occur within the larger society. Within organizations conflict – and therefore politics – is a routine feature of everyday life' (Salaman 1979, pp. 50–1).

Thus not only is it necessary to recognize control and conflict as the fundamental and contradictory bases of organizational life (and thus the focus for research and theorizing), it must also be taken into account that both forms of social process consist of individual actors and groups of actors seeking to impose their will on others or further their interests and concerns over and against the interests and concerns of others. Conflict and control are not merely reified qualities of organizational functioning but the effects and outcomes of deliberate planning and face-to-face interactions. Organizational politics is in practice a strategic, material and inter-personal process.

> any analysis of organizational relationship must attend to the ways in which actors protect or develop their positions within the enterprise. This requires consideration of, on the one hand, those overt strategies, involving explicit reference to some version of the organizational goal, by which members may defend or advance their interests in organizational bargaining; and on the other those less explicit manoeuvres which are also important in defining the position of members, but which avoid reference to the jurisdiction of organizational mandates. (Elger 1975, p. 101)

Such a view has two direct implications. First, we must recognize that schools as organizations are frequently marked by disputes around competing versions of the organization's goals – these are essentially matters of value and ideological commitment. Secondly, such a focus will inevitably take us into what Hoyle (1982) calls the 'organizational underworld' or 'the dark side of organizational life'. Micro-politics are decidedly not confined to the formal and obvious arenas of decision-making.

Here then are the starting points for a sociology of school organization. I shall attempt to develop this outline more fully and specifically later. But first I want to address my second task of explaining why no account of this kind has been developed and in doing so consider Salaman's second criterion more fully, that is the legitimations used for the forms of control employed in organizations, specifically again in schools.

2. Why no sociological theory of school organization thus far?

I want to suggest that the absence of sociological theory in this field has two interrelated causes. First, the theory of school organizations may be seen as a victim of the theoretical disputes in the development of the sociology of education since 1971. With a degree of crudity this development can be characterized in terms of the dialogue, sometimes deaf, sometimes acrimonious, usually self-defeating, between the macro and micro, structure and agency perspectives of neo-marxism and interactionism. These disputes have tended to polarize the forms of analysis employed in the theorization of schools into accounts which either stress and privilege economic and political structures or which rely almost exclusively on the perceptions and interpretations of individual teachers and students. School organization has been viewed either from out of the classroom gazing upward or from the heights of the economy looking downward. The terrain of the organization itself has been, by default, ignored or misrepresented or dismissed as epiphenomenal.

Clearly though, this polarization is weakening, there have been some recent attempts to link the macro and the micro which have provided conceptual development. The organization is now more likely to be viewed as a necessary link between classroom and social structure, but the nature of its mediation still remains under-theorized. Three contributions are worth mentioning. One lies in the area of the sociology of the curriculum, so excellently pulled together and discussed in the recent book by Whitty (1985). As Whitty points out, referring to the work of Hindess (1982), 'Power relations within particular arenas are the outcome of practices in those arenas rather than an automatic product of resources held elsewhere' (p. 36). Whitty suggests that 'Such a perspective, when applied to the analysis of education, clearly implies a need to re-examine the possibilities inherent within schools as sites of ideological and political practice' (p. 36). This links directly with the grounds set out previously. Another contribution may be found in Pollard's (1982) attempt to formulate a 'Model of Classroom Coping Strategies'. He argues that classroom strategies must be related to their organizational context, to the 'institutional bias' (Bachrach and Baratz 1962) which imposes limits upon the scope of the political process in the organization via taken-for-granted social and political values and routine institutional practices. He goes on to say, 'In a sense it (institutional bias) conceptualizes understandings at school-level which are some-thing similar to the working consensus of the classroom. By this I mean that it is actively produced by negotiation among school staff each with particular interests, and it reaches a stability of understandings which reflect power differentials among such staff' (p. 26). The third contribution to mention is the corpus of work produced by Apple. In a series of papers on the labour process of teaching he has sought to identify changes in the technology of teaching and in the developing relationship between schools and corporate needs (Apple 1982). 'The language of efficiency, production, standards, cost effectiveness, job skills, work discipline, and so on – all defined by powerful groups and always threatening to become the dominant way we think about schooling – has begun to push aside concerns for a democratic curriculum, teacher autonomy, and class, gender and race inequality' (1986, p. 4). Apple's basic approach can be described as a form of Bravermania, with primary emphasis upon the effects of proletarianization and deskilling. He offers a telling analysis of the links between control over teachers, curriculum innovation and economic change. But for the purposes of theorization here the analysis remains over-generalized (1986, p. 12): it addresses teaching as a whole, and general tendencies in curriculum change. While its organizational relevance is undeniable, the impact of and struggles over such changes in particular schools are glossed. For the most part the responses and resistances which he explores are not related to actualities but to possibilities.

These contributions have done something at least in pointing to the significance of 'the school as an organization' for the sociology of education. However, they pale into insignificance when set alongside the 'theorizing' done on 'the school as an organization' by other disciplines in the vacuum left by the absence of the sociology of education, notably that derived from 'organizational science'. For the most part that vacuum has been filled by various versions of 'management theory' (which has increasingly come to replace the previous 'theories' of teacher professionalism). As a result analysis of the nature and processes of organizations as they are or might be have been displaced by accounts which both legitimate and prescribe the nature of organizations as they should be or can only be.

These management theories are, for the most part, rooted in versions systems theory and humanistic psychology. They are focused on individual participants on the one hand, and as part of a complex, inter-related, interdependent structure on the other. In a nutshell systems theory 'starts with a view of society and social life as inherently ordered and searches for shared agreements and convictions through an analysis of apparently mutually interlocked and adjusting systems and structures' (Salaman and Thompson 1973). That is to say, 'The systems notion posits an organizational force or framework which encompasses and gives order to people and events within it. The system – unseen behind everyday affairs – is real; it *is* the organization' (Barr-Greenfield 1975, p. 65). Dissensus or conflict are not necessarily totally ignored in this work but are regarded, within the logic of the paradigm, as aberrant and pathological. The emphasis is upon remediating or managing conflict, treating it as though it were a disease invading and crippling the body of the organization. In some versions of management theory where motivations and psychologies are to the fore, any manifestations of conflict or contestation are taken to be indications of individual mal-adjustment or personal dissatisfaction. They offer particular interpretations of how to understand such occurrences. Thus, Hannan (1980, p. 6) says of Richardson's (1973) study of Nailsea school, 'Conflict or disagreement is interpreted as deviation from the task prompted by emotional reaction rather than the opposition of those who define the task of the school differently.' In this way oppositional activity within the organization is defined in terms of the perspectives of the dominant groups as inherently irrational. The 'subject', the individual worker or practitioner, is constructed in terms of sameness and individuality (Macdonell 1986). The 'problem' is taken to be 'in' the person rather than the system, and collective interests, other than those of 'the system', are in effect deconstructed.

> it is conceded that there will be differences of outlook, disagreement, argument and opposition; but these are understood as taking place within a broader basic framework of agreement – 'the consensus' – to which everybody sub-scribes, and within which every dispute, disagreement or conflict of interest can be reconciled by discussion, without recourse to confrontation ...
>
> (Hall *et al.* 1978, p. 56)

Theories of management reflect the particular interests and needs of administrators. (Also at the present time they align with crucial aspects of the political and economic project of Thatcher-ism.) They are top-dog theories; they contain a view of the organization looking down from the position of those 'in control'. They are inherently biased and distorted by this partiality. They are in Foucault's terms 'technologies of power'. There is the tendency to slip almost imperceptibly from analysis to prescrip-tion. The distinction between 'is' and 'ought' becomes blurred. Rather than explanation, such theories provide justification. In this way theories of organization actually become ideologies, legitimations for certain forms of organization. They deploy arguments in terms of rationality and efficiency to provide control. The limits that they impose upon the conception of organizations actually close down the possibility of considering alternative forms of organization. Management both intends itself as *the* real world of organizational life and it acts to exclude other versions, 'any discourse concerns itself with certain objects and puts forward certain concepts at the expense of others' (Macdonell 1986, p. 3). Concepts like efficiency are treated as though they were neutral and technical matters and scientific categories rather than being tied to the advantage of particular interests. The question of 'efficiency for whom?', is rarely asked. Efficiency itself is taken as self-evidently a good thing. The costs involved for workers in achieving greater efficiency (intensification, loss of autonomy, closer monitoring and appraisal, non-participation in decision-making, lack of personal development through work) are rarely considered.

Such an approach also has the effect of rendering issues of value and matters of justice and equality (which underlie much of the decision-making in social welfare agencies) as technical decisions. The discourse of management (as a system of possibility for knowledge) eschews, or marginalizes the problems, concerns, fears and difficulties of the 'subject'. Management intends and constructs 'subjected and practised bodies'; in Foucault's terms it 'increases the forces of the body in economic terms of utility and diminishes these forces in political terms of obedience' (1979, p. 130). As such efficiency becomes the sole or pre-eminent criterion for decision-making; arguments which do not articulate with the efficiency agenda can be ruled as irrelevant. Thus management theories as discourses with a scientific status, as 'regimes of truth', empower the manager, as Foucault suggests. Knowledge, power and the body are interrelated in the achievement of subjugation.

All of this is beginning to be evident in the current application of management theories to schools. Such theories are coming to be widely accepted by administrators and teachers as the 'one best way' of organizing and running schools. And they are increasingly evident in the 'measurement of outputs' (effectiveness) and in forms of appraisal, what Foucault would describe as 'normalizing judgements'. Through staff reviews the 'normalizing gaze' is being turned upon individual teachers; they are to be made specifically visible in the conduct of their work and are to be differentially encoded in written reports and files. Concepts of excellence and incompetence are increasingly employed to refer to and differentiate types of teacher. This involves a ranking and grading which in effect 'marks the gaps, hierarchizes qualities, skills and aptitudes but it also punishes and rewards' (Foucault 1979, p. 181).

Management theories as modes of objectification make human beings into subjects, to be managed. This is a 'discourse of right' which legitimates the exercise of power. (The basis of this is disciplinary and it is a 'fundamental instrument in the constitution of industrial capitalism and the type of society that is its accompaniment' (Foucault 1980, p. 105). Its primary instrument is a hierarchy of continuous and functional surveillance.)

Now it could be argued that the systems perspective is no longer predominant, or at least unchallenged, within management theory. Gray (1982) suggests a shift of emphasis. 'In recent years there has been a reaction against the hard line approach in management and administration and an interest in the so-called qualitative aspects of organizations' (p. 29). Drawing on humanistic psychology and phenomenological sociology, a subjective theory of organizations has grown in popularity among management theorists, this 'provides a way of looking at organizations so that the uniqueness of individual perceptions is held in focus and becomes their major concern' (Gray 1982, p. 30). However, it is important not to mistake the effects of such theoretical reconsideration. For the most part the insights and possibilities of subjective theory (like those of micro-political theory: Hoyle 1986; Stephenson 1985) have been incorporated into the existing 'knowledges' of the management perspective. In a sense such theoretical diversity and willingness to accommodate criticism only strengthens the claims to scientific status of management theorists, consultants and practitioners. Ribbins (1985) makes the point that 'If there is to be a profession of educational management there must be a body of relevant knowledge in which its practitioners are superior to non-managers' (p. 223). An understanding of contrasting or multi-theoretical perspectives is, it is claimed, a development of the skills of the manager and management theorist. It further enhances and extends the possibilities of and the repertoire of control. Ribbins again, 'To be able to conceptualize schools as organizations in a variety of ways is not an esoteric luxury for the student and the manager. Rather it is to be liberated from the embrace of a particular vision which probably obscures as much as it reveals and constrains as much as it enables' (p. 256). Significantly in virtually all of these accommodations the meanings and interpretations of 'the managed' are presented in theory rather than in substance. Where they are represented, these interpretations are viewed as an alternative rather than an oppositional reality. The basic ideology of management remains unbreached – indeed it is enhanced and re-legitimated. The aim remains that of greater efficiency and improved control. 'It is through the informed attempts of practising managers (with such assistance and encouragement as are appropriate) to apply different templates or paradigms to situations of practice, that management can become more purposeful and more effective' (Hughes, Ribbins and Thomas 1985, p. 475).

Most of the work which counts as the theory of school organizations has failed to address either the diversity of interests which constitute the school or the strategies employed by particular interest groups to further their concerns. Neither control nor conflict are adequately theorized. Even within the sociological field, as I have indicated, major absences are evident. King's reference to work on the effects of group practices (while itself worth while) also indicates a deflection from the question of how the decisions about such practices are arrived at. Essentially his view of schools as organizations is pupil centred; it fails to address the organizational experiences of the teachers and other employees of the organization, that is teaching as work! Furthermore, his reference to the issue of the distribution of authority accepts the concept of authority as unproblematic. Such an acceptance produces theoretical closure and totally obscures basic questions of power, domination and conflict. In effect the experiences of organizational actors and their purposive action in pursuit of their interests are defined as irrelevant. The school as an organization is taken to be determined by technology and commonly agreed goals. Analysis and theorizing are thus replaced by the stultifying assumption of an inevitable and benign structure.

3. A micro-political theory of school organization

The third task then is to outline an alternative (and indeed oppositional) theory which meets the criteria outlined above. As Macdonell (1986) argues discourses take shape antagonistically, out of clashes with one another, 'what is thought in one discourse is in effect related to what is unthought elsewhere in another'

(p. 47). I want to suggest that a *micro-political theory of school organization best fits the bill.*

In Hoyle's (1982) definition:

> Micropolitics can be said to consist of the strategies by which individuals and groups in organizational contexts seek to use their resources of authority and influence further their interests.

In Harold Lasswell's simple terms it can be reduced to the issue of who gets what, when and how. The concept of interests is crucial here and must not be over-simplified.[1]

I want to advance and develop micro-political theory in a specific way. Such a theory can provide an account of both the processes involved in the maintenance, reproduction and extension of *control,* and of the processes of *conflict, opposition and struggle* which are set against this control. As adumbrated here micro-politics is focused both upon the interrelated and concomitant aspects of *material* conflict (access to resources) and conflict and competition over the *definition of the school* (access to policy) (Lacey 1977). In schools the field of micro-politics arises and exists in the nexus between professionalism (and its discourse of autonomy and responsibility) and management (and its discourse of monitoring and control). The medium is frequently that of the interpersonal (as is the lay discourse), but the context and the consequences are collective and structural. As noted in section one both vertical relationships of control and lateral relationships of competition are involved. In part at least micro-politics is a field of struggle over control of the labour process of teaching. I have not the space here to outline such a theory in detail and would refer you to a more detailed exposition (Ball 1987). However, I shall attempt to trace some key features of the theory here through a general and illustrative discussion.

In many cases where the concept of micro-politics is envoked (Bacharach and Lawler 1980; Pettigrew 1978; Pfeffer 1981) to explain organizational processes, it is access to resources, the lateral and internecine competition among sub-groups or interest sets (Hoyle 1986) that is the prime focus. Where vertical relationships are of concern there is a concentration on the one-way strategies of control employed by management. Indeed Hoyle (1986) argues that micro-political processes become such an essential form of control in school precisely because the professional norms of teacher autonomy limit the use or the effectiveness of more overt forms of control. Thus, he says, 'the head's administrative control must depend to a considerable degree on the exercise of latent power and of influence. This would seem to be likely to encourage the head's deployment of micro-political strategies in the somewhat gaping interstices within the management structure' (p. 135). This assumption, that micro-politics is the prerogative, albeit a dubious one, of management, is held by most of the management theorists who have attempted to take up the micro-political perspective. Micro-politics is seen in these terms as a form of control to which managers must turn, however unfortunately, when other forms of control are ineffective. Writers from the field of business management are less coy. Stephenson (1985), for example, argues that managers function within what he calls a micro-political network, and 'Within this network the manager acts in an accommodative and manipulative manner, seeking to restructure the conditions in which the manipulated operates, so that the course of action he [*sic*] desires is accepted' (p. 37).

However, I want to give equal emphasis to both the lateral and vertical dimensions of micro-politics, thus both material and ideological decision-making *and* to the use of micro-political strategies to both assert and resist control.

I will discuss the concept of micro-politics in general terms via the several dimensions already indicated. I recognize the complex interrelatedness of these dimensions in practice, their separation here is purely for heuristic purposes. And for the purposes of exposition I will focus specifically on the issues of headship, dominance and opposition. These offer particular insight into the nature of micro-political processes.

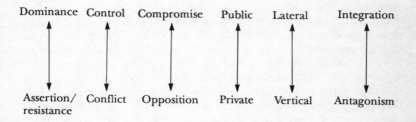

Figure 9.1

230   *Stephen J. Ball*

Headship: dominance and opposition

In the case of vertical relationships micro-politics is the channel
for and means for the antithetical processes of dominance and
opposition. In the school this focuses particular attention on the
Headteacher and/or senior management team. As licensed
autocrats and like many other organizational leaders, headteachers
are faced with a basic micro-political conundrum (at least when
they define their task in conventional terms). On the one hand they
seek the achievement and maintenance of control (the problem of
domination), on the other they work at encouraging and ensuring
social order and commitment (the problem of integration). This is
what Duverger (1972) refers to a the 'janus-face' of power.

> Under their dual aspect of antagonism and integration,
> political phenomena occur within many kinds of human
> communities – nations, provinces, cities, international so-
> cieties, associations, trade unions, clans, bands, cliques and
> other assorted groups. From our point of view political
> sociology is the study of power in every human grouping, not
> just the nation state. Each of these groups therefore serves as a
> structure, a framework for the enactment of conflicts and
> integration. (p. 21)

The contradictions of these demands are most acute in
organizations like schools where 'responsible autonomy' is
employed as a management strategy, as opposed to or in addition
to 'direct control'. (Claims for professional autonomy can at times
facilitate management and at other times inhibit the assertion of
management.) The solutions attempted by heads to resolve this
basic political contradiction, the strategies they employ and
construct, may be interpreted as being realized in terms of a
particular leadership style. I use style here to refer to a form of
social accomplishment, a particular way of enacting headship. A
style embodies a definition of the situation, a proposed or claimed
or perhaps imposed version of the possible modes of social
interaction between leader and led. To the extent that a particular
style is tenable, that it has some joint credibility, and is brought off
effectively, then a specific framework for control is achieved. (My
interest in styles of leadership is not to identify fixed, substantive
types as such but rather as a heuristic, analytical tool for
investigating different possibilities for control, the practical
achievement of domination.) Accordingly most leadership styles

require a greater or lesser degree of mutual alignment between the leader and the led. And the need on the part of the leader to maintain this mutual alignment offers possibilities to lower participants, to teachers, of involvement in some form of micro-political activity. As Stephenson (1985) puts it, the Headteacher like the manager must 'recognise that support is achieved at a price; his [*sic*] relations with others are based upon interdependence' (p. 37). By negotiation and compromise, individually or collectively, in public or in private, depending on the prevailing style of headship, teachers can seek to exchange aspects of commitment, forms of social stability (agreement, acquiescence, support, loyalty) for concessions of control (influence over policy, issue concessions, material benefits, promotion, autonomy). The cracks opened up in the fabric of the organization as a result of the tension between order and control, between task and consideration, may be filled by bargaining, trade-offs, and deals. Here tactics and ploys, caucusing and lobbying, the building of coalitions and alliances are important devices and skills on both sides. The use of influence will be critical on both sides. Dominance is thus always partial and changing and always tentative. Paradoxically, compromise, bargains and trade-offs, by their very nature, most often tie micro-political activity back into the autocracy and the dominance of headship. They act informally to reinforce and underpin the power of heads whose formal authority is flawed or incomplete. (There is as always a crucial difference between having the capacity to reject something and having the power to change it. It is only when micro-political activity in the form of opposition addresses the question of power itself that autocracy is called into question and alternative forms of control are put on the agenda.) Micro-politics can both undermine and confirm the claims for power made by the organizational leader.

It is important to be clear that micro-politics are lived processual moments and aspects of structure. I am not simply erecting again the age-old distinction between the formal and the informal aspects of organization. When such a distinction is employed the informal so often becomes merely a convenient residual category for the messy, interpersonal 'bits and pieces' that do not fit the neat systems erected elsewhere. Indeed the formal–informal distinction employed here is heuristic, for in practice there is no distinction. The arenas of formal structure and the arenas of micro-politics overlap and interpenetrate. They may differ in interactional style but they are not mutually exclusive. For example, committee decisions may be carefully set up in advance by compromise, meetings may be packed, votes canvassed and favours exchanged, formal promotions and appointments may be settled by personal influence and sponsorship. In some headship performances the distinction is entirely or deliberately blurred.

However, micro-politics is an arena of strategy rather than procedure; it can evince interpersonal rivalries and misplaced trust, bitterness and envy. Corridors, closed offices and staffroom corners are the key sites where decisions are arrived at, compromises arranged. Micro-politics here is about relationships not positions, knowledge rather than information, skills rather than roles, talk rather than paper. The hint, the guarded reference and the euphemism are often the lexicon of conflict. It is the stuff of tacit understandings and later denial, of informed sources and second-hand accounts. It typically deals in short-term gains, expediency and pragmatism rather than long-term goals, principles and ideals (although these may be attempted through such channels). As such micro-politics is a way for the dominant to get by and the assertive to deride. Here power is a goal, an outcome, rather than a precondition. And structure is also in effect an outcome, it is the totality of relationships and moments that constitute the organization, the negotiated order. The organization is thus essentially a 'set of events' – these may be discontinuous, divergent, plural and unpredictable but also intersecting, serial and conditional (Foucault 1971).

It is in this arena of micro-politics that the headteacher seeks in Stephenson's terms to 'manipulate other members through the use of political language and symbols, trade-offs and the like, and in turn they seek to manipulate him [*sic*]' (p. 39). The onus is upon the head to attempt to realize the leadership style to which he or she makes claims, and thus 'to be powerful', to become the critical reality definer in the organization. I give little credence here to analyses which rely upon un-theorized assumptions about the authority of headship. Power is an active, penetrating and flexible concept in this context, and the concept of power employed is a particular one. It does not involve reference to position or capacity as such but to performance, achievement and struggle, 'the struggles over divergent objectives really are struggles, not the play-out of some pre-ordained script (Hindess 1982, p. 506). Power is a result of micro-political activity not its pre-condition.

Unfortunately, as noted above, writers like Hoyle (1986), locked into a management perspective, tend to see micro-politics as pre-eminently a top-dog strategy. He sees the rewards to the teacher as limited and suggests that micro-political activity 'is probably inhibited to the degree that their preoccupations are with their classroom activities rather than school policy' (p. 136). That may describe some, even most teachers most of the time, but certainly not all or most all of the time. The opening up of the micro-political arena is possible from both ends; it is a vehicle for dominance *and* assertion. For example, policies like anti-racism or anti-sexism, when given 'official' support by influential moral entrepreneurs, can empower grass-roots activists. Paper structures may be subject to a vocabulary of critique which is legitimated by the vocabulary of policy, i.e. anti-racism. Also while micro-politics contains and mirrors other inequalities and unfair advantages it is also a potential equalizer, for it works aside from (though in relation to) formal hierarchies and relies on skills and insights which may be distributed more evenly across the organization. In this way it can be a channel to articulate and effect opposition as well as control and as well as sectional or personal advantage. I want to go on now to consider opposition further.

It is important also to recognize that the vertical and lateral dimensions of competition and conflict frequently inter-link. Compromise may involve gaining advantage over others or obtaining privileged access to scarce resources. Where policy change involves a redistribution of resources, policies may be addressed head on and fought out in terms of principles or pragmatics, or resource control may be employed to blunt or enact policy without direct confrontation over general principles. Then again resources may be tied to policy change, funding being made dependent on new and specific working practices.

Micro-politics is multi-faceted. One aspect of micro-political struggle is denoted by compromise and negotiation. This often involves the private use of informal relations and contexts, and interpersonal influence. The emphasis is on minor adjustments rather than major reforms, on the redistribution of rewards and benefits rather than the reconstruction of reward structures and reallocation of control over policy-formation. However, the effects of such compromises and the outcomes of negotiations are not necessarily always trivial and not always limited to the furtherance of vested interests. And not all micro-political activity within the organization is conducted behind the hand or via mutually acceptable trade-offs or bargains. Micro-political theory also encompasses those struggles which present a more profound challenge to the established order or to the dominant definition of the school, those struggles that cannot or will not be accommodated through corridor exchanges of favour or advantage. On occasion struggle becomes visible, heated and bitter via direct, publicly articulated opposition.

If the private struggles indicated above are primarily a matter of compromise, then the public struggles of opposition are most often denoted by confrontation, by challenges to formal authority and to the status quo or by deliberate attempts to subvert or by-pass the accepted, formal and informal channels of policy-making. Opposition in these terms may be rooted in an objective and collectively held sense of differing interests, arising out of the gaps between 'them and us', management and line, employer and employee, black and white, men and women, or articulated by issue-based 'interest sets', coming together and fading away in relation to very specific concerns. On occasion such sets lead to alliances of 'strange bedfellows'.

Opposition is, in varying degrees, a failure of integration. And it is also more likely to occur when control is incomplete or ineffective. Paradoxically it may arise most vehemently through those forms of participation (or pseudo-participation) which are intended to increase and facilitate integration and commitment (e.g. staff meetings). Thus in its two basic aspects it is possible to see opposition as both occasional and specific, and as fundamental and structural.

As regards the latter, the objective and contemporary conditions for and occurrence of opposition in schools is recognized by a number of commentators and can be linked to fundamental changes taking place in the labour process of teaching via the assertion of forms of qualitative and quantitative efficiency articulated in the discourse and technology of management. Morgan, Hall and MacKay (1983), for example, argue that 'Heads in the 1980s cannot promote their policies without contest, or impose their values or ethos without debate, bargaining and compromise' (p. 11) and Pratt (1984) opines that:

> They key issues no longer surround the question as to whether teachers can be helped to respond, in their own self-interest, to the initiatives of enlightened benevolent heads. Today we need to understand the interaction between

superordinates defending the interests of the providers of the education service, and the subordinates defending their opposing interests. (p. 303)

In other words the micro-politics of the school can be set in relation to the processes of de-skilling and proletarianization experienced by teachers and matters of ideological dispute over the processes of education and the definition of the school, although again not all cases of oppositional conflict can be adduced as these. For example, depending on the context and the issue at hand opposition may be analysed as either reactionary or radical. Opposition may be examined in relation to attempts to impose greater control over conditions of work and the 'act of production' or to cut or alter the financing of particular teaching programmes. It may be seen to be part of a struggle to introduce more egalitarian forms of schooling or to hang on to cherished traditional forms. Material, ideological and self-interests will come into play in different relations to one another and in differing priorities. As Salaman (1979) suggests, 'Within organizations members are constantly trying to control each other, or to avoid such control' (p. 51). This cuts both ways, schemes of teacher appraisal may be opposed, so too may schemes to monitor teacher racism. The same arguments and tactics can be mobilized in each case against 'the management'.

Opposition is, however, a problematic stance for organizational members. Typically, as soon as any group or individual acts outside of the accepted channels of decision-making or beyond the fixed agenda of officially defined legitimate discussion – what has been called the 'inferential structure' – then they open themselves up to criticisms of being subversive and/or disloyal. Opposition is indulgence in the politics of the profane. This is evident in the following extract from an interview with a comprehensive head.

I certainly would accept that when the authority of the headmaster is challenged and that's the area of disloyalty that would be most obvious, I object vehemently and strongly. I see it as undermining the fabric, but I also see it probably as a challenge to me as a person. Now that has happened. Eight or nine years ago it didn't happen at all ... There has crept in a whole new social atmosphere now, not only do teachers say they are under pressure, 'Why should it be asked of me?', and demand the answer before they will do it, but there are

236 Stephen J. Ball

certain subversive elements in the staffroom who will actually work to undermine the authority so that they can have a little more authority themselves. Now that sounds quite bitter but it would be quite false if I did not say it was there... You can learn new tricks when this sort of thing happens; it means you change your whole tack; now when decisions are to be taken policy is to be changed, we think as a management team about all the things that could be raised in opposition before we introduce it.

These comments are telling in a number of ways. They highlight the extent to which consultation and decision-making is, in the Head's own words 'a trick'. The autocracy of the Head is to be asserted in one way or another (Hoyle's point above). There is no place for opposition. The parameters of legitimate 'participation' are set by the Head; what can be said and how are carefully demarcated. Open discussion and the airing of views is only acceptable when the views aired are not damaging to the policy intentions of the senior management team. 'The primary definition sets the limit for all subsequent discussion by framing what the problem is' (Hall *et al.* 1978, p. 59). These intentions are presented as those that represent the best interests (in all three senses: self, ideological and material) of the whole collectivity. As soon as these intentions are threatened the opportunities for free discussion are closed down. Any challenge to these intentions or their integrity is defined as oppositional – subversion and disloyalty are very powerful concepts here. (Here we see the dialectical relationship of opposition and control.) Such definitional work by the leadership acts to factionalize the staff and stigmatize and isolate opponents. Saunder's (1983, p. 63) makes the point that 'definition of acceptable behaviour will often reflect not so much the inherent qualities of the behaviour in question, but more the assessment by those in power of the desirability of the demands being made'. However, there clearly is a real category of oppositional practice as far as its practitioners are concerned. But equally many heads appear to regard *any* form of dissent as opposition and as a threat to the stability and authority of their leadership and will go to virtually any lengths to avoid or diffuse open conflict. In this way public utterance of opposition may lead to a 'privatization' of contested issues and interests. Actions which challenge or breach the performance of the 'collective' definition of the school are pushed into the backstage. Opposition may be driven by default into unresolved frustration or grumbles or again into the realm of closed-door compromise.

The dominant political culture in schools as in society generally rests upon a limited conception of democracy and participation. Two strongly held conceptions of political possibility are embedded in this culture. First, there is the presentation and conceptualization of political problems as technical problems. Such problems need to be left in the capable hands of professional experts; the ordinary teacher like the ordinary citizen, it is argued, lacks the skills, information and resources to deal with problems or participate effectively in the decision-making processes (Barker 1978) (this notion is embedded in *and* serves to underpin the hegemony of management). The second major assumption is the emphasis on empiricism characterized by a prime and over-whelming concern with maintaining the stability of the system – a concern in which there is 'neither starting-place nor appointed destination. The enterprise is to keep afloat and on an even keel' (Oakeshott 1962, p. 127). The emphasis is almost exclusively on the survival of the system itself and the objectives of the system, so to speak, are lost sight of. Ends are displaced by means. Again efficiency is a key concept here. These elements of the political culture of the school provide in effect a clear definition of opposition. It is illegitimate to attempt to dispute the framework within which 'legitimate' activity takes place. Thus in the official view opposition is that which is disruptive and threatening, concomitantly it is regarded as 'unhelpful', 'misguided', and dubiously 'motivated', as in the extract above. In effect opposition is seen as attempts at participation by inappropriate persons acting in inappropriate ways. Strict interpretations of legitimacy are employed to label and exclude those who challenge the root paradigms of the organization. Spurious claims to collective interest are used to 'demonize' dissenters.

I want to underline again the dual conflicts and contradictions which lie at the heart of this conception of micro-politics and which define the two major arenas of organizational struggle. The first dimension of conflict is the vertical relation of dominance and resistance. Domination is intended to achieve and maintain particular definitions of the school over and against alternative, assertive definitions. The resistance to control and the assertion of alternatives are voiced in terms of opposition. The stake is policy. (Micro-politics is a channel for the maintenance of control; it is also a channel through which control may be challenged or resisted.) The second dimension of conflict cuts across the first and highlights lateral rather than vertical relationships. Here the primary stake is normally articulated in terms of control over or access to key resources – time, materials, territory, personnel, capitation, information or influence. The conflicts here often occur between constituent units within the organization or permanent or transitory 'interest sets', based on age, race, gender, career position etc. But as indicated already these two arenas of conflict are never mutually exclusive either in terms of action or objective. Clearly policy is never insulated from resource allocations; the budget is always a critical focus for micro-political activities (Wildavsky 1968). Material and ideological interests are thus frequently interrelated. Thus, on occasion basic transformation of the definition of the school, of its cultural meaning, may be achieved through battles won for control over resources. However, space does not permit exposition of lateral conflicts here (see Ball 1987, chapters 2 and 9).

Conclusion

The micro-political perspective provides a vehicle for linking individual careers, ideological commitments and actions with organizational structures, and forms of control with forms of resistance and opposition. The processes of micro-politics are achieved via the skilful (or unskilful) participation (or non-participation) of the members of the organization. The stress is upon those 'moments' and 'events' which constitute and reconstitute structure. The stress is upon struggle and conflict as against dominance and conformity. The stress is upon invisible compromises and visible confrontations rather than formal and benign procedures. But this is not simply an argument for reversion to the primacy of agency. Rather it serves to 'maintain the elements of choice, doubt, strategy, planning, error and transformation' (Connell 1985, p. 266) that are the stuff of practical politics and ideological struggle. The constraining power of the organization that people confront daily is real. But this constraint is embedded in and reproduced in the actions of others with all their ambiguities and complexities.

Acknowledgements

I am indebted to Brian Davies and Andy Hannan for their helpful comments on previous drafts of this chapter. The inadequacies which remain are most certainly mine.

Note

1. Material or vested interests refer to the material concerns of teachers as related to working conditions: rewards from work, career and promotion. Access to and control of resources in the school are central here: time (timetabled lessons or free periods), materials, capitation allowances and special monies and grants, personnel (the definition and control of appointments and the formation of specialist teams) and territory (particularly offices and dedicated teaching rooms and suites). These vested interests will be a matter of contention between individuals and between groups (e.g. departments, pastoral-care staff, administrative and non-teaching staff), especially when resources are scarce and promotion prospects limited. Ideological interests refer to matters of value or philosophical or political commitment – views of practice and organization that are preferred and advanced in debate and discussion. These interests often relate practical issues to fundamental political or philosophical positions. Self-interest employs the term 'self' in a particular way to refer to the sense of self or identity claimed or aspired to by the teacher; the sort of teacher a person believes themselves to be or wants to be (e.g. subject specialist, educator, pastoralist, administrator). The satisfactions associated with this sense of self may be directly related to certain sorts of work, work with particular groups of pupils, or even the use of specific resources or settings (e.g. laboratories, sports facilities, studios). (In this way it is easy to see the close interrelationships between the different types of interests; in the analysis of specific events it is often difficult or impossible to separate one set of interests out or give priority to one set).

References

Albrow, M. (1968) 'The study of organizations – objectivity or bias?' in J. Gould (ed.), *Penguin Social Science Survey 1968*. Harmondsworth, Penguin.
Apple, M. (1982) *Education and Power*. Boston, Routledge & Kegan Paul.
Apple, M. (1983) 'Work, class and teaching' in S. Walker and L. Barton (eds), *Gender, Class and Education*. Lewes, Falmer Press.
Apple, M. (1986) 'Mandating computers: the impact of the new technology on the labor process, students and teachers', paper

240 *Stephen J. Ball*

presented at the International Sociology of Education Conference, Westhill College, Birmingham.

Ball, S.J. (1987) *The Micro-Politics of the School*. London, Methuen.

Bacharach, S. and Lawler, E. (1980) *Power and Politics in Organizations*. San Francisco, Jossey Bass.

Barchrach, P. and Baratz, M. (1962) 'Two faces of power', *American Political Science Review*. 56, 4.

Barker, R. (1978) *Political Ideas in Modern Britain*. London, Methuen.

Barr-Greenfield, T. (1975) 'Theory about organization: a new perspective and its implications for schools' in V. Houghton, G. McHugh and C. Morgan (eds), *Management in Education Reader 2*. London, Ward Lock.

Connell, R. (1985) 'Theorizing gender', *Sociology*. 19, 2, pp. 260–92.

Duverger, M. (1972) *The Study of Politics*. London, Nelson.

Elger, A.J. (1975) 'Industrial organizations: a processual perspective' in J.B. McKinlay (ed.), *Processing People*. London, Holt, Rinehart and Winston.

Foucault, M. (1971) *L'Ordre du Discours*. Paris, Gallimard.

Foucault, M. (1979) *Discipline and Punish*. Harmondsworth, Penguin.

Foucault, M. (1980) *Power/Knowledge: Selected Interviews and other Writings 1972-1977*. C. Gordon (ed.). Brighton, Harvester Press.

Giddens, A. (1984) *The Constitution of Society*. Oxford, Polity Press.

Gray, H. (1982) (ed.) *The Management of Educational Institutions: theory, research and consultancy*. Lewes, Falmer Press.

Hall, S. *et al.* (1978) *Policing the Crisis: Mugging, the state and law and Order*. London, Macmillan.

Hannan, A. (1980) 'Problems, conflicts and school policy: a case study of an innovative comprehensive school', *CORE*, 4, 1. Microfiche.

Hindess, B. (1982) 'Power, interests and the outcomes of struggles', *Sociology*. 16, 4, pp. 498–511.

Hoyle, E. (1982) 'Micropolitics of educational organizations', *Educational Management and Administration*. 10, pp. 87–98.

Hoyle, E. (1986) *The Politics of School Management*. Sevenoaks, Hodder and Stoughton.

Hughes, M., Ribbins, P. and Thomas, H. (1985) *Managing Education, the System and the Institution*. London, Holt, Rinehart and Winston.

King, R. (1984) 'Educational administration and organizational theory', *Educational Management and Administration*. 12, pp. 59–62.

Lacey, C. (1977) *The Socialization of Teachers*. London, Methuen.

Macdonell, D. (1986) *Theories of Discourse*. Oxford, Basil Blackwell.

Morgan, C., Hall, V. and MacKay, H. (1983) *The Selection of Secondary School Heads*. Milton Keynes, Open University Press.

Oakeshott, M. (1962) *Rationalism and Politics and other Essays*. London, Methuen.

Pettigrew, A. (1978) *The Politics of Organizational Decision-Making*. London, Tavistock.

Pfeffer, J. (1981) *Power in Organizations.* Mass, Pitman.

Pratt, S. (1984) 'Subordinates' strategies of interaction in the management ship. Lewes, Falmer Press.

Pollard, A. (1982) 'A model of classroom coping strategies', *British Journal of Sociology of Education,* 3, 1, pp. 19–38.

Ribbins, P. (1985) 'The role of the middle manager in the secondary school,' in M. Hughes, P. Ribbins and H. Thomas (eds.), *Managing Education, the System and the Institution.* London, Holt, Rinehart and Winston.

Richardson, E. (1973) *The Teacher, the School and the Task of Management.* London, Heinemann.

Salaman, G. (1979) *Work Organizations: Resistance and Control.* London, Longman.

Salaman, G. and Thompson, K. (1973) *People and Organizations.* London, Longman.

Saunders, P. (1983) *Urban Politics: A Sociological Interpretation.* London, Hutchinson.

Stephenson, T. (1985) *Management: a Political Activity.* London, Macmillan.

Whitty, G. (1985) *Sociology and School Knowledge.* London, Methuen.

Wildavsky, A. (1968) 'Budgeting as a political process', in D. Sills (ed.), *International Encyclopaedia of the Social Sciences,* 2, 192–99 New York, Cromwell, Collear and Macmillan.

Index

All references to public schools indicate state schools.

Barr-Greenfield, T., 224
Barrett, M., 105
Barthes, R., 210
Barton, L., 1-6, 3
Bates, I., 2
Beattie, A., 52
Beauvoir, Simone de, 180
Beazley, Kim, 174
Benn, C., 10
Bessant, B., 103, 104
Best, R., 7, 8, 10
Bevan, J., 37
Beynon, J., 5, 191-216
Birmingham Feminist History Group
  (BFHG), 36, 39
Blackburn, K., 7
Bland, 33, 35
Bluestone, B., 127-8, 129
Blumhagen, 45
'bodybuilding' (standing up to teacher
  violence), 200, 204
Bolton, E., 60
Braverman, Harry, 131
Brent (London Borough of), anti-racist
  education, 60
Bullivant, B., 68, 69
Burgess, Hilary, 5, 10, 26
Burgess, R., 7-30
Buroway, Michael, 131
Byrne, 194

Calabrese, 43
Cambridge, influence of university, 88,
  91
Cambridgeshire,
  establishment of village colleges in,
    84-92
  strength of Church in, 88-9
caning, 11
  see also violence in school
capitalism, and assessment of
    educational success, 226
  attitudes underpinning, 131, 132
  relationship with education, 98, 102-3
Carby, H., 60
  Multi-Cultural Fictions, 60-1
career breaks, 170, 187
career choices,
  of boys, 135-8
  of girls, 144-8
careers, sex segregation in, 148, 159-60

Catholic schools,
  enrolment rates, 108
  retention rate of pupils, 101
  role of governors, 26
Cauthery, P., 40, 41
Centre for Contemporary Cultural
  Studies, 93, 97
  'Unpopular Education', 87
character, assessment of in school,
  113-22
character building, 107-8
  and maintenance of structure of
    power, 111
Chesser, Elizabeth Sloan, 35
Chevanne, M., 67
childcare, women's responsibility for,
  138-41, 150-6, 187-8
children, as object of community
  education intervention, 95-6
Chodorow, N., 105
Christianity,
  and character training, 110-11
  varying place in curriculum, 110
classroom strategies, 222
Coard, B., 67
Cohen, 195
Cohen, L. and Cohen, A., *Multi-
  cultural Education*, 67
Cohen, L. and Mannion, L., *Multi-
  cultural Classrooms*, 67
college education, American pupils
  belief in, 135-8
Colwill, 167
Comfort, A., *The Joy of Sex*, 41-2
Commission for Racial Equality, 62
'common code' of beliefs, 78-9
  and multi-cultural education, 68
Commonwealth aid to private schools
  in Australia, 103-4
community,
  concept of applied to Australian
    education, 104
  public school serving interests of, 112
community education,
  1924 Memorandum, 84-92
  in 1970s and 1980s, 92-7
  and access, 90
  development of, 82-3
  future of, 97-8
  'Innovation Time Lag' theory (Ree),
    86

246 *Index*

role of, 15-16, 20-2, 26-7, 94, 229-31,
  232, 234-7
selection of, 184
Health Education from 5 to 16 (HMI
  1986), 39-40
Health Education in Schools
  Department of Education 1977), 39
Helman, C., 45, 49
Herzlich, C., 49
heterosexuality, representation in
  education, 41-2
'hidden curriculum' in multi-cultural
  education, 96
higher education, access to, 108
Hindess, B., 222, 232
Hogan, M., 101, 108
Homans, H., 31-58, 48, 53
homosexuality,
  as arrested development, 40, 41
  in school sex education, 42
  seen as cause of AIDS, 32, 43-5
Honeyford affair, 60
Hoyle, E., 9, 26-7, 221, 226, 228, 232-3,
  236
Hughes, M., 227
humanities teaching, and multi-
  cultural education, 69-77
Humphries, M., 194
Hyams, B., 103, 104

'ideology of romance' (McRobbie), 144,
  149-50
India, study of in school, 70-7, 78
individual choice, in education, 100
individualism, and youth culture, 130
individualist values, and protectionist
  international scene, 102-3, 105
inequality in education,
  affirmative action against, 176-8
  programmes to combat, 174-5
infant teaching, 171
information campaigns, on AIDS,
  31-2
Inner London Education Authority, 42
'Innovation Time Lag' theory (Ree), 86
INSET courses, 68
institutional context of education,
  191-2
International Sociology of Education
  Conference, 1
International Women's Year (1975), 171

Jackson, M., 41, 42
Jarvis, C., 7
Jeffcoate, R., 60, 78-9

Kapferer, B., 102, 123
Kapferer, J., 5, 100-25, 105, 109
Karmel, P., 101
King, Ronald, 218, 219
Kurtz, Z., 48

Lacey, C., 195, 228
'lads' culture' (Willis), 130-1
Lasch, C., 105
Lasswell, Harold, 228
lateral relationships in micro-political
  theory, 228-9
Lawler, E., 228
leadership styles, 230-31
Lee, C., 33-4, 34-5
Levi-Strauss, C., 210
Levine, M., 36
Lips, 167
Little, A., 77
'lived contradiction' in attitude to
  education, 158, 162
Llewellyn, 194
Lloyd, 167
London, Howard, 131
Louden, D., 67
Lynch, *The Multi-cultural Curriculum*,
  67

McArthur, M., 109
MacDonald, B., 20
Macdonell, D., 224, 225, 227
MacFarlane-Burnett, 37-8
McGoldrick affair, 60
McIntosh, M., 105
Mackay, H., 234
McMillan, 170, 179, 182
McQueen, Humphrey, 124
McRobbie, Angela, 144, 149-50, 194
Malinowski, B., 210
Malloch, M., 5, 166-90
management goals, 1-2, 4
management theory, 223-7
  and distribution of power, 225
  incorrectly applied to sociology of
    school organization, 218
  qualitative approach, 226-7
  subjective theory, 226

O17983
21.3.89